FEMINISM BEYOND MODERNISM

FEMINISM BEYOND MODERNISM

Elizabeth A. Flynn

Southern Illinois University Press
Carbondale and Edwardsville

Library of Congress Cataloging-in-Publication Data

Flynn, Elizabeth A., 1944–
    Feminism beyond modernism / Elizabeth A. Flynn.
        p. cm. — (Studies in rhetorics and feminisms)
    Includes bibliographical references and index.
        1. Feminist criticism. 2. Feminism. 3. Feminism and literature.
4. Rhetoric. 5. Reader-response criticism. I. Title. II. Series.

HQ1190 .F593 2002
305.42—dc21
ISBN 0-8093-2434-2 (alk. paper)
ISBN 0-8093-2435-0 (pbk. : alk. paper)   2001041077

To John (1943–2000) and Kate

Contents

Preface

*T*his book represents my attempt to comprehend feminism's diverse traditions as I have encountered them in my reading, writing, and teaching. I began my career exploring ways in which three different literary critical approaches—Marxist, archetypal, and neo-Aristotelian—could be used in the practice of feminist literary criticism and illustrating each through three different readings of Virginia Woolf's *Mrs. Dalloway.* Feminism itself, however, remained a fairly monolithic concept in my mind. As I shifted my attention to feminist reader-response criticism and feminist rhetoric and composition, though, and as I began to teach graduate courses in feminist theory, I could not ignore feminism's contradictions and complexities. However, my attempts to find satisfying descriptions of feminist traditions were often frustrated by treatment of feminism as if it were a monolithic ideology, by counterproductive disputes, and by discussions of feminism from disciplinary perspectives that resulted in a proliferation of names that prevented interdisciplinary comprehension and exchange.

The provisional map I provide here is the result of my circuitous inquiry and of my personal and professional situations. I have a hybrid academic appointment—professor of reading and composition—and hybrid affiliations and commitments. My home base is English studies, defined broadly to include both literary studies and rhetoric and composition, and much of my work has been in feminist reader-response criticism and feminist rhetoric and composition. My department, however, is an interdisciplinary one, and the presence of faculty in fields such as philosophy, communication, linguistics, and modern languages has considerably broadened my perspective over the years. My conceptual map has also expanded as I have taught the work of writers such as Adrienne Rich, Alice Walker, and Louise Rosenblatt in undergraduate and graduate courses. It became historical in emphasis as a result of attempting to contextualize the reading notebooks of Virginia Woolf and to determine how Woolf's feminism was related to her modernism. I have also had the good fortune over the years of being assigned to teach graduate seminars and a few undergraduate ones in feminist theory, and the contributions of the students in these classes have been invaluable.

My approach, then, is historical, but I attempt to move beyond linear accounts of historical periods and beyond positivistic investigative methods. The feminist traditions I present here—modern, antimodern, and postmodern—though often associated with familiar historical periods, are evolving and are often found in hybrid forms and in a number of different historical eras. The boundaries of these traditions are fluid rather than fixed. The methods I employ, including archival research, interviews, and textual analysis, do not aim to provide definitive historical accounts based on rigid periodization. I represent the traditions I name as provisional constructions rather than static essences. I also suggest that modern, antimodern, and postmodern traditions coexist and frequently overlap, collide, and converge, especially within the twentieth century, and do not have clear delimitations.

I see the researcher and the material being analyzed as necessarily interconnected. Researchers bring their own perspectives to bear on the material, because all research is situated, and researchers are often in positions of power. They have an ethical obligation, however, to the authors they are reading to read as accurately as possible. That readers have historically produced multiple and contradictory readings of the same text does not absolve researchers of an obligation to read responsibly and ethically. I also assume that researchers necessarily select material from an overabundance of potentially useful material. I represent my analyses, therefore, as tentative readings rather than conclusive findings. They are what Michel Foucault in *The Archaeology of Knowledge* (1972) calls "rewriting"— "a regulated transformation of what has already been written" rather than a return to "the innermost secret of origin" (140). I am less interested in defining terms and historical eras once and for all than in suggesting directions for future inquiry. My study makes clear, I hope, that re-viewing and re-naming feminist traditions are productive moves at this moment in the development of the feminist movement and the fields of literary studies and rhetoric and composition. I leave it to numerous others to continue this work.

The book also evolved as a result of work on *Gender and Reading: Essays on Readers, Texts, and Contexts* (1986), which I coedited with Patrocinio P. Schweickart and its sequel, *Reading Sites: Social Difference and Reader Response* (forthcoming). My first sabbatical project, an investigation of Virginia Woolf's reading and critical practices, took me to Stanford University and to the University of Sussex in England. On my second sabbatical, I visited The Ohio State University where I presented a lecture that became "Feminism and Scientism," an essay I have reworked here in chapter 6. The book has also been indirectly influenced by my work on a reader for first-year English courses, *Constellations,* coedited with John Schilb and John Clifford; my work as founding editor and then coeditor of the journal *Reader* (1983–2000); and a five-year, collaborative writing project with engineering faculty at Michigan Tech funded by the Whirlpool Foundation and the National Science Foundation. A Creativity Grant from Michigan Tech supported my research on Virginia Woolf. Two Faculty Scholarship Grants from

Michigan Tech supported editorial assistance, purchase of materials, and funds for indexing the book. A grant for my project, "The Genders of Rhetoric," from the Research Foundation of the National Council of Teachers of English allowed me to do research on relationships between feminism and rhetoric.

Several sections of the book are substantial revisions of essays published elsewhere. Portions of "Rescuing Postmodernism" (*CCC* 48 [1997]: 540–55) are included in the introduction: copyright 1997 by the National Council of Teachers of English, reprinted with permission. All quotations from the Holograph Reading Notes of Virginia Woolf are published by the kind permission of the Society of Authors as the Literary Representative of the Estate of Virginia Woolf and of the Curator and Trustees of the Henry W. and Albert A. Berg Collection, the New York Public Library, Astor, Lenox and Tilden Foundations. Quotations from the Monks House Papers in the Manuscript section of the University of Sussex Library are also published by the permission of the Society of Authors as the Literary Representative of the Estate of Virginia Woolf. An earlier version of chapter 5 was originally published as "Rosenblatt and Feminism" in *The Experience of Reading: Louise Rosenblatt and Reader-Response Theory,* edited by John Clifford and published by Boynton/Cook Publishers, Inc., a subsidiary of Reed Elsevier, Inc., copyright © 1991 by Boynton/Cook Publishers, Inc. It is reprinted by permission of the publisher. Portions of "Feminism and Scientism" (*CCC* 46 [1995]: 353–68) are included in chapter 6: copyright 1995 by the National Council of Teachers of English, reprinted with permission. Also included in chapter 6 and reprinted with permission is a revision of my portion of "Interaction across the Curriculum," written collaboratively with Kathryn Remlinger and William Bulleit and published in *JAC* (17.3 [1997]: 343–64).

A number of people have helped in significant ways. I dedicate the book to my late husband, John, who provided encouragement, support, conversation, and sources despite a busy schedule of teaching and, then, an extended illness. He read many of the chapters in draft form, though I regret that he did not live to see the book published. It is no coincidence that he was trained as a historian and had interests in Enlightenment modernism and in relationships between the sciences and the humanities. For many years, he did most of the family shopping and cooking and shared child care responsibilities until his death of bile-duct cancer in September of 2000. I also dedicate the book to my daughter, Kate, who has lived with this book since her birth in September of 1988 and who now writes books of her own.

Cheryl Glenn, coeditor of the Studies in Rhetorics and Feminisms series of Southern Illinois University Press, read the entire manuscript three times and was wonderfully able to see its potential while pointing out its limitations. Her patience and energy helped make disparate chapters a book. Dale Bauer also provided very insightful feedback on a draft of the manuscript. Karl Kageff, acquisitions editor at Southern Illinois University Press, very expertly administered negotiations with the publications board, kept me well informed at every stage of the process, and has also been very enthusiastic and supportive. Carol Burns and Mary Lou Kowaleski did excellent copyediting work.

James Kincaid, Marlene Longenecker, and Mildred Munday, mentors at Ohio State, provided invaluable assistance in my initial investigation of literary studies from a feminist perspective. Herbert Lindenberger and Lucio Ruotolo of Stanford University, Elizabeth Inglis of the University of Sussex Library, and Lola Szladits, curator of the Berg Collection of the New York Public Library, were very helpful in my investigation of Woolf's reading and critical processes. My sister, Alice Hayes, housed me for several weeks when I did research on Woolf at the New York Public Library. John Clifford solicited the essay on Louise Rosenblatt for the collection of essays he was editing on her work, and Rosenblatt herself has been generous with her time in conversations as I have revised that essay. Andrea Lunsford and Suellynn Duffey arranged for my talk on feminism and scientism at Ohio State on my second sabbatical. The many faculty and graduate students who attended that talk helped focus my thinking on relationships between feminism and scientism within rhetoric and composition.

Lisa Ede read numerous chapters in their early stages and encouraged me to keep going. More recently, she provided very helpful feedback on a version of the introduction. David Bleich, Suzanne Clark, and Gesa E. Kirsch read and commented on several chapters and have also provided support and encouragement over the years. Carol Brown, Beth Daniell, Laura Gray-Rosendale, Michael Kearns, Jonathan Loesberg, Steve Mailloux, Laura Micciche, Krista Ratcliffe, Joy Ritchie, Mehdi Semati, Kurt Spellmeyer, and Marilyn Urion read and commented on drafts of particular chapters. Christa Albrecht-Crane read and provided very helpful feedback on a draft of the entire manuscript, and Denise Heikinen edited and also made very helpful suggestions for revision on three drafts of the book. Joe Harris, as editor of *College Composition and Communication,* responded to several drafts of "Rescuing Postmodernism" and "Feminism and Scientism" as did *CCC* reviewers Susan Jarratt, Sharon Crowley, Kurt Spellmeyer, Peshe Kuriloff, and Mary Minock. In addition, I benefited from the comments of Jennifer Slack and Rob Wood on drafts of the *CCC* essay "Feminism and Scientism." Jennifer Slack also became my sounding board for titles, though ironically the one I selected was not on one of those many lists I sent her via e-mail. Susan Stanford Friedman, Herbert Lindenberger, Ann Lowry, Patrocinio P. Schweickart, and Louise Yelin read and provided very helpful commentary on drafts of the book proposal. Colleague Patty Sotirin participated in several of the graduate seminars on feminist theory and helped me sort through a number of issues. I commiserated on numerous occasions with John Schilb when he was struggling with his book *Between the Lines* (1996). Carol Berkenkotter has been very interested over the years in the book's progress as have Glenda Gill, Bill Powers, Tim Whitten, and my mother, Elizabeth Sherry. Department chair Bob Johnson has also been very supportive.

I could not have progressed on the book at all without technical support, the time to complete it, and the assistance of local librarians and child care providers. Stuart Selber, Alwood Williams, Jeremy Bos, Karla Kitalong, Matt Yeager, and Keith West provided help with computer hardware and software as did the staff of the Department of Humanities' Center for Computer-Assisted Language Instruction. Scheduling coordinator Jean Blanning assigned me flextime in academic years 1997–98, 1998–99, and 1999–2000 so that I did not have to teach winter terms. Sabbatical leaves in 1986, 1994, and 2001 also provided much-needed time. I also appreciate the help provided by librarians at the Van Pelt Library of Michigan Tech, especially Janet Locatelli, Ellen Seidel, Stephanie Pepin, and Dave Bezotte. I could not have worked on the book when my daughter was young had she not had excellent child care from a number of individuals including Martha Pekkala, Ardith Homola, and Tami Bessner. Many others nurtured and cultivated her talents in preschool, school, after-school, and summer activities.

I appreciate the support and encouragement of members of my interdisciplinary women's writing group. Eunice Carlson, Sandra Harting, Carol MacLennan, Betzi Praeger, and Christa Walck have provided encouragement on a regular basis and have read chapters and provided references and books and articles. Their disciplinary perspectives, which include biology, business, and the social sciences, have broadened my own, though it is their interdisciplinarity that I have appreciated even more. At dinner once a year at the annual convention of the Conference on College Composition and Communication, Lynn Bloom, Lisa Ede, Anne Ruggles Gere, Linda Peterson, and Louise Smith have listened to my frustrations and celebrated my successes. I've also benefited greatly from a newly formed, feminist, reading-and-writing group within the Department of Humanities. Vicky Bergvall, Heidi Bostic, Diane Shoos, and Patty Sotirin have introduced me to new material and provided stimulating commentary on it. Countless others helped as well in direct and indirect ways.

I should add that the book was written before the tragic events of September 11, 2001. Those events make evident the urgency of the need to develop alternatives to Western modernism that will lessen the divide between Western and non-Western cultures discussed in chapter 2.

FEMINISM BEYOND MODERNISM

Introduction

Despite our desperate, eternal attempt to separate, contain, and mend, categories always leak.

—Trinh T. Minh-ha, *Woman, Native, Other: Writing
Postcoloniality and Feminism*

modernism. On the longest view, modernism in philosophy starts out with Descartes's quest for a knowledge self-evident to reason and secured from all the demons of sceptical doubt. It is also invoked—with a firmer sense of historical perspective—to signify those currents of thought that emerged from Kant's critical revolution in the spheres of epistemology, ethics, and aesthetic judgement. Thus "modernity" and "enlightenment" tend to be used interchangeably, whether by thinkers (like Habermas) who seek to sustain that project, or by those—the post-modernist company—who consider it a closed chapter in the history of ideas.

—Christopher Norris, "Modernism"

Modernism. [F]rom about the middle of the nineteenth century—and even this date is arbitrary—the foundations of an earlier understanding of the nature and place of humanity were so shaken that, by the end of the century, a great many artists and writers throughout the Western world had developed a kind of future-shock, a sense that one view of the world and the meaning and place of human existence had been taken from them, and that a replacement had not yet arrived, or that a sometimes bewildering array of possible replacements were contending for sovereignty. The broadest view of modernism is that, unconsciously as well as consciously, technically as well as thematically, it encompasses not only comprehensions and accommodations, but also the initial apprehensions of this change, and that the range of its works extends from George Moore and George Gissing to Joyce and Wyndham Lewis, from Browning and Arnold to Eliot and Pound.

—David Brooks, "Modernism"

*T*he feminist movement is composed of a number of different social, political, and intellectual perspectives and institutions in a number of locations that intersect and overlap in complex ways. It is also a movement that has been influenced by and that influences other traditions, including ones focusing on related concerns such as class, race, ethnicity, culture, sexual orientation, and age. Given this complexity, it is not surprising that there is considerable confusion, both within or beyond the movement, about what feminism's traditions are and how they relate to one another or to other traditions.

However, complexity is not the only factor that contributes to the confusion. Because feminism is a liberatory movement that directly challenges existing institutional arrangements, those who feel threatened by it often respond by representing it in negative and often hostile ways. Such representations pervade the media and even the academy. Feminists have been cast as destroyers of families and other cherished institutions. They have been blamed for problems such as the delinquency of adolescents, the inability of qualified males to find jobs, and the erosion of standards in the professions, the schools, and the academy. If women would only embrace traditional roles, the argument seems to go, there would be far fewer societal problems.

Feminists have devoted considerable time and energy to refuting unfounded attacks and making clear that much work still needs to be done if women are to achieve equality. Feminist responses to the problems of misunderstanding and negative representations of its traditions, however, have sometimes been problematic. At times, feminists have seen strategic value in representing feminism to a resistant audience as a unified movement with clearly identifiable goals. Presenting feminism as a unified ideology, though, oversimplifies a complex movement and reinforces the modernist idea that its traditions and goals must be consistent and without contradiction.[1] Some feminists have also sometimes resisted naming feminist traditions because they feel doing so commits them to rigid categories with firmly delineated boundaries,[2] or they have indirectly contributed to the confusion by engaging in counterproductive internal disputes.[3]

Another response has been the production of a proliferation of names for feminist traditions, often a result of discussions within disciplinary contexts.[4] Philosopher Rosemarie Tong in the first edition of *Feminist Thought* identifies liberal, radical, Marxist, psychoanalytic, socialist, existentialist, and postmodern feminisms, for instance.[5] Historian Alice Echols in *Daring to Be Bad,* a historical account of radical feminism within the United States in the 1960s and 1970s, distinguishes among liberal, cultural, and radical feminisms. Maggie Humm in *Modern Feminisms* speaks of first-wave feminism and second-wave feminism, both of which she sees as modern. According to Humm, first-wave feminism began in the eighteenth century with the work of Mary Wollstonecraft and includes the work of feminists such as Olive Schreiner, Virginia Woolf, Rebecca West, and Simone de Beauvoir. Humm sees Kate Millett, Shulamith Firestone, Susan Brownmiller, Susan Griffin, and Andrea Dworkin and other 1970 or post–1970 writers as second-wave feminists. For Humm, first-wave feminism is principally concerned with equalities, second-wave feminism with using "women's difference to oppose the 'legalities' of a patriarchal world" (11). Linda Alcoff's frequently cited "Cultural Feminism versus Post-Structuralism" dismisses cultural feminism and post-structuralist feminism and calls for an alternative, what she calls *positionality.* Proliferating names have the advantage of accounting for a diversity of traditions and enable explanations in a variety of contexts and with specificity. They can present a problem, however, if there are no attempts to relate them to one another and if they convey the impression that feminism is an entirely incoherent movement. The named traditions are often meaningful in disciplinary contexts but not in interdisciplinary ones.

A promising interdisciplinary approach, and one that is fairly widespread within feminist studies, is to distinguish between modern and postmodern feminisms. The approach is promising because the terms *modernism* and *postmodernism* are used in a variety of fields to identify broad intellectual, political, and social movements. There is by no means agreement on what these terms mean, however, and so using them might create more problems than it solves. I am especially concerned about the consequences for feminism of the tendency to identify postmodernism as modernism's binary opposite and as relativist and subjectivist because defining the relationship between the two terms in this way is almost always accompanied by an easy dismissal of postmodernism and of postmodern feminism. I am also concerned about the discrepancy between the way modernism is defined within literary studies and the way it is defined within a number of other fields including philosophy, history, and the social sciences. As David Brooks's definition in the epigraph makes clear, within literary studies, modernism is a late-nineteenth- and twentieth-century movement associated with a departure from realism. As Norris's definition that precedes it in the epigraph indicates, however, within other fields modernism describes a constellation of ideas and projects associated with the late-seventeenth- and eighteenth-century Enlightenment.

In *Feminism Beyond Modernism,* I take the risk of using the terms modernism and postmodernism to describe feminist traditions, but I do so by describing postmodernism as a critique of modernism rather than a complete rejection of it. In order to clarify the relationship between modernism and postmodernism, I introduce a third term, *antimodernism,* and suggest that it, rather than postmodernism, is relativist and subjectivist and directly opposed to modernism. In making a distinction among modern, antimodern, and postmodern feminist traditions, I should emphasize that these three tendencies are related in complex ways, are rarely separate and distinct, and are not necessarily limited to a single historical era or geographical location. Also, brief summaries necessarily obscure the depth, complexity, and contradictions inherent in any movement and the extent to which these are highly contested terms. I nevertheless take the risk of providing brief explanations of the three traditions.

I associate modernism with the Enlightenment and suggest that doing so can lead to new understandings of traditions within English studies. Although I have a broad focus including the interdisciplinary field of feminist studies, an important concern is the development of feminism within literary studies, especially the subfield reader-response criticism, as well as rhetoric and composition defined broadly to include technical communication. I provisionally describe the complex relationships among modern, antimodern, and postmodern feminisms, point out problems with some representations of postmodern feminism, and explore some ways in which postmodern feminists, recognizing that modernism is deeply implicated in sexism, racism, classism, colonialism, and other forms of oppression, have attempted to find alternatives to modernist assumptions, methods, and practices without completely rejecting the modernist project. I also investigate ways in which postmodern feminists challenge modernist beliefs in the objectivity and the neutrality of the observer or interpreter, positing instead that all observation and interpretation are necessarily situated and value laden. If traditional academic discourse is modernist in its pretense of objectivity and neutrality, postmodern feminist discourse asks what difference do race, class, gender, and sexual orientation make in the processes of reading and writing? Postmodern feminists, without resorting to relativism or subjectivism, also investigate the role of the reader in the interpretive process. If objective detachment is an impossibility, they suggest, fairness is not. Interpreters have an ethical obligation to read and write in ways that are accurate and that attend to the nuances and complexities of that which they are interpreting.[6]

In naming and provisionally describing three broad, feminist movements—modern, antimodern, and postmodern—I associate liberal and Marxist feminisms with modern traditions, radical and cultural feminisms with antimodern traditions, and postmodern feminisms with traditions that challenge modern ones without repudiating them. I also associate modern feminism with Western Enlightenment rationality and empiricism, Marxism, and psychoanalysis and suggest that postmodernists and postmodern feminists do not reject rationality and science but, rather, critique it. I relate antimodern feminism, in contrast, to the Romantic movement with its emphasis on nature, spirituality, and irrationality and with some late-twentieth-century intersubjective approaches to language. I also acknowledge, however, that modern, antimodern, and postmodern feminisms are orientations rather than clearly delineated traditions. Their boundaries blur, they are never found in pure form, and they are often found in diverse geographical locations. My aim, then, is not to define three clearly distinct feminist movements but to chart three dynamic perspectives, tendencies, or impulses that often overlap and intersect and that are plural rather than singular. In defining relationships between modern and postmodern feminisms I attempt to reclaim both. I suggest that feminist traditions will be better understood if they are named, at least provisionally, if they are related to other intellectual and historical traditions, and if they are represented in nonreductive ways. Following is a brief overview of the ways in which I am using the terms modern, antimodern, and postmodern within the context of modern, antimodern, and postmodern feminisms in this book. First, though, I make the case that postmodern feminism and postmodernism have been misread and misrepresented as being opposed to modernism and as subjectivist and relativist.

Misreading Postmodern Feminism and Postmodernism

Feminists themselves often misread postmodern feminism by seeing it as modernism's opposite. Martha C. Nussbaum in *Sex and Social Justice,* for instance, in defending what she calls a liberal approach to equality for women, speaks of the postmodern feminists who oppose her position as "antiessentialists" and "anti-universalists" (35). Such attacks are tame, however, compared to those on post-modern feminism by individuals outside the feminist movement, often by scientists or historians of science in what has come to be called the science wars. In such attacks, postmodern feminists are often cast as opponents of science and as relativists or worse. Physicist and historian of science Gerald Holton in *Science and Anti-Science,* for instance, accuses postmodernists and postmodern feminists of being against science (154) and associates them with astrology, attacks on relativity theory,[7] scientific illiteracy, and support of Creationism (145). In casting postmodernists and postmodern feminists as opponents of science, Holton has aligned them with the superstitious and the ignorant. The work of feminist philosopher Sandra Harding is often the object of attack. Life scientist Paul R. Gross and mathematician Norman Levitt in *Higher Superstition: The Academic Left and Its Quarrels with Science,* for example, in disparaging the work of postmodernists and postmodern feminists, accuse Harding of megalomania (132) and incoherence (130).[8]

Critics within rhetoric and composition are often considerably more careful and restrained in their critiques of postmodernism and postmodern feminism. Davida Charney in "Empiricism is Not a Four-Letter Word," for instance, speaks appreciatively of Harding's work and of the work of feminist compositionists such as Gesa E. Kirsch and Joy S. Ritchie. Charney reserves her criticism for postmodern and feminist critics who "conflate methods and ideologies in simplistic ways that have been challenged by others sharing their political commitments" (568). Charney's attack is like that of Holton and Gross and Levitt in an important way, however. She tends to construct the debate in terms of a binary opposition, seeing those who critique objective research methods as advocating subjective methods (569). She devotes considerable attention to pointing out the limitations of the perspectives of "subjectivists" (586) and argues that subjectivist methods, if they are truly local and context bound, cannot "extend a discipline's repertoire of methods or deepen its knowledge" (589). She does not seem to recognize that many of the individuals whose work she critiques are postmodernists rather than subjectivists and are interested in critiquing objectivism, not in replacing it with subjectivism.[9]

The misunderstanding of postmodern feminism is closely related to the misunderstanding of postmodernism in general within and beyond the academy. In both, postmodernism is often associated with subjectivism and relativism. A good example of such a misunderstanding is Darryl S. L. Jarvis's article "Postmodernism: A Critical Typology." Like many others, Jarvis sees postmodernism as antimodernist, a rejection of the tradition of the Enlightenment thought (97). He speaks of postmodernism as negating modernism (100), as antilogocentric (101), as myopic and ahistorical (103), and as relativistic (118). He argues, further, that postmodernists such as Jacques Derrida and Michel Foucault "abandon objectivity, embrace perspectivism and relativism, and deny the privileging of any one narrative over others" (125). In the essay, Jarvis invokes terms often associated with modernism such as "rationality," "progress," "justice," and "emancipation" (126) without providing a critical perspective on them. As Jarvis's essay makes clear, postmodernism is too often seen as the opposite of modernism and as relativist.[10]

The representation of postmodernism as modernism's binary opposite, despite postmodernism's problematizing of binary oppositions, is widespread within English studies. Such representations are often accompanied by a belief that Romanticism is a modernist tendency. Lester Faigley's *Fragments of Rationality,* for instance, a critique of the field of rhetoric and composition, defines modernism broadly to include Romanticism and sees modernism as in opposition to postmodernism. Faigley says that many of the practices in the contemporary teaching of writing follow from the ongoing debate within modernism between those "who wish to preserve the rational, coherent subject of the Enlightenment and those who advocate the self-expressive subject of Romanticism." For Faigley, modernism is comprised of both Enlightenment rationality and Romantic expressivism. He equates the field's modernist orientation, including expressivism, with its conservatism. His own perspective, in contrast, is a postmodern one. He sees that postmodernism, despite its limitations, can become one of the primary venues of critical pedagogy (xii).

The tendencies to define postmodernism as a binary opposite of modernism and to subsume Romanticism into modernism are also common within literary studies, a field in which postmodernism has been a familiar term for decades. Ihab Hassan's representation of postmodernism's relationship to modernism has been very influential. In his "Postlude" to the second edition of *The Dismemberment of Orpheus,* Hassan provides a chart that makes evident that he sees Romanticism as a modernist movement. The first item under modernism is "Romanticism/ Symbolism." Opposite it, under postmodernism, is "'Pataphysics/Dadaism." Hassan includes Romanticism as a form of modernism and creates a binary scheme in which modernism and postmodernism are opposed.[11] Brian McHale's *Constructing Postmodernism,* another exploration of postmodernism within the context of literary studies, reproduces Helmut Lethen's bipolar scheme that depicts modernism as characterized by, among other things, hierarchy and presence, postmodernism as characterized by anarchy and absence (7–8), thereby suggesting that Lethen, like Hassan, is advocating a dichotomous scheme. Lethen, however, is critical of bipolar portrayals, seeing them as inherently modernist, and argues that there is no abrupt discontinuity between modernism and postmodernism (236).[12] Following are brief and tentative descriptions of the modern, antimodern, and postmodern traditions, including feminist ones, that form the basis for subsequent discussions. Those discussions make clear the usefulness as well as some limitations of these constructions. I provide more specific and fully developed descriptions in chapter 1.

Modern/Antimodern/Postmodern

Modernism

I am provisionally defining modernism as it is frequently understood in feminist studies,[13] philosophy, the social sciences, and sometimes rhetoric and composition[14] rather than art history and literary studies.[15] Philosophers, historians, and social scientists often see modernism as arising out of the Enlightenment and as associated with the scientific revolution and rationalism. Within art history and literary studies, in contrast, modernism is usually associated with a late-nineteenth-century and early-twentieth-century movement emphasizing aesthetic innovation and departure from realism. David Brooks's definition of modernism in the *Encyclopedia of Literature and Criticism* quoted in the epigraph above is typical of definitions within literary studies in that he defines it as a radical departure from previous traditions and makes no mention of the Enlightenment. Feminist literary studies often identify a female modernist tradition but usually within the parameters of modernism as it has been traditionally defined within literary studies. I suggest, however, that feminists, including those in literary studies, can benefit from thinking of twentieth-century manifestations of modernism in the context of the Enlightenment. I ask how our conceptions of late-nineteenth-century and twentieth-century modernisms change if those conceptions are contextualized in relation to late-seventeenth- and eighteenth-century commitments to rationalism and empiricism. John Trimbur in "Agency and the Death of the Author," an essay about debates about modernism and postmodernism within rhetoric and composition, defines modernism in this way.

Historical benchmarks of the Enlightenment include the English Glorious Revolution of 1688, the American Declaration of Independence of 1776, and the French Revolution of 1789. Often associated with the work of Descartes, Locke, Voltaire, Diderot, Mendelssohn, Lessing, and Kant, the Enlightenment emphasized reason and was optimistic about the ability of humans to progress to perfection. It also affirmed an inductive approach to the study of nature as well as individual liberty and equality and de-emphasized nonrational aspects of human experience. The Enlightenment had two related emphases, rationality and empiricism. Stephen Toulmin in *Cosmopolis* speaks of these two emphases as "twin founding pillars," consisting of modern science, an intellectual movement that he traces to Isaac Newton, and modern philosophy, an intellectual movement that he traces to Descartes (ix).

The Cartesian conception of the rational mind as distinct from the body was paralleled by the development of the physical sciences with their emphasis on observation of material reality by a neutral, objective observer. Faith in the ability of humans to rise above passion is paralleled by the emergence of the scientific method, which aims to rid the scientist of bias and enable accurate observation and the development of authoritative knowledge. Although originally intended to understand physical reality, the scientific method later was modified for use in attempting to understand human reality. Language, in a modernist context, is seen as a transparent medium that plays a relatively minor role in the process of scientific investigation or as an impediment to the achievement of understanding. Communication is understood as a fairly unproblematic process of transmitting information or as a process of overcoming obstacles to accurate transmission of information. Communicators are seen as having relatively stable identities and as producing and transmitting relatively stable meanings. The Enlightenment modernist tradition persists in the nineteenth and twentieth centuries, though in somewhat different forms. Some common characteristics of later modernist developments include a belief that science and technological developments will bring about positive societal changes and a belief that human behavior can be described in scientific terms. Sometimes, too, modernism is characterized by a belief that scientific investigation of human behavior necessitates attention to structures and forms as foundational principles divorced from social context. Such tendencies can be seen within modernist traditions such as utilitarianism, formalism, and structuralism.

Enlightenment literary criticism and rhetoric focus on realism and on the text as a mirror, a mimetic reflection of reality, terms M. H. Abrams uses in *The Mirror and the Lamp*. Abrams says, "Through most of the eighteenth century, the tenet that art is an imitation seemed almost too obvious to need iteration or proof" (11). To illustrate the point, Abrams discusses French art critic Charles Batteux and German poetry critic Gotthold Ephraim Lessing. Abrams also emphasizes, however, that Enlightenment criticism sometimes also focuses on the relationship between work and audience (14). Enlightenment rhetoric focuses on the importance of reason and logic in persuasion, emphasizing inductive reasoning, the approach taken in experimental science. In focusing attention on the human mind, it begins to develop psychological explanations of reality. In their introduction to the section on Enlightenment rhetoric in *The Rhetorical Tradition*, Patricia Bizzell and Bruce Herzberg conclude, "In the eighteenth century, then, rhetoric could offer a link to the classical period, an analysis of taste and literary judgment, instruction in correct and effective speaking, and a respectable scientific theory of psychological persuasion" (638).

The Enlightenment can be credited with the development of democratic institutions and processes and with commitments to universal human rights and equality. The Enlightenment also contributed, however, to dissociation of mind from body, colonial expansion, and the continued enslavement of peoples of color. The optimistic belief in rationality, human perfectibility, and scientific progress provided the basis for imperialist policies and a belief in the superiority of Western cultures and traditions. The Enlightenment also gave rise to the Industrial Revolution that in turn resulted in population growth, the emergence of an underclass of unprotected and exploited workers, and the creation of urban centers characterized by poverty and disease. This dark side of the Enlightenment set up the conditions necessary for the development of progressive, modernist scientific explanations of social and economic reality—Marxist explanations, for example—as well as antimodern theories and practices that repudiate rationality and empiricism.

Modern feminists, including Wollstonecraft in the eighteenth century, John Stuart Mill and Charlotte Perkins Gilman in the nineteenth century, and Beauvoir in the twentieth century, were committed to equal opportunities and equal rights for women and focused on ways in which women, despite having capacities equal to men, had been discriminated against and excluded from the public sphere and from opportunities to develop their intellects. Modern feminism tends to be universalistic and to see hope for women's liberation in scientific and technological development. Liberal feminists focus on providing women economic, social, and political equality with men. The Suffrage Movement arose out of liberal feminist commitments to democratic principles and sought to provide women a voice in democratic political structures. Marxist feminists focus on the economic exploitation of women as workers within and outside the home and call for the elimination of oppressive working conditions. Psychoanalytic feminists focus on imbalances in familial and interpersonal relationships and call for equality with men in the home and in relationships.

Antimodernism

I prefer the term *antimodernism* to *Romanticism* because I think antimodernism makes clearer the relationships I am attempting to establish among the three categories. It is also a term that is not primarily associated with the literary movement of the early-nineteenth century. Antimodernism includes Romanticism but is not limited to it. It is admittedly not usual within literary studies and rhetoric and composition to use the term antimodernism to describe what is more often referred to as Romanticism or expressivism. There is some precedent for doing so in other fields, however. Historian Jackson T. Lears in *No Place of Grace: Antimodernism and the Transformation of American Culture, 1880–1920,* for example, describes a Romantic tradition that reacted against the central tenets of modernism. Although Holton's *Science and Anti-Science* is limited by a tendency to conflate antimodernism and postmodernism and to repudiate the latter, as I suggested earlier, his book is useful for its identification of characteristics of antimodernism. He constructs two lists, one the modern perspective, which he favors, and a countervision, which he argues against. Some of the modern characteristics he lists are: objective, quantitative, extra-personalized, universalized, anti-individualistic, rational, problem-oriented, proof-oriented, meritocratic, functional, skeptical with respect to authority, secular, antimetaphysical, evolutionary, cosmopolitan, active, and progressive (173–74). Some of the characteristics of the countervision are: subjective, qualitative, personalized, ego-centered, moralistic, accessible to all, purpose-oriented, faith-based, systems based on individual authority, power prior to and determining knowledge, and fields of knowledge as equally authoritative (174–75).[16]

Antimodernism directly challenges the basic tenets of modernism. Some present-day manifestations include subjectivism—Romanticism or expressivism—and sometimes forms of intersubjectivism or weak social construction, what postmodernist Thomas Kent in *Paralogic Rhetoric* calls communitarianism. Subjectivism, which I describe in the context of Romanticism, often emphasizes irrationality, the instability of the self, and the uniqueness of the individual, whose psychological depths are mysterious and ultimately unknowable. History is often portrayed as a series of catastrophic or sublime events that are uncontrollable, and the future is often seen through either visionary or pessimistic rather than optimistic lenses. Emphasis is often placed on nature, the ideal, transcendence, and political revolution. From an expressivist perspective, truth is unattainable, unfathomable, and has spiritual dimensions. Knowledge is subjective and relative. Because individuals are unique and because perceptions of reality are entirely subjective, scientific knowledge has very limited authority, and the ability of scientific projects to lead to valid or reliable truth claims is questioned.

The antimodernist tradition I identify is sometimes intersubjectivist as well as subjectivist. James A. Berlin in *Rhetoric and Reality* identifies a strong subjectivist or expressivist tradition within the field of rhetoric and composition. I suggest, however, that some intersubjective perspectives are closely associated with subjectivist ones and that taxonomies that make a distinction between work that focuses on the individual language user and work that situates the act of composing within a social context (Faigley "Competing Theories"; Berlin "Rhetoric and Ideology") sometimes fail to take this into account. The important issue is not whether the language user is an individual or a member of a community but whether the individual or the community is seen as perceiving things objectively as in a modernist world view or subjectively as in an antimodernist world view.

Radical and cultural feminist perspectives are often antimodern in orientation. For radical feminists, the world of men, of economic, social, and political activity, is seen as the cause of women's problems rather than the solution to them as in modern feminism. Radical feminists argue that traditional institutions are patriarchal, alienating, and hostile to women, and need to be overthrown entirely or radically transformed in order to bring about the emancipation of women. Cultural feminists also emphasize the differences between women and men but place greater emphasis on the positive aspects of women's experience. Women are seen as belonging to a common culture and hence as having common strengths and capacities including nurturing, child rearing, and an ability to connect with others. If women were placed in positions of authority, some cultural feminists might argue, there would be less competition and less warfare. Men are often portrayed within cultural feminism as being competitive, aggressive, and combative.

Writers whose works can usefully be contextualized in relation to radical feminism include Kate Millett, Tillie Olsen, Dale Spender, Robin Morgan, Adrienne Rich, and Susan Brownmiller. Writers whose works can be contextualized in relation to cultural feminism include Dorothy Dinnerstein, Deborah Tannen, Nancy Chodorow, Carol Gilligan, and the *Women's Ways of Knowing* collective, Belenky, Clinchy, Goldberger, and Tarule. Many of these writers, however, often exhibit characteristics of both tendencies because the two are closely related. These writers also sometimes exhibit characteristics of liberal feminism and postmodern feminism because the categories of radical, cultural, liberal, and postmodern feminisms are not mutually exclusive. Antimodern feminists often reject Enlightenment modernist projects and male writers and thinkers and associate them with patriarchal culture.

Postmodernism

I am provisionally defining *postmodernism* broadly to include the many perspectives that had emerged in a number of different fields in the twentieth century and continue to emerge that place language and interpretation at the center of their inquiry, that recognize truth as contingent and provisional rather than absolute and determinate, and that question the universal subject of the Enlightenment and foundational approaches to language and to knowledge. I do not deny the differences in the diverse perspectives that comprise postmodernism as I am constructing it. Rather, I emphasize their commonalities for strategic reasons. If denunciations of postmodernism define it broadly, there is, in defending postmodernism, some value in defining it broadly as well. I represent postmodernism, therefore, as encompassing a number of different movements and a number of different theorists including the postformalism of Mikhail Bakhtin, the poststructuralism of Foucault, Derrida, Jean-François Lyotard, and Julia Kristeva,[17] the neopragmatism of Richard Rorty, the new historicism of Thomas Kuhn and Hayden White, the neo-Marxism of Louis Althusser, the "postfeminist" perspectives of Judith Butler and Donna Haraway,[18] and the social-epistemic rhetoric of Berlin, Faigley, and Susan Miller. Although postmodernism has been defined in a number of different ways by a number of different people and although it is sometimes seen, as a result, as a term that has outlived its usefulness, I argue that it is a term that can be refigured and reclaimed.

Postmodernists and postmodern feminists question the neutrality of the humanistic and scientific researcher and the uncritical acceptance of concepts such as rationality and objectivity.[19] They critique the modernist orientation of much work in the humanities and the sciences for constructing subjects who are universalized, rational individuals, often implicitly Western, white, privileged, male, and presumably impartial. A metanarrative of postmodernism is difficult to construct because postmodernism resists the creation of metanarratives, has arisen in diverse locations, and has been defined in relation to a number of different intellectual, social, and political traditions. There is also little agreement on the merits of postmodernism. Accounts of postmodernism are often favorably disposed

(Hutcheon "Poetics of Postmodernism," "Politics of Postmodernism;" McHale) or critical (Jameson, Eagleton), and those that are critical are often dissatisfied with postmodernism's tendency to insufficiently attend to Marxist and materialist concerns. Debates within feminism about the relative merits of postmodernism often arise out of commitments to Marxism.[20] I describe postmodernists as recognizing that criteria and norms are applied in the making of judgments but those criteria and norms are, in turn, context-specific, hence subject to scrutiny and revision. Conclusions are arrived at, and preferences are expressed, but those conclusions and preferences are uncertain rather than certain, contingent rather than definitive. Professionals and nonprofessionals, experts and nonexperts are seen as interpreters rather than as objective presenters of facts, results, conclusions, and representations. Their perspectives are necessarily partial and situated.

Postmodernists critique foundational approaches to language and often attempt to reconceptualize objectivity rather than to reject it entirely or to replace it with subjectivity. Such reconceptualization necessitates calling into question the possibility of impartiality, of detachment of the observer from that which is observed, or of identifying a principle or principles that will provide a firm foundation, ground, or cause upon which to base an analysis. Considerable postmodernist problematizing of science has arisen out of feminist reconsiderations of the aims and methods of science. Haraway in "Situated Knowledges: The Science Question in Feminism and the Privilege of Partial Perspective," for instance, tries to find a middle way between accounts of work in science and technology that reduce it to power moves on the one hand or to "scientific, positivistic arrogance" on the other (179). Haraway sees that the alternative to relativism is "partial, locatable, critical knowledges sustaining the possibility of webs of connections called solidarity in politics and shared conversations in epistemology" (182). She calls for a commitment to mobile positioning and to passionate detachment and to a split and contradictory self who can interrogate positionings and be accountable (183).[21]

Postmodernists often emphasize that there is no clear boundary between modernism and postmodernism, and discussions of postmodernism are often characterized by ambivalence. Lyotard's well-known assertion in *The Postmodern Condition* that the postmodern is "that which, in the modern, puts forward the unpresentable in presentation itself" (81) provides a good example of the blurred boundaries between modernism and postmodernism. Fredric Jameson in *Postmodernism* interprets Lyotard's position as celebrating postmodernism while continuing to value modernism (60).[22] This attempt to have it both ways is characteristically postmodern. In repudiating either/or and binary thinking, postmodernists make possible the emergence of a movement that is not necessarily set on replacing or repudiating its precursors.[23] A postmodern perspective also suggests that intellectual movements do not have essences but are always limited, partial, and embedded in contexts that have a bearing on whether they are politically progressive, reactionary, or some combination of the two. A consequence of this emphasis on partiality is an attention to the local circumstances that give rise to events.

Postmodern feminists problematize and question the assumptions of modern feminisms without repudiating them. They are not antimodern. They do not oppose modern intellectual and social traditions or repudiate the sciences or other Enlightenment projects. Rather, they are critical of them and attempt to find alternatives to them. Often this involves reconceptualizing objectivity and calling into question the possibility of impartiality, that is, of detachment of the observer from that which is observed. Considerable postmodernist problematizing of science has arisen out of feminist reconsiderations of the aims and methods of science. Postmodern feminism also attempts to find alternatives to literary traditions such as realism, formalism, and structuralism without denouncing them. It questions the traditional literary canon and values noncanonical genres, styles, and media. It also attempts to move beyond modern feminism with its white, liberal, humanist agenda. Ann Brooks in *Postfeminisms* emphasizes that postmodern and poststructuralist critiques of the essentialism, ethnocentrism, and ahistoricism of much feminist theory were instituted initially by women of color. According to Brooks, critics such as Hazel Carby, bell hooks, and others observe that the feminist movement is essentially white, middle-class, and heterosexual (16).

Focusing on postmodern feminism as a critique of modern feminism rather than its binary opposite invites explorations of relationships between Anglo-American feminism and continental feminism. It is difficult, for instance, to discuss either Anglo-American or continental feminisms without discussing Marxism or psychoanalysis, traditions that were initiated by continental theorists but that have had a significant impact on Anglo-American traditions as well. I also attempt to disrupt the binary way in which Western and non-Western feminisms are often discussed.

Beyond Modernisms

I suggest that antimodern and postmodernism feminisms are forms of resistance to modernist projects, though antimodern feminism opposes modernism directly and attempts to subvert its aims and goals whereas postmodern feminism resists modernism without attempting to negate it. The broad movements I provisionally name, modern, antimodern, and postmodern feminisms, bear some resemblance to the movements outlined in French feminist Kristeva's "Women's Time," first published in 1979. Toril Moi, in her introduction to this essay in *The Kristeva Reader,* says that it is one of Kristeva's most important essays because it is one of the few in which Kristeva addresses the issue of feminism directly (187).[24] "Women's Time" makes evident that there are parallels between the traditions of the French women's movement and the Anglo-American women's movement and that neither is monolithic. Kristeva sees that the first generation of feminists, in struggling for equality, aspired to gain a place in linear time as the time of project and history. I see this approach as corresponding in some ways to modern feminism. A difficulty with this approach, however, according to Kristeva, is that the increase of women in positions of power has not radically changed the nature of that power because women in high positions become guardians of the status quo. A second generation of feminists, according to Kristeva, focuses on the specificity of female psychology and its symbolic realizations and seeks to give a language to the intrasubjective realizations left mute by culture in the past. I see this movement as in some ways resembling radical feminism, which I see as antimodern. The creation of a counter-society, however, according to Kristeva, results in a kind of inverted sexism. Kristeva calls for a third generation that can be interwoven with the other two (209). This third generation, which I associate with postmodern feminism,[25] questions the dichotomy of man/woman as an opposition of two rival entities (209) and attempts to replace scapegoating with the analysis of the potentialities of victim/executioner that characterize each identity, each subject, each sex (210).

I posit that whereas modern feminists focus primarily on equality and antimodern feminists focus on creating a women's culture that opposes male culture, postmodern feminists move beyond both by questioning representations of women and men as binary opposites and by making evident that both women and men are capable of being victims and executioners. I also suggest that whereas modern feminists emphasize commonalities between women and men and antimodern feminists focus on differences between them, postmodern feminists problematize binary conceptions of difference. If modern feminists see women as the equal of men rather than their opposite, postmodern feminists emphasize the limitations of dichotomous representations of relationships between women and men or women's culture and men's culture. They also see that gender is only one variable in a complex matrix. Factors such as race, class, ethnicity, age, culture, and sexual orientation must be taken into consideration as well, and doing so makes evident the limitations of explanations and representations that focus exclusively on gender.

In the first section of the book, "Reconfigurations," I define modernism, antimodernism, and postmodernism provisionally as broad intellectual, social, and political movements. I also situate feminist traditions, especially liberal feminism, radical feminism, cultural feminism, and postmodernism feminism, in relation to modern, antimodern, and postmodern traditions and suggest that these traditions have relevance beyond Anglo-American feminism by demonstrating their usefulness in understanding feminism within global contexts. In the next two sections of the book, "Opposing Modernisms" and "Critiquing Modernisms," I describe feminist perspectives that move beyond modernism either by opposing it or by critiquing it. In "Opposing Modernisms," I focus on the complex and partial antimodernisms of Virginia Woolf, Adrienne Rich, and Alice Walker. In "Critiquing Modernism," I discuss perspectives within literary studies and rhetoric and composition that move toward or are postmodern critiques of modernism.

This book, then, explores relationships among modern, antimodern, and postmodern feminisms as they have been understood within a number of fields in the humanities and the social sciences in a number of locations, focusing especially on antimodern and postmodern feminisms as moving beyond modernism, though in different ways. I devote considerable attention to the ways in which these traditions have been represented within the fields of literary studies, especially reader-response criticism and rhetoric and composition. I do so however in order to disrupt the opposition that frequently characterizes the relationship between these two fields. I therefore focus on the activities of reading and writing that are common to both. When I discuss the work of individuals usually associated with literary studies, for instance, Virginia Woolf in chapter 3, and Adrienne Rich and Alice Walker in chapter 4, I attend to their essays rather than their novels or poetry. The work of Louise Rosenblatt, which I discuss in chapter 5, is situated between, within, and beyond literary studies and rhetoric and composition because she is mainly concerned with literature but her focus is often pedagogical, and much of her work is in English education. Feminists in English studies, I suggest, have not adequately explored relationships between feminist literary studies and feminist rhetoric and composition.

Chapter 1, "Modern/Antimodern/Postmodern: Rewritings," provides a provisional map of modern, antimodern, and postmodern traditions, including feminist traditions, and situates them historically. I briefly discuss modern writers such as Descartes, Locke, Mill, Immanuel Kant, Karl Marx, and Friedrich Engels, Ferdinand de Saussure, William James, and Sigmund Freud and modern feminist writers such as Wollstonecraft, Mill, Gilman, and Beauvoir. I also associate antimodernism with the early-nineteenth-century Romantic movement and with writers such as William Wordsworth and Samuel Taylor Coleridge as well as with the present-day intersubjectivism of writers such as Stanley Fish and with radical and cultural feminisms. Finally, I discuss postmodern and postmodern feminist writers Bakhtin, Derrida, Lyotard, Foucault, Kristeva, Haraway, Butler, and others as inheritors as well as critics of the Enlightenment. Chapter 2, "Reading Global Feminisms," demonstrates that the names I have selected are useful within the context of an important issue within feminist studies, how to develop feminist perspectives in cultures that have suffered the consequences of Western colonialism and imperialism.

In chapter 3, "Woolf's (Anti)Modern Reading," I suggest, by examining Woolf's observations about the activity of reading in her essays and by examining her reading notes, that her perspective is a complex combination of the modern and antimodern. Influenced by modernist formalism, Woolf nevertheless develops accounts of reading that emphasize women's separate literary tradition and women's different writing and reading styles. Chapter 4, "Rich and Walker on Writing and Mothering: Radical/Cultural Feminist and Womanist Perspectives," provides a description of the radical and cultural feminist perspectives of Adrienne Rich and the womanist perspective of Alice Walker, focusing especially on their struggles to reconcile within modern patriarchal culture the activities of writing (an activity traditionally reserved for men) and mothering (an activity traditionally associated with women).

In chapter 5, "Pragmatic Reading and Beyond: Rosenblatt and Feminism," I demonstrate the usefulness of the reconfigurations I describe in analyzing the work of literacy theorist Louise Rosenblatt. I suggest that her work, though modern in many ways and not usually directly concerned with feminist issues, resists modernism through attention to the aesthetic components of reading and through an insistence that reading has an important emotional dimension. Her work is useful, therefore, in the development of cultural feminist and postmodern feminist perspectives on reading and writing. Most importantly, in her conception of transactional reading, she moves toward a postmodern nonfoundational approach to reading. Chapter 6, "Toward Postmodern-Feminist Rhetoric and Composition," suggests that as the field of rhetoric and composition has struggled for legitimacy within the academy, it has sometimes embraced modernist scientism and positivism, but it has become increasingly critical of these tendencies as it has matured, thus enabling the development of a postmodern feminist perspective. An important step along the way has been the emergence of transactional or interactional approaches to reading and writing influenced by theorists such as Rosenblatt. I describe postmodern feminist strategies that make productive use of student resistance in chapter 7, "Employing Resistance in Postmodern-Feminist Teaching." I also suggest that feminist rhetoricians and compositionists can have an impact on the academy through the creation of pedagogies of resistance and conceptions of modernism and postmodernism that enable interdisciplinary connections.

Postmodern feminism has been represented as the binary opposite of modernism and as relativist and subjectivist. I ask, however, how our understanding of the movement changes if it is distinguished from antimodern feminism. Exploring how antimodern and postmodern traditions move beyond modern ones necessitates finding alternatives to those definitions of postmodernism that are pervasive within and beyond the academy and to those definitions of modernism that arise out of literary studies. Associating postmodern feminism with a critique of the Enlightenment enables new historical accounts of and perspectives on the activities of reading, writing, and teaching.

PART ONE: *Reconfigurations*

1

Modern/Antimodern/Postmodern:
Rewritings

A cultural domain has no inner territory. It is located entirely upon boundaries, boundaries intersect it everywhere, passing through each of its constituent features.
>   —M. M. Bakhtin, "Content, Material, and Form in Verbal Art"

To live in the Borderlands means to
>   put *chile* in the borscht,
>   eat whole wheat *tortillas,*
>   speak Tex-Mex with a Brooklyn accent;
>   be stopped by *la migra* at the border checkpoints;
>   —Gloria Anzaldúa, *Borderlands/La Frontera: The New Mestiza*

Deconstruction was very harmful in this respect because it was misunderstood. One does not deconstruct before having constructed. Those who are
not capable of a certain classicism should return to Cartesian ideas, to max-
ims like "Ce que l'on conçoit bien s'énonce clairement" ("What is clearly
conceived is clearly expressed")—and afterward produce an effect of flux, of
orchestration, and of polyphony. But as enrichment, not as confusion.
>   —Julia Kristeva, "Cultural Strangeness and the Subject in Crisis"

*T*he following descriptions make clearer some ways in which antimodern and
postmodern traditions move beyond modern ones. These descriptions are meant
to be suggestive and metonymic rather than definitive and exhaustive. I have
chosen strong examples, though other selections could have been made as well,
and certainly the examples I provide need fuller development in subsequent studies. In describing modernism, for instance, I have included discussions of both
rational and empirical traditions and of important contributors to these traditions, though these discussions are brief. Defining modernism as it is usually understood outside English studies enables scholars within English studies to participate in interdisciplinary exchange.

Modernisms

Here I sketch out some of the parameters of Enlightenment modernism in its
late-seventeenth-century and eighteenth-century, nineteenth-century, and twen-

tieth-century manifestations in areas such as philosophy, the social sciences, literature, rhetoric, and feminist studies. The individuals I have selected to discuss—including René Descartes, John Locke, Immanuel Kant, Mary Wollstonecraft, John Stuart Mill, Karl Marx and Friedrich Engels, William James, Ferdinand de Saussure, Sigmund Freud, and Simone de Beauvoir—have diverse interests and concerns but are nevertheless optimistic about the ways in which reason, empiricism, or democracy can solve intellectual, social, or political problems. Two traditions that are sometimes distinct—rational and empirical—emerge. Although modern or liberal feminism is often criticized for its association with humanism and for emphasizing outmoded conceptions of the self and of identity, I suggest here that it is related in important ways to other forms of feminism such as Marxist feminism. Enlightenment-modern feminists see women as oppressed because they have been restricted to the domestic realm and have not been granted the same opportunities or rights as men. Modern feminism is universalist, insisting that men and women have the same innate capacities but that women have been deprived of a right to develop those capacities because of prejudicial laws and policies.

Emphasizing that humans can arrive at truth through rational processes necessitates, for Descartes, a distinction between perception and thought. He sees that whereas perception is always in danger of being flawed and unclear, thought can achieve clarity and coherence. Errors arise, according to Descartes, from the will rather than the understanding, though the understanding can constrain the will (*Discourse* 143). In *Discourse on Method,* Descartes asserts that reason is found "whole and entire" in each man because individuals of the same species have the same natures (37). He also asserts that individuals are persuaded by evidence that the reason accepts (66). Here he affirms that the truth "I think, therefore I am" is the first principle of philosophy (61). He concludes that he is resolved to spend the rest of his life acquiring a knowledge of nature that will enable him to establish rules of medicine (97). For Descartes, thought, as distinct from perception, leads to truth. Rationality also depends on a conception of the mind as distinct from the body, which becomes an impediment to rational thought.

John Locke's approach is empirical rather than rational. He privileges perception rather than understanding because, for him, the mind functions as a perceiver of external reality. Locke begins *An Essay Concerning Human Understanding* by establishing that knowledge is not innate. One of the arguments he uses to make this point is that ideas are not known to children; hence, individuals are not born with truths. Rather, knowledge is imprinted on the mind through perception (96). For Locke, all ideas come from sensation or reflection, hence from experience (121), but language gives us imperfect descriptions of things (290). Despite the imperfections of language, however, it is necessary in communicating to another person as easily and quickly as possible, thereby conveying knowledge of things (298). In order to attempt to counter the imperfections of language and hence to convey "dry truth and real knowledge," speakers should avoid figurative language (299). His *Of Civil Government* explains how empiricism plays itself out in the realm of government and demonstrates that Enlightenment empiricism was not limited to the natural sciences. Locke's perspective partakes of Enlightenment optimism in that he affirms that in a state of nature, humans are in a state of perfect freedom and equality (4), and the laws of municipalities and countries are right in that they are founded on the laws of nature (11). Government exists, according to Locke, in order to restrain violence (11), but the purpose of laws is not to abolish or restrain but to preserve freedom (44). Locke concludes *Of Civil Government* by affirming that in joining society, individuals give over their power to the community (205) and that conflicts between the prince and the people should be adjudicated by the body of people (204).

Kant's *Critique of Pure Reason* (1787) attempts to rescue Cartesian reason from empiricists who would minimize its importance. He explores "pure" reason or reason that is distinct from experience (12) and speaks of *a priori* knowledge as pure "when there is no admixture of anything empirical" (43). He also speaks of keeping pure reason free from errors (59) and reserves the study of rationality for metaphysics, which he calls the "science of reason" (21). Kant distinguishes between reason and feelings, elevating reason and denigrating feelings by associating them with empirical sources of knowledge (61). Like Descartes, he distinguishes between mind and body, speaking of his existence as a thinking being as distinct from "other things outside me—among them my body" (370). For Kant, reason can be tempted to abandon itself to skeptical despair or dogmatically commit itself to certain assertions, refusing to grant a fair hearing to the arguments for the counterposition (385). Either attitude is the "death of sound philosophy" (385). Human reason is by nature architectonic, belonging to a possible system (429).[1]

Mary Wollstonecraft's *A Vindication of the Rights of Woman* is a classic example of Enlightenment feminism, placing emphasis on the value of providing women an education aimed at developing rational faculties. Wollstonecraft holds Enlightenment beliefs in progress and argues that women should be given the same education as men. She begins the treatise by affirming that an individual's nature and happiness are dependent on reason, virtue, and knowledge, which are also the basis for the laws that bind society (39). Women, though, have been deprived of an opportunity to acquire human virtues because of their subordination to men. They must therefore "be permitted to turn to the fountain of light, and not forced to shape their course by the twinkling of a mere satellite" (50). According to Wollstonecraft, women must receive the same education as men, and this education must take place within society rather than the home, because "Men and women must be educated, in a great degree, by the opinions and manners of the society they live in" (52). The aims of an education should be to "enable the individual to attain such habits of virtue as will render it independent" (52). Wollstonecraft sees that women are not inherently inferior to men; rather, women have been subjugated, deprived of an opportunity to develop their abilities (73).

Nineteenth-century manifestations of modernism reflect the influence of the early-nineteenth-century Romantic Movement and illustrate a concern for the development of the human sciences in addition to the natural sciences. Mill works in the empirical tradition of Locke, though Mill's perspective differs in a number of ways from that of Locke, and he looked to Romanticism for answers to personal crises. Abandoning Locke's concept of the state of nature, he focuses on the importance of individual liberty. He speaks in *On Liberty* of human reason as allowing the world to challenge our beliefs and allowing better truths to replace the beliefs we hold (28). He places considerably more emphasis than does Locke, however, on the potential for the tyranny of rulers. In *On Liberty* he speaks of the danger not only of the tyranny of the magistrate but also of the tyranny of prevailing opinion and feeling and of the tendency of society to impose its own ideas and practices on those who dissent from them (7). He says that individuals are not accountable to society for their actions in matters that concern only them, though they are accountable if their actions affect others (120). He also emphasizes that wives should have the same rights as their husbands (133). Freedom of speech is important to Mill because he recognizes that truth is always partial and incomplete (61). Progress consists only in the new fragment of truth being "more adapted to the needs of the time, than that which it displaces" (61). Rational assurance of being right arises out of a climate in which there is liberty to contradict and disprove opinions (26). In *On Liberty* he calls for the "greatest dissemination of power consistent with efficiency; but the greatest possible centralization of information, and diffusion of it from the centre" (145). Mill nevertheless sees that mechanical inventions have the potential to "effect great changes in human destiny" (328).[2]

In "The Subjection of Women," he argues for equality between men and women, seeing that the legal subordination of one sex to the other is a hindrance to human improvement and should be replaced by "a principle of perfect equality" (196).[3] Women are not forced slaves but willing ones, with the result that their minds have become enslaved (202). Mill insists that human society will only progress if the system of unequal rights is eliminated (202–3). Mill also suggests that the differences between men and women is "an eminently artificial thing" (203). If women were allowed to develop their capabilities, they would no doubt be able to achieve what men have achieved. Women should have the right to vote, Mill insists (217), and to govern (219). Restraints on the freedom of human fellow creatures reduces that which makes us human (238).

If Mill exemplifies liberal approaches to social, political, and economic problems, Marx exemplifies radical ones. Marx's approach is nevertheless modernist and empiricist in his faith in science, in his representation of the relationship between historical circumstances and consciousness, and in his belief that history is progressing in a positive direction.[4] In his preface to the first German edition of *Capital,* Marx shows that he conceives of his investigation as a science. He speaks, for instance, of his analysis of economic forms as minutiae and compares them to the minutiae that anatomists see under a microscope (192). He also compares his work to that of a physicist who observes physical phenomena where they occur in their most typical form and where they are free of disturbing influence. Marx, too, will examine economic phenomena in their "classic ground," England (192). Later in the book *Capital,* he speaks of a scientific analysis of competition necessitating an understanding of the "inner nature of capital" and compares such analysis to attempting to understand the apparent motions of the heavenly bodies without knowledge of their real motions, motions that are not directly perceptible by the senses (268). In *The German Ideology,* Marx and Engels speak of empirical observation bringing out "without any mystification and speculation" the connection of the social and political structure and production (118). "Where speculation ends—in real life—there real, positive science begins" (119), and this belief in empiricism is directly tied to Marx and Engels's belief in materialism. In *The German Ideology* they make clear their belief that material reality leads to changes in consciousness: "Life is not determined by consciousness, but consciousness by life" (119). They distinguish their position from that of German idealist philosophy that "descends from heaven," whereas Marx and Engels ascend "from earth to heaven" (118). Their inquiry, then, begins with a study of men in "their actual, empirically perceptible process of development under definite conditions" (119). They clearly see themselves as scientists.

Liberation from oppressive circumstances, too, is tied to empiricism, materialism, and technological advancement. Marx and Engels say in *The German Ideology,* "It is only possible to achieve real liberation in the real world and by employing real means, that slavery cannot be abolished without the steam-engine and the mule and spinning-jenny, serfdom cannot be abolished without improved agriculture" (133). For Marx and Engels, liberation is historical rather than mental and is brought about by historical conditions (133), especially the exploitation of the proletariat. They also are concerned, though, about the exploitation of women in society, speaking in *The German Ideology* of the bourgeois seeing his wife as a mere instrument of production (350). Marx and Engels are optimistic, however, that the proletariat will coalesce as a class and overthrow its oppressors. In *The German Ideology* they see the communist revolution as overthrowing the ruling class and creating a new society (157). They affirm in *The German Ideology* that in order for the proletarians to assert themselves as individuals, they must overthrow the state (164).

In the nineteenth century, modern feminism continued to be universalistic, to emphasize equal rights between men and women (now referred to as universal suffrage), to fight discrimination against women despite abilities that are the same as those of men, and to champion the importance of education for women.[5] Later-nineteenth-century manifestations of liberal feminism often reflect the influences of Marx and of Charles Darwin. Charlotte Perkins Gilman's *Women and Economics* is a good example. Gilman's indebtedness to Marx and Darwin is evident in her emphasis on women's economic dependency. Gilman's perspective is also liberal or modern feminist in its attention to the potential symmetry between the sexes despite women's thwarted development. According to Gilman, although they have the ability to be equal to men, women have been deprived of opportunities afforded men to develop their capacities and become independent (5). This situation of dependency results in stifled development so that women become incapable of working outside the home and achieving economic independence. Gilman explains that women's incapacities are not a result of "inherent disability" but of the situation in which they find themselves (9). She also insists, "Women work longer and harder than most men, and not solely in maternal duties" (20), but, unfortunately, her hard work does not improve her economic status (21).

Twentieth-century modernism extends even further the contexts within which empiricism and rationality become pertinent through the development of disciplines outside the natural sciences in areas such as linguistics, psychology, and pragmatic philosophy. The modernism and empiricism of Ferdinand de Saussure are evident in his commitment to creating a science of linguistics. In the introduction to his *Course in General Linguistics,* a reconstruction of notes delivered in lectures from 1906–1911, Saussure demonstrates that he considers linguistics to be a science. He traces its development from the study of grammar, which was unscientific, to the study of philology, which was a scientific movement that originated at the end of the eighteenth century (1). Saussure sees the scope of the science of linguistics as describing and tracing the history of all observable language, determining the forces that are permanently and universally at work in all languages, deducing the general laws to which all specific phenomena can be reduced, and delimiting and defining itself (6). In determining what the science of linguistics is, Saussure has to determine how it differs from other sciences such as sociology or the physiology of sounds. In order to advance the study of linguistics to that of a science, Saussure had to provide a foundational principle. His solution is to place language *(langue)* at the center of his system and to distinguish it from speech *(parole).* Saussure says that speech is many sided and belongs both to the individual and to society, whereas language is a self-contained whole (9). Because it is distinct from speech, language can be studied separately (15). Saussure works hard to maintain rigid distinctions between the two domains, though he is unsuccessful at a number of points, resulting in contradictions that he is ultimately unsuccessful in resolving.

William James, like Saussure, sees himself working within an empiricist tradition, as evident in *Pragmatism* (1907). In emphasizing his commitments to empiricism, he rejects the rationalist philosophical tradition, seeing it as always monistic, starting from wholes and universals and emphasizing the unity of things whereas empiricism starts from the parts and "makes the whole a collection." It is pluralistic (21). He calls rationalists tender minded and empiricists tough minded (22). Pragmatism avoids static conceptions of truth and is concerned instead with how truth is realized and what difference an idea's being true makes in actual life (133). Truth is made, he emphasizes, in the course of experience (143). It is therefore always changing; it is mutable (146–47) and conditional (150). Distinguishing between rationalism and empiricism, James says, "for rationalism reality is ready-made and complete from all eternity, while for pragmatism it is still in the making, and awaits part of its complexion from the future" (167).

Although I am representing Freud as a modernist and hence aligning him with Saussure and James, he is sometimes associated with Romanticism (Kristeva, *Strangers* 181). Such an association is understandable given Freud's emphasis on irrationality, the unconscious, dreams, and sexuality. Freud's focus on the subjective aspects of experience directly challenged optimistic beliefs in the ability of rationality to solve problems in a variety of spheres. Psychoanalysis no doubt contributed in significant ways to the emergence of postmodernism because it eroded modernist optimism. Freud, however, quite clearly considered himself to be a scientist and is optimistic about the ability of science to solve problems. This becomes evident in his essay "On the History of the Psycho-Analytic Movement." In the essay, he speaks positively, for instance, of a "cool and scientifically objective spirit" and sees his work as a contribution to the history of science (24). He sees psychoanalysis as not being restricted to the medical field alone but as capable of being applied to a variety of other "mental sciences" (26). He also speaks of the relationship between psychiatry and other sciences dealing with activities of the mind (36) and makes connections between "medical psycho-analysis and other fields of science" (38). He compares the upheavals and dissensions in psychoanalysis with those that occur in "other scientific movements" (49). Although Freud focuses primarily on psychic disorders and unconscious processes, he does so in a systematic way, making use, primarily, of scientific observation. He distinguishes in "On Narcissism: An Introduction," for instance, between speculative theory and "a science erected on empirical interpretation," clearly preferring the latter. Speculative theory may be based on a "logically unassailable foundation," but science is based on "observation alone" (77). He also compares the development of knowledge in psychoanalysis to the development of knowledge in physics, both of which are based on "basic notions" that are debatable (77). His aim is to systematize, to confirm, or to alter hypotheses on the basis of careful observation. Freud quite clearly considers himself to be a scientist and an empiricist. His perspective is decidedly modern.

Twentieth-century modernism can also encompass philosophies such as existentialism, as Beauvoir's *The Second Sex* demonstrates. Beauvoir makes use of the existentialist emphasis on otherness, arguing that throughout time, women have been defined as other, as inferior to men. For Beauvoir, woman represents "only the negative, defined by limiting criteria, without reciprocity" (xv). Her perspective is rooted in existentialist ethics, which casts liberty in terms of exploits or projects that lead to transcendence, to a "continual reaching out toward other liberties" (xxviii). Women, though, are not free to choose their projects but are condemned to immanence or stagnation (xxvii). Beauvoir had also been influenced by Marx and focuses attention on women's economic oppression and on the denial of opportunities to participate in activities that would make her more fully human. According to Beauvoir, women's oppression is different from the oppression of other groups because, unlike the proletariat, women have no solidarity of work (xix). They "have no past, no history, no religion of their own" (xix). Like Gilman, Beauvoir focuses on women's dependency upon men, calling them man's dependent "if not his slave" (xx). Beauvoir also sees similarities between the situation of women and the situation of blacks in that both have suffered from the paternalism of their masters (xxiii); she emphasizes that she is interested not in women's happiness but in their liberty (xxix). Beauvoir has also clearly been influenced by psychoanalysis, and much of her analysis of the unfortunate situations of women in traditional roles draws heavily on the work of Freud.[6]

Later-twentieth-century manifestations of liberal feminism are Betty Friedan's *The Feminine Mystique,* Eleanor Emmons Maccoby and Carol Nagy Jacklin's *The Psychology of Sex Differences,* the guiding principles of the National Organization of Women, Cynthia Fuchs Epstein's *Deceptive Distinctions,* Drucilla Cornell's *At the Heart of Freedom,* Susan Hartmann's *The Other Feminists: Activists in the Liberal Establishment,* Martha Nussbaum's *Sex and Social Justice,* and Seyla Benhabib's "Sexual Difference and Collective Identities: The New Global Constellation." Friedan explores the oppressive situation of middle-class, suburban housewives who have been denied opportunities to fulfill themselves through meaningful work outside the home. Maccoby and Jacklin aim to demonstrate that the differences between men and women are minimal. The National Organization of Women focuses especially on creating equality between women and men. In *Deceptive Distinctions,* Epstein takes issue with recent work in sociology and psychology arising out of the cultural feminist tradition that emphasizes the differences between women and men; she argues, instead, that we should be emphasizing that women and men have similar abilities and should therefore be afforded an equal place in the world of work. In *At the Heart of Freedom,* Cornell, drawing on the work of Kant and John Rawls, provides a feminist reinterpretation of liberal feminist commitments to equality and rights. Hartmann in *The Other Feminists* documents the considerable achievements of liberal feminists in improving the situation of workers, in litigating feminist principles, and in establishing feminism's moral authority. Feminist philosophers Martha Nussbaum and Seyla Benhabib take a modernist stance in defending universalism and coherence in the face of postmodern emphases on local contexts and decentered selves.

In feminist literary studies, modern feminism was especially pronounced in the early 1970s at the beginnings of the contemporary feminist movement and has taken the form of examinations of images of women in literature. According to the images-of-women approach, reading necessitates a repudiation of stereotypical and therefore oppressive representations of what it means to be a woman or a man and a celebration of portrayals of women that demonstrate that women and men are equal. A number of essays in Susan Koppelman Cornillon's *Images of Women in Fiction,* for instance, address the stereotypical treatment of women in literature from a variety of historical periods. Perspectives taken in the book are diverse, and topics covered are numerous including Lillian S. Robinson and Lise Vogel's Marxist one.[7] The predominant mode, though, is liberal feminist.

Within feminist rhetoric and composition, work expressing a liberal feminist perspective focuses on eliminating sexist language and sexist practices in composition classrooms and on examining the status of teachers of composition as a feminized, marginalized group. In the early 1970s, there was a strong commitment on the part of leaders within the National Council of Teachers of English and the Conference on College Composition and Communication to eliminate sexist language, and this commitment was an essentially modern-feminist impulse. The goal of eliminating sexist language and promoting gender neutral language was related to eliminating barriers to the achievement of equal rights for women. The first anthology to provide a discussion of composition from a feminist perspective had a modern-feminist emphasis. Cynthia L. Caywood and Gillian R. Overing's *Teaching Writing: Pedagogy, Gender, and Equity* includes essays that focus on teachers of composition as marginalized and discriminated against within the academy[8] (Bechtel), women students as discriminated against in composition classes (Barnes), and bias in writing classes such as inequality in classroom interaction, sex segregation, and differences in feedback male and female students receive from teachers (Sadker and Sadker). Theresa Enos's *Gender Roles and Faculty Lives in Rhetoric and Composition* focuses on equity issues for faculty in rhetoric and composition, including discrimination and sexual harassment and provides considerable and graphic evidence that many women in rhetoric and composition have been treated unfairly by male colleagues and male-centered departments and universities.

Modernism is obviously valuable in attempting to formulate generalizations and make predictions about phenomena or human behavior. In attempting to determine what is universal, it seeks out commonalities and unities. The contributions of the various scientific and technical fields to all of our institutions are everywhere evident. In addition, our legal system is based on conceptions of rationality that derive from modernist methods and procedures. Antimodernists and postmodernists alike have pointed out, however, that rationalism and objectivist empiricism are limited when they place too much faith in objectivity and quantification and become positivistic, ignoring the reality that observation is necessarily interpretive. For positivists, the variables in scientific experiments are accurate descriptions of reality rather than constructs. In focusing on what can be tested empirically, they also ignore large areas of experience. Literary modernism has also come under attack recently for its elitism and political conservatism.[9] Modernism is often associated with disciplinarity, universalism, political repression, sexism, imperialism, racism, and colonialism.[10]

Modern feminism has been the inspiration for the struggle for equality for women in a number of historical eras and geographical locations. The contributions of the various scientific and technical fields to the improvement of the situation of women are everywhere evident. As a result of technological developments, large numbers of women have been able to make choices about pregnancy and childbearing as well as birth control and abortion. In addition, women have definitely benefited from modernist legal procedures and principles including laws that prohibit rape and violence against women and sanctions against sexist language, discrimination, and unequal pay. Radical, cultural, and postmodern feminists alike have pointed out, however, that struggling for equality and inclusion is not always sufficient for improving the situation of women; deeper structural changes are often necessary. A modern-feminist perspective does not adequately account for differences between men and women. Nor does it always allow for women's different history and different societal roles and for the effects these differences may have had in the shaping of consciousness. It also tends to ignore differences within the category *woman* that result from different racial, class, and sexual positionings. It can, therefore, contribute to rather than mitigate the oppression of women of color in colonizing and colonized countries. Too often it does not question the oppressive nature of patriarchal structures of power. The goal becomes the elimination of discriminatory practices rather than the transformation of society.

Antimodernisms

Antimodernism tends to be relativist and subjectivist and to directly oppose modernist values and procedures. If modernists privilege rationality, antimodernists explore irrationality. If modernists privilege empiricism, antimodernists focus on the ways in which empiricism distorts reality and ignores large areas of human experience. M. H. Abrams in *The Mirror and the Lamp,* in attempting to identify distinguishing characteristics of Romantic critical theory, identifies expressive theory as seeing the work of art as essentially the internal made external, the attributes and actions of the poet's own mind (22). In expressive theories, according to Abrams, the poet becomes the hero, the chosen one who is a force of nature and serves as a measure of the reader's piety and taste (26).

Early-nineteenth-century Romantic writers such as William Wordsworth and Samuel Taylor Coleridge responded to Enlightenment rationalism and empiricism by criticizing the mechanistic nature of scientific approaches to reality and emphasizing the importance of feelings, pleasure, the imagination, solitude, poetry, and nature. In the "Preface" to *Lyrical Ballads,* Wordsworth contrasts the poet with the man of science. The poet writes with the "necessity of giving immediate pleasure to a human Being" (257). In contrast, numerous obstacles stand between truth and the lawyer, physician, mariner, astronomer, and natural philosopher (257). The poet connects us with our fellow beings whereas the man of science "seeks truth as a remote and unknown benefactor" and "cherishes and loves it in his solitude" (259). Wordsworth thinks it is possible that the work of the men of science will create a material revolution in the condition of their fellow beings and will become "flesh and blood," but clearly they had not yet done so, and it is possible that they would never do so (259–60). In *The Prelude,* Wordsworth repeatedly returns to nature for restoration after he had spent periods of time at Cambridge or in cities in England or France. In book 9, for instance, he describes his attempt, during a period of depression, to find solace in "abstract science" (419). Luckily, though, his sister Dorothy provided him a "saving intercourse" and restored him to his "true self," reminded him of his calling as a poet, and encouraged him to seek his "office upon earth" beneath that name and nowhere else (419–20). He also speaks in *The Prelude* of the historian's pen delighting in "power and energy detached / From moral purpose" whereas he has learned to "look with feelings of fraternal love / Upon unassuming things that hold / A silent station in this beauteous world" (457).

Coleridge discusses more extensively than does Wordsworth the work of individual philosophers such as Descartes and Locke, providing a more complex analysis of the relationship between nature, poetry, the imagination, and Enlightenment thought. Coleridge tells us in *Biographia Literaria* that he was so taken by the associationist psychology of David Hartley, which derived from the work of Locke, that he named his son after him (121). He also tells us in *Biographia Literaria,* however, that he came to repudiate Hartley's position as "mechanical" (74). Coleridge is also critical of Descartes's dualism. He finds that Descartes was the first philosopher to introduce the idea that the mind and the body are heterogeneous, the mind being associated with intelligence, the body with matter (88). Descartes, in turn, influenced Baruch Spinoza who influenced Gottfried Wilhelm Leibniz. For Coleridge, though, dissociating the mind from the body is "absurd" (89). Coleridge is dissatisfied with the philosophies of Locke, Hartley, and others because he finds that the human mind is capable of activities other than merely observing, collecting, and classifying (93). Coleridge found that his own perspective coincided, instead, with German idealist philosophers such as Johann Gottlieb Fichte (101) and Friedrich Schelling (102). Coleridge in *Biographia Literaria* speaks of the "restorative atmosphere" created by the "undisturbing voices" of a wife or sister (154) and feels that a woman's place is in the home (157).

Recent manifestations of antimodernism sometimes take the form of intersubjectivism, which can become an extension of expressivism. Sometimes called communitarianism, it emphasizes that language users are members of discourse communities that determine what their opinions, attitudes, and interpretations will be. Like expressivism, communitarianism directly challenges modernism, suggesting that scientific work is neither objective nor neutral but, rather, communal and collective and that scientists reflect the interpretive frameworks of the communities to which they belong. Communitarian work in rhetoric and composition, like expressivist work, challenges the positivism of current-traditional rhetoric or objectivist, empirical research. Writers are not single individuals who transmit information in a simple and direct way but, rather, belong to relatively stable discourse communities that determine what interpretive strategies they will employ as they read and write. Because academic writing amounts to writing in academic disciplines, the task of the writing instructor becomes one of initiating students into the conventions of the various discourses they will encounter as they progress through the university and beyond. Learning is seen as a collaborative and intersubjective process, and students are encouraged to participate in group work, to receive feedback on their work from peers, and to learn the conventions of the discourse communities they will have to write within.

Thomas Kuhn's *The Structures of Scientific Revolutions,* though not itself antimodern, is often invoked by communitarians to support intersubjectivist claims. Kuhn contends that paradigms, which are discrete and in fundamental disagreement with each other (15), compete with one another and succeed one another through scientific revolutions and evolutions. Communitarians, however, place considerably more emphasis than does Kuhn on paradigms as entirely discrete structures. If it is not clear, however, how legitimate claims can be distinguished from illegitimate ones, intersubjectivist work becomes little better than subjectivist work in the difficult process of attempting to determine which truth claims have more legitimacy than others.

The connection between subjectivism and intersubjectivism is obvious in the work of Stanley Fish, who began his career as a subjectivist but later became an intersubjectivist. Fish's *Self-Consuming Artifacts* is subjectivist in its emphasis on the individual reader's subjective processes, though his *Is There a Text in This Class?* is intersubjectivist in its emphasis on the importance of interpretive communities in the interpretive process. He develops this perspective in the antiformalist and antifoundationalist *Doing What Comes Naturally:* "Meanings that seem perspicuous and literal are rendered so by forceful interpretive acts and not by the properties of language" (9). Fish exhibits relativist tendencies in directly challenging and inverting modernist assumptions about language and knowledge, though he denies that his work is relativist, claiming that interpretive communities authorize knowledge. It is not clear, however, how judgments can be made when the claims of different interpretive communities conflict. As Ronald Dworkin observes in "My Reply to Stanley Fish," "If Fish has not made interpretation wholly subjective, the difference is not noticeable to the naked eye" (295). Kenneth Bruffee, also an intersubjectivist, speaks of nonfoundational knowledge, of collaboration, and of learning as a communal process. He says in *Collaborative Learning,* "College and university education should help students negotiate their membership in the knowledge communities they come from while it helps them reacculturate themselves into the academic communities they have chosen to join" (191). Like Fish, Bruffee emphasizes that language communities are discrete groups with separate identities and conventions, and like him, he has difficulty moving beyond relativism.

Feminist antimodern perspectives tend to be radical or cultural feminist in orientation. A familiar slogan associated with radical feminism is "the personal is political," a phrase that arose out of the women's liberation movement outside the academy in the United States in the 1970s. Although the phrase establishes a connection between personal life and political life, the emphasis it places on the personal belies a radical feminist concern with personal oppression and personal solutions to problems. From a radical feminist perspective, women and men constitute distinct classes: a dominant masculine or patriarchal order that controls public life and a subordinate feminine order relegated to the private sphere. Some radical feminists provide revisionary historical accounts that claim that an egalitarian matriarchal era preceded the present patriarchal one. They also sometimes envision an androgynous future in which the differences between men and women will be maintained but a balance will be achieved resulting in cooperation rather than competition. Too often there is little emphasis within radical feminism, though, on differences within the category *woman,* and generalizations about women as a whole are often based on the experiences of white, middle-class women.

Mary Daly's work tends to be radical feminist in emphasis. *Gyn/Ecology,* for instance, is a radical feminist exploration of the ways in which all-pervasive androcentric thinking and patriarchal thinking are damaging to women; it is also a call for a program for healing and renewal. Daly focuses especially on spirituality and on religious ritual. She suggests, though, that the "dis-ease" she speaks of cannot be escaped. The journey she charts involves both discovery and creation of a world other than patriarchy. Daly invites her readers to join with her in an otherworld journey that involves exorcism of the internalized godfather in his various manifestations (1). Daly's journey is a spiritual one that necessitates breaking through a maze/haze of deception into free space, what Daly calls an "a-mazing" process (2). The feminist hero/reader who undertakes Daly's journey moves through the stages of demystifying patriarchal myth, encountering misogynistic institutions and structures such as genital mutilation and witch burning, and finally spinning new space and time through processes of escaping, female bonding, and moving through and beyond the realm of multiply split consciousness (386). Daly's book is antimodern in that it identifies modernist institutions and methods with patriarchy and repudiates them. She uses Romantic language such as the "Self's own integrity" (387) or "inner reality" that invaders yearn to destroy but cannot even find (386).

Radical feminist Dale Spender argues in *Man Made Language* that language has been made by men and supports a male-dominated social structure. A semantic rule that results from male domination is "male-as-norm . . . Hence our fundamental classification scheme is one which divides humanity not into two equal parts . . . but into those who are plus male and those who are minus male" (3). Spender speaks of sexism in language and of the semantic derogation of women. She argues, too, that "a masculinist bias has been implanted in the very methods of inquiry" (60). Women, if they speak at all, must speak the language of the group that has oppressed them, language that is inflected in such a way that words such as *spinster* are pejorative whereas its counterpart, *bachelor,* is not. Spender argues, further, that women have been silenced but should be encouraged to write, to read, to speak, and to enter into linguistic exchange. Language itself must be transformed so that it no longer reflects the domination of men.

Although radical feminists emphasize differences in the situations of men and women, seeing men as victimizers and women as victims, those differences are not necessarily biological but may result from environmental conditioning. Gender roles are often seen not as innate characteristics but as learned through socialization into institutions that are harmful to women. Those roles have considerable tenacity, though, and are relatively unchanging over time and space. Constructing gender roles as binary opposites as radical feminists tend to do can have powerful therapeutic and transformative effects. Consciousness raising whereby women get together and share their experiences with others arises out of radical feminism. Such talk becomes a way of dealing with the frustrations that result from being a member of an oppressed group and of gaining a feeling of empowerment in the face of feelings of powerlessness.

Radical feminists are antimodern in that they tend to reject traditional intellectual and social traditions and institutions. Often they reject science, technology, and the perspectives of male intellectuals such as Marx and Freud. Freud's work is often singled out as supporting the domination of men over women, as supporting traditional roles for women, and as presenting women very unfavorably.[11] The family is often represented as reinforcing male domination and female inferiority. Radical feminists also often see technology as enslaving rather than liberating women.[12]

Whereas radical feminism emphasizes the problems that have resulted from male domination, cultural feminism emphasizes the positive characteristics of women's culture such as cooperation and an ability to collaborate effectively. Male culture is identified as the problem and female culture as the solution. The attempt within literary studies to identify a female literary tradition by scholars such as Elaine Showalter, Susan Gubar, Sandra Gilbert, and others also arises out of a cultural feminist impulse.[13] Numerous books and articles have argued that women are influenced by other women writers, that the influence is nurturing rather than anxious, and that the literary traditions that women writers constitute are distinctly different from that of men. As I observe in chapter 3, scholars such as Bonnie Kime Scott have argued that examining the work of female modernists results in new conceptions of the modernist movement as a whole. Cultural feminist thought has also influenced the work of scientists such as Evelyn Fox Keller whose book *A Feeling for the Organism* (1983) argues that women such as Nobel Prize–winning geneticist Barbara McClintock have a different relationship to their research subject than do male scientists.

Like radical feminists, cultural feminists implicitly privilege subjective experience over objective analysis. Women are seen as intuitive, emotional, and connected to one another, whereas men are seen as abstract, rational, and hierarchical in their thinking. Cultural feminists emphasize that although men often see themselves as having objective perceptions, in fact they are highly subjective, a result of their gender conditioning that blinds them to other perspectives. They also emphasize that women and men constitute two distinctly different cultures and hence have different interpretive processes and ways of developing and behaving.

For cultural feminists, fighting for equality within such a social order, which is the liberal feminist solution, is unacceptable. The exclusion of women from dominant man-made institutions has resulted in women's different and better ways of perceiving reality and of behaving. Like radical feminists, cultural feminists tend to see these differences as relatively enduring; hence gender identity becomes a fairly stable concept. Usually cultural feminists speak of centuries of acculturation that have resulted in strongly demarcated roles and differential status. Gender differences may have originally been historically constructed, but the result has been the development of a gendered consciousness that resists change. Men and women have had different roles and so have different attitudes, ways of learning, and ways of interacting with others. Women's experience is seen as different from men's and as preferable to it. Mothering is valued highly and held up as an alternative to masculine activities such as warfare. Sara Ruddick in *Maternal Thinking: Toward a Politics of Peace* promotes the activity of maternal thinking as a way of bringing about world peace. Carol Gilligan in *In a Different Voice* values the relationality and connectedness of women's approaches to moral reasoning, and the *Women's Ways of Knowing* collective values connected knowing and cooperative learning (Belenky et al.). Nel Noddings in *Caring* affirms the value of caring within our educational institutions, an activity she sees as closely akin to women's nurturing of children.

A number of articles in rhetoric and composition are also cultural feminist in orientation in that they emphasize that women and men have different ways of writing or arguing and tend to valorize women's ways. Catherine Lamb's "Beyond Argument in Feminist Composition," for instance, demonstrates that cultural feminist theory is helpful in developing a mode of argument that privileges negotiation rather than contention. Andrea Lunsford and Lisa Ede's essay, "Rhetoric in a New Key: Women and Collaboration," makes a connection between cultural feminist theory and collaborative writing. David Bleich's "Genders of Writing" argues for interpersonal, collaborative writing in writing classes, seeing such writing as gendered feminine. Linda H. Peterson, in "Gender and the Autobiographical Essay: Research Perspectives, Pedagogical Practices," asks us to reexamine our pedagogical practices because the genre of autobiography has frequently been associated with women; and my own essay, "Composing as a Woman," suggests that women's ways of writing may be different from those of men. Other examples include Anne R. Gere's *Intimate Practices,* which provides a historical account of the literacy practices of women who belonged to women's clubs in the United States between 1880–1920. Lynn Z. Bloom's *Composition Studies As a Creative Act: Teaching, Writing, Scholarship, Administration* contains essays such as "Teaching College English as a Woman" that are overtly cultural feminist and numerous others that explore cultural feminist themes indirectly. Shirley W. Logan's *With Pen and Voice* (1995) provides a very valuable historical account of the women's contributions of African American women to literacy development.

Cultural feminism is antimodern in that it opposes androcentric traditions and replaces them with gynocentric ones. Men's ways, which have dominated Western culture, are associated with warfare, competitiveness, and aggression whereas women's ways, which have been suppressed in Western culture, are associated with cooperation and collaboration. Cultural feminist solutions include shared parenting and recognition of the value of traditional women's roles such as mothering and caretaking. Cultural feminists call for a transformation of alienating educational and legal institutions by replacing them with woman-centered approaches to the solving of problems.

Antimodernism is valuable in that it directly challenges and inverts modernism thereby helping contain its considerable power and authority. It focuses attention on experience and nature thereby providing alternatives to scientific and rationalistic ways of knowing. It is often limited, however, by its relativism and its inability to generalize beyond the individual or the particular language community. Postmodernist Thomas Kent in *Paralogic Rhetoric* critiques both expressivism and social construction as forms of what he calls "internalism," a belief that a conceptual scheme or internal realm exists anterior to an external realm of objects and events (98). Kurt Spellmeyer in *Common Ground* also critiques weak social construction, what he calls "constructionism," which he sees as providing oversimplified images of knowledge and community (158). According to Spellmeyer, Kenneth Bruffee, in defending social construction, demonstrates a desire for knowledge exempt from contradiction and change (159).

A problem with radical and cultural feminist perspectives is that they tend toward essentialism, toward too rigid a conception of gender identity, one resistant to the influences of history or language. Also, antimodern feminists do not always adequately take into consideration differences within the category *woman* and too often ignore the effects of race and class on gender-identity formation. They tend, too, to place so much emphasis on difference that they ignore similarities between the genders. Difference is essentialized, reified. And in reacting so vehemently against modern institutions and structures, antimodern feminists sometimes overlook the ways in which those structures can be reclaimed to accomplish feminist goals.

Postmodernisms

My suggestion that postmodernism is not modernism's binary opposite and is neither relativist nor subjectivist is supported by a reading of the work of Mikhail

Bakhtin, Jean François Lyotard, Jacques Derrida, Michel Foucault, Julia Kristeva, and other postmodernists and postmodern feminists. Bakhtin is clearly critical of Enlightenment rationalism and of the sciences, speaking in *Problems of Dostoevsky's Poetics* of monologism being promoted by "European rationalism, with its cult of a unified and exclusive reason" (82). He is also critical of the faith that is too often placed in the self-sufficiency of a single consciousness (82) and speaks in "Content, Material, and Form in Verbal Art" of the dangers of superficial imitation of science (258). Bakhtin sometimes speaks appreciatively of Einsteinian science, though, comparing polyphony with an Einsteinian multiplicity of systems of measurement in the conclusion of *Problems of Dostoevsky's Poetics* (272). According to Bakhtin, dialogic relationships are absolutely impossible without logical relationships or relationships oriented toward a referential object, but they are not reducible to them, and they have their own specific character (184). If Bakhtin is critical of modernist projects,[14] he does not revert to antimodernism, and he often expresses his dissatisfaction with Romanticism. In *Problems of Dostoevsky's Poetics,* Bakhtin contrasts the Hegelian dialectic, which arises out of philosophical idealism, with dialogism. He emphasizes that dialogic interrelationships cannot be reduced to thesis, antithesis, and synthesis (26). For Bakhtin, the unified, dialectically evolving spirit, understood in Hegelian terms, gives rise to a philosophical monologue (26). He says, "The soil of monistic idealism is the least likely place for a plurality of unmerged consciousnesses to blossom" (26), and Bakhtin emphasizes that the image of a unified spirit was "deeply alien" to Dostoevsky (27). In *Rabelais and His World* Bakhtin also emphasizes the limitations of a Romantic world view. He contrasts grotesque realism with the Romantic grotesque, associating the former with folk culture and a carnival spirit that is shared by many and the latter with an individual, private carnival and with isolation (37).

In its attempt to find alternatives to modernist approaches to discourse without directly opposing them, the work of Bakhtin bears some resemblance to that of Lyotard. In an interview with Gary A. Olson published in *JAC,* for instance, Lyotard insists that he is not interested in replacing rationality with absurdity but, rather, replacing rationality with another rationality and says he considers himself to be "a completely rational thinker." He also claims that he likes the sciences (408). He does not denounce scientific ways of knowing, university structures, or technological innovation, though he is critical of them. In *The Postmodern Condition,* Lyotard explores relationships between scientific knowledge and power. The important questions are: Who decides what knowledge is, and who knows what needs to be decided (9)? His answer is that in the computer age, "the question of knowledge is now more than ever a question of government" (9). Lyotard sees that knowledge, in particular scientific knowledge, is in a state of crisis because traditional means of legitimation no longer have authority. Increasingly, knowledge becomes the "production of proof" driven by money and power, a process that is self-legitimating (47). "Scientists, technicians, and instruments are purchased not to find truth, but to augment power" (46), though he makes a distinction between power and terror. In *The Postmodern Condition,* force does not take the form of totalitarianism. He is concerned, instead, with agonistic "language games" in which players attempt to make better moves than other players. If players threaten other players and attempt to harm or destroy them, the social bond is broken, and the realm of the game is replaced by the realm of terror (46).

Derrida is similar in that he moves beyond modernism by critiquing rather than completely rejecting it. In an interview with Olson in *JAC,* Derrida explains that his deconstructive method is often misunderstood as calling for the overthrowing of tradition. On the contrary, deconstruction depends on an understanding of traditional norms: "I don't start with disorder; I start with the tradition. If you're not trained in the tradition, then deconstruction means nothing. It's simply nothing" (11). He says that in the dispute between philosophy and rhetoric, contrary to what Habermas and others might think, he is on the side of philosophy, logic, truth, and reference (16). He is also suspicious of the opposition between philosophy and rhetoric, and he tries not to remain within this opposition (559). Although Derrida is highly critical of the logocentrism of traditional science and philosophy, calling in *Of Grammatology* for the end of linear writing, he also explains in *Of Grammatology* that he is not calling for a regression to myth (87). Rather, he is calling for metarationality or metascientificity (87). If the conception of writing he is calling for leaves behind our traditional idea of science, it does not leave science itself behind. Indeed, he entitles one of his chapters "Of Grammatology as a Positive Science." Derrida makes evident that his "undoing" of logocentrism does not have to mean the destruction of science. He will not venture up to the "perilous necessity" of defining grammatological knowledge outside of science (74). Rather, he is working within "the traditional norms of scientificity" (74). His complaint against traditional science, with its commitment to conceptions of objectivity, is that it ignores writing, the reality of the written signifier (88). He speaks of the "incompetence" of science and of the incompetence of philosophy but he does not invoke

> a return to a prescientific or infra-philosophic form of discourse. . . . This unnameable movement of *difference-itself,* that I have strategically nicknamed *trace, reserve,* or *differance,* could be called writing only within the *historical* closure, that is to say within the limits of science and philosophy. (93)

He is calling for the creation of a science or a philosophy of writing within the limits of science and philosophy (93).

Foucault places greater emphasis than does Derrida on the dark side of the Enlightenment, speaking in *Discipline and Punish* of the Enlightenment's egalitarian juridical framework made possible by the organization of a parliamentary, representative regime but also of the concomitant development of nonegalitarian and asymmetrical disciplinary mechanisms that worked against formal frameworks designed to ensure freedom and equality (222). He says, "The 'Enlightenment', which discovered the liberties, also invented the disciplines and sees the disciplines as a kind of counter law (222). Although Foucault is dealing with discipline in the context of the penal system, the central subject of his study, he is also concerned with disciplines within educational institutions. He speaks, for instance, of the examination in the fields of the human sciences as remaining "extremely close to the disciplinary power that shaped it" (226). He concludes part 3 of *Discipline and Punish* by asking, "Is it surprising that prisons resemble factories, schools, barracks, hospitals, which all resemble prisons?" (228). Foucault is critical of science in *The Archaeology of Knowledge* though he is by no means antiscience. In the chapter entitled "Science and Knowledge," he indicates that science is ideological and that identifying its ideological functioning necessitates questioning it as a discursive formation (186). Science should be treated as "one practice among others" (186). His archaeological method involves questioning the sciences by examining their history, their unity, their dispersion, and their ruptures (195). He says that archaeology as he defines it is not a science, but it is related to the sciences and to analyses of a scientific type or to theories "subject to rigorous criteria" (206). He says in the foreword to the English edition of *The Order of Things* that his archaeological method involves exploring scientific discourse from the point of view of "rules that come into play in the very existence of such discourse" (xiv). He tells us that he is not interested in developing a theory of the knowing subject but, rather, a theory of discursive practice (xiv). The book is an attempt to analyze "the pure experience of order and its modes of being" (xxi). John Trimbur in "Agency and the Death of the Author" speaks of Foucault's "qualified appreciation of the Enlightenment" (292).

Julia Kristeva's work, to the extent that it is feminist, tends toward postmodern feminism. As the epigraph to this chapter demonstrates, Kristeva resists developing her perspective in opposition to modernism and remains committed to finding alternatives to rationality and empiricism rather than repudiating them entirely. Her work builds on structuralist principles even as it attempts to alter them. Also, Kristeva is critical of theories of meaning rooted in Cartesian principles, though her work is greatly indebted to these theories. Like Bakhtin, who was an important influence on her work, she provides an alternative to the static descriptions of literary transactions provided by structuralism in literary studies. In "Word, Dialogue, and Novel," an essay in which her indebtedness to Bakhtin is pronounced, she speaks of literary structures as generated in relation to other structures rather than a fixed point or a fixed meaning (65). The literary word becomes a dialogue among several writings, that of the writer, the addressee, and the contemporary or earlier cultural context (65).

Critical of the science of linguistics because it ignores play, pleasure, and desire, she speaks in "The System and the Speaking Subject," first published in the *Times Literary Supplement* in 1973, of transforming the science of linguistics into semiotics. According to Kristeva, semiotics derives from Saussurean and Peircean linguistics while altering Saussurean and Peircean linguistics, the linguistics of the Prague School, and structuralism (27). Semiotics is concerned with what is outside metalinguistics, the speaking subject as the subject of a heterogeneous process (30), emphasizing "heterogeneity with respect to system" (31). Describing some ways in which semiotics moves beyond rationalist and scientific projects in her essay, "Semiotics: A Critical Science and/or a Critique of Science," she speaks, as her title illustrates, of semiotics as both a science and a critique of science and is critical of approaches to linguistics that are scientific without also being critical of science. She sees Noam Chomsky's generative or transformational grammar as positivist and as being indebted to Descartes (*Language* 260).

She is careful to distinguish semiotics from idealism on the one hand and from vulgar sociologism on the other, both of which affirm some form of transcendence, and neither of which takes the sociology of the speaking subject into consideration ("System" 26). She also distances semiotics, or what she sometimes calls the semiology of signifying processes, from Marxism. Although Marxism is useful in understanding the economic determinants of social relations, it is limited because it is not a theory of meaning or of the subject: "There *is* no subject in the economic rationality of Marxism" ("System" 31). She credits Freud, however, with enabling the conception of language that resulted in semiotics. Kristeva speaks of Freud's research as elucidating linguistic specificities that sciences that do not take discourse into account will never attain (*Language* 272).

Kristeva provides a theoretical account of the linguistic subject and desire in language in her essay "Revolution in Poetic Language." She once again makes the point that modern linguistics lacks a subject or tolerates one only as a *"transcendental ego"* (90) [Kristeva's emphasis]. The subject Kristeva identifies is a divided one comprised both of semiotic drives or energy charges, which she calls *chora,* and of symbolic signification processes. When Kristeva translates these semiotic and symbolic processes into explanations of how texts function, she creates the terms *genotext* and *phenotext.* Kristeva emphasizes, however, that individual signifying practices do not encompass the infinite totality of the signifying process, because there are always multiple constraints that "knot" it and "lock it into a given surface or structure" (122).

Kristeva's project, then, and the project of semiotics, are to instate the speaking (or writing, or reading) subject into scientific studies of language that have heretofore developed abstract, objective systems that ignore individual utterances or practices. To instate the subject is to introduce desire, emotion, subjectivity, specificity, and singularity. Instating the subject challenges structuralist, formalist, rationalist, or modernist projects in significant ways without abandoning a commitment to the scientific study of language. Kristeva's project is not a Romantic one. Rather, she is adding a consideration of the speaking subject, hence of desire, of the body, and of history, to semiological or structuralist approaches and in so doing transforming them in dramatic ways. She distances semiotics from transcendental and idealist approaches to language and attempts to move beyond rationalist and scientific ones.

Postmodern feminists, including Kristeva, problematize the category *woman*, emphasizing its contradictions and inconsistencies. They raise questions about modernist projects, especially their commitments to searching for "objective" knowledge and stable meaning. Within a postmodern frame of reference, names and categories are seen as fluid rather than rigid, their boundaries permeable rather than fixed. Names and categories become limiting though necessary to describe partial and historically situated knowledge. A work that in many ways exemplifies a postmodern feminist approach to a particular interpretive problem is Donna Haraway's *Modest_Witness@Second_Millennium,* an exploration of the dangers of uncritical acceptance of what Haraway calls "technoscience." Haraway was trained as a scientist, though her work over the past twenty-five years has become increasingly interdisciplinary and increasingly critical of the scientific enterprise. She speaks in *Modest_Witness* of racism and colonialism flourishing in the Enlightenment and of the "intensified misery" of billions of people as a result of the so-called freedoms of transnational capitalism and technoscience (3). She also acknowledges her allegiance to interdisciplinary inquiry by speaking of the "grammar" of feminism and technoscience and by using linguistic categories—syntactics, semantics, and pragmatics—as headings for the sections of her book. She does not reject technoscience, however. Quite the contrary. She says the goal of her book is to "put the boundary between the technical and the political back into permanent question" (89). The problem as she sees it is that technoscientific knowledge has not been recognized as situated knowledge; its interpretive and political dimensions have been ignored. Her book demonstrates persuasively that scientific investigation is not politically neutral but is deeply implicated in decision making that affects in significant ways the lives of individuals in marginal positions. For her, postmodernity is characterized by the collapse of distinctions between sign and referent, of that which is real and that which is represented (74). She also makes clear that the constructivist position she espouses is not relativistic (99).

The work of Judith Butler is also in many ways postmodern feminist in approach, though her context is continental philosophy rather than technoscience. The problem of categorization and naming is at the center of much of Butler's work. An aim of *Gender Trouble,* for instance, is to attempt to determine what feminist politics might mean once we move beyond the categories of identity that have constrained them. Although gender has traditionally been represented, according to Butler, as stable and relatively determinate, she emphasizes its instability and indeterminacy. Butler identifies her task as attempting to decenter the institutions of phallogocentrism and compulsory heterosexuality (ix). Influenced by the work of Foucault, Butler attempts to effect a critical genealogy of gender categories (ix). For her *female* and *woman* are relational rather than fixed terms (ix). Her postmodern feminist perspective results in a problematizing of traditional gender categories rather than in a dismissal of them. In *Bodies That Matter,* Butler focuses on the abjection of lesbians and gays and suggests that terms such as *queer* that have been used to subject a group can be reclaimed to enable social and political resignification (231).

The importance of naming and renaming in postmodern feminist work is also highlighted by the situation of feminists who are neither middle class nor white. Kadiatu Kanneh, for instance, in "Black Feminisms" devotes considerable attention to exploring how she is using the term *black feminism* and provides a historical account of its various uses within the feminist movement including a discussion of *This Bridge Called My Back,* an early collection by Cherrie Moraga and Gloria Anzaldúa of essays devoted to women of color.[15] Kanneh explains, for instance, that within the United States, *black* is used when referring to the African American population whereas Asian Americans, Latinas, and Native Americans are referred to as "people of color" (86). However, in Britain *black* is a considerably more inclusive category that is often used to describe Asians, Africans, and Afro-Caribbeans (86). Postmodern feminists with non-European heritages have struggled with the problem of naming the perspectives they embrace.[16]

Other postmodern feminist work makes evident that postmodern feminism is a contested site and that there is no agreement on how feminism articulates with postmodernism. Patricia Waugh in "Postmodernism and Feminism" suggests that mapping the relationship between postmodernism and feminism necessitates distinguishing between postmodernism as an aesthetic practice, which she sees as "weak postmodernism," and postmodernism as a critique of knowledge, which she sees as "strong postmodernism." Waugh finds that making such a distinction allows feminism to take a "strategic stance" on postmodernism, selecting those aspects that might be useful to a particular goal at a particular time (182). Linda Hutcheon in *The Politics of Postmodernism,* though, argues that feminist practices have had a powerful impact on postmodernism but that feminism and postmodernism should be discussed as distinct traditions (142). For her, postmodern feminism is not a useful category.[17]

As I indicated in the introduction, resistance to postmodern feminism within feminist studies as well as beyond it has existed as long as postmodern feminism has been named as such. Philosopher Linda J. Nicholson's edited collection, *Feminism/Postmodernism,* for instance, though containing contributions by individuals such as Jane Flax, Butler, and Haraway who have subsequently published books that have a postmodern perspective, also contains a number of essays by skeptics such as Susan Bordo, Nancy Harstock, and Christine Di Stefano. Nicholson herself, however, sees postmodern feminism as I do as critiquing without repudiating modern feminism. In the introduction to the book, for instance, she says, "A postmodern feminism could thus both support certain procedural aspects of natural science or other reflexive criteria of validity claims . . . while acknowledging such support as political and grounded in a particular cultural context" (11).[18] A collection of essays published four years after Nicholson's, *Feminism and*

Postmodernism coedited by Margaret Ferguson and Jennifer Wicke is more consistently receptive to postmodern approaches to feminism and explores ways in which postmodern perspectives are productive in the analysis of literature.

Postmodern feminists have diverse orientations, work in diverse fields, have diverse emphases, and configure the relationship between modern and postmodern feminism in diverse ways. Regardless of orientation, however, their work usually makes evident that postmodern feminism moves beyond modernism by critiquing it rather than opposing it. Chandra Talpade Mohanty's introduction to her, Ann Russo, and Lourdes Torres's *Third World Women and the Politics of Feminism,* a cultural studies approach to postmodern feminism, is a good example. Mohanty differentiates between white, Western, middle-class, liberal feminism and the feminist politics of women of color. Liberal feminists, according to Mohanty, focus exclusively on gender as the basis for equal rights whereas she focuses on "gender in relation to race and/or class as part of a broader liberation struggle" (11). Mohanty aims, however, to broaden the goals of liberal feminism rather than to reject them. She argues that gender and race are relational terms that are not reducible to binary oppositions. Multiple, fluid structures of domination intersect to locate women differently in particular historical eras (13). A problem that Mohanty sees is that feminist historians too often focus on gender as the sole determinant of struggle and omit discussion of racial struggle (12).[19]

Postmodern feminist work such as Susan Stanford Friedman's "Beyond White and Other: Relationality and Narratives of Race in Feminist Discourse" provides a postmodern feminist perspective on cultural studies that moves beyond the modernist-white/other binary. The essay is postmodern feminist in that it examines gender and race as well as other components of identity as "interactive systems of stratification" (4). Flax's work illustrates that postmodern feminists attempt to find alternatives to modernist approaches without repudiating them completely by rethinking modernist, Anglo-American, object-relations psychology. Flax in *Thinking Fragments* insists that gender is a social relation (182). Like Nancy Chodorow, who also derives her position from object-relations psychology, Flax sees that humans are formed in and through social relations and that family social relations cannot be understood apart from other forms of social relations, especially class and gender (162). She is critical, however, of Chodorow, whose work I have characterized as cultural feminist, for not adequately placing childbearing and childrearing into a political, economic, and social context (165). Whereas Flax's postmodern feminist perspective is primarily Anglo-American in orientation, Butler's has been influenced primarily by continental philosophy, especially the work of Foucault. In *Gender Trouble,* Butler sees that "gender is always a doing" (25); gender identity is always a process in motion rather than a stable category. For both Flax and Butler, androcentric traditions such as object-relations psychology and analytic philosophy need not be repudiated entirely but can be altered to serve postmodern feminist goals. Postmodern feminists have also demonstrated that the work of male postmodernists such as Bakhtin can serve feminist ends. A good example is Dale Bauer's "feminist dialogics" (x), discussed in her book by the same title, which focuses explicitly on feminist approaches to language and draws heavily on the work of Bakhtin. Recognizing that Bakhtin did not write about feminist issues, Bauer is nevertheless able to productively reread his work within a feminist context.

Postmodern feminist approaches to rhetoric and composition often emphasize pedagogy and attempt to develop ways to reconceptualize the student writing and reading self in light of postmodern critiques of identity and agency. The approaches also often attempt to reread the history of rhetoric, providing revisionary approaches to classical rhetoric, Enlightenment rhetoric, and contemporary rhetoric. Some approaches are indebted to French theory and criticism or to the work of Americans in French feminist literary studies. Susan C. Jarratt in *Rereading the Sophists* calls for a "feminist sophistics" (xii), a method of revising logic through narrative. Invoking the work of Gayatri Spivak, Mary Jacobus, and Nancy K. Miller, Jarratt calls for resistant "misreadings" in order to disrupt received readings (76). Lynn Worsham, in "Writing against Writing: The Predicament of *Écriture Féminine* in Composition Studies," recontextualizes the work of Kristeva, Hélène Cixous, and Luce Irigaray, especially their conception of *écriture féminine,* for rhetoric and composition. Miriam Brody in *Manly Writing* demonstrates that postmodern feminists often work to develop alternatives to androcentric traditions, in this case classical rhetoric and Enlightenment rhetoric, by tracing their dislocative moments (7). Pamela L. Caughie's essay "Let it Pass: Changing the Subject Once Again" defines postmodernism as a shorthand for the social, cultural, and theoretical movements of the 1980s and 1990s that erode any faith in a stable, coherent self, in a universal foundation for knowledge and truth, and in language as a transparent medium of communication (130). Nedra Reynolds in "Interrupting Our Way to Agency: Feminist Cultural Studies and Composition" resists versions of postmodernism that deny agency to the subject and leave it fractured or dispersed (58). In "Beyond Anti-Foundationalism to Rhetorical Authority: Problems Defining 'Cultural Literacy,'" rhetorician Patricia Bizzell critiques the modernist foundationalism of individuals such as E. D. Hirsch who think that students should be acculturated into an academic discourse community, an apparently stable, unchanging construct. For her, discourse communities are not stable but, rather, fraught with contradiction and polyvocal (662–63).

Cheryl Glenn in *Rhetoric Retold* takes a postmodern feminist approach to the history of rhetoric, providing resistant readings of paternal narratives. Such readings, according to Glenn, acknowledge that they are written from a particular angle and avoid linear plottings, thus charting previously unseen and unmeasured contours of landscape (5). Her aim is to trace the routes where communities of women reside, resurvey the territory, and locate and position women rhetoricians on the map (4). Jacqueline Jones Royster in *Traces of a Stream* provides what she calls an "afrafeminist" approach to the study of the literacy of nineteenth-century African American women, an approach that has more affinities with postmodern feminist perspectives than with cultural feminist ones. She carefully avoids an essentialized perspective by acknowledging that individuals who are not African American can contribute in important ways to "afrafeminist" scholarship (277), though she argues, as well, that African American women should be central to the formation and development of knowledge production (276). Nancy Maloney Grimm in *Good Intentions* demonstrates the usefulness of a postmodern perspective in writing-center work.

Postmodernism is valuable because it moves beyond modernism without repudiating it entirely. It explores the limitations of rationality and empiricism and attempts to provide alternatives to them. It challenges the elitism of much academic work and explores modes of resistance to institutionalized power and authority. It is committed to the inclusion of multiple voices and hence to the creation of heterogeneous cultures. In many areas, however, it has pointed out the limitations of modernist and antimodernist perspectives before having worked out satisfactory alternatives. Much recent work in feminist theory with a postmodern orientation, for instance, critiques essentialized conceptions of gender and identity without explaining adequately how nonessentialized conceptions can accomplish political goals or produce meaningful knowledge. The postmodern emphasis on the local also can work against the formulation of generalizations that have global implications. Also, the writing of postmodernists is sometimes so abstruse that, despite its anti-elitist sentiment, it becomes exclusionary.

This overview is necessarily highly selective and condensed and does not emphasize the extent to which modern, antimodern, and postmodern perspectives have blurred boundaries or the extent to which works in feminist studies, literary studies, or rhetoric and composition are often manifestations of a number of different and often contradictory tendencies. In the next chapter, I illustrate the usefulness of the perspectives through a discussion of global feminisms. In the analysis, some limitations of both modern and antimodern approaches to the development of feminist perspectives, in this case within non-Western cultures, are explored.

2

Reading Global Feminisms

[C]ategories often invoked disparagingly by feminist theorists—equality, reason, history, modernity—are not stable, uniform entities but are reproduced and changed by the specific context of their articulation. It is here that much of feminist philosophy, with its sweeping vision of the *longue durée* of Western history as a history of pathological phallocentrism, reveals its limitations.

—Rita Felski, "The Doxa of Difference"

As the history of Western women makes clear, there is no validity to the notion that progress for women can be achieved only by abandoning the ways of a native androcentric culture in favor of those of another culture.

—Leila Ahmed, *Women and Gender in Islam: Historical Roots of a Modern Debate*

It is another form of oppression and colonialism, the colonialism of Western feminists.

—Nawal Saadawi and Mary E. Willmurth, "A Feminist in the Arab World"

*A*s I have suggested, postmodern feminism moves beyond modernism by challenging and problematizing it rather than replacing, opposing, or nullifying it. Theorists, such as Bakhtin, Lyotard, Derrida, Foucault, and Kristeva, and postmodern feminists influenced by their work criticize modernist projects but do not directly oppose them. They do not repudiate science, rationality, epistemology, or liberal democracy but make clear their serious limitations. Postmodern feminists criticize modernist tendencies to universalize, to focus on the individual divorced from social context, and to ignore the ways in which local situations affect interpretive processes. They also attempt to find alternatives to modern feminisms and sometimes draw heavily upon the work of male theorists and practitioners. It is antimodern feminists who, more often, associate male institutions and discourses with androcentrism and patriarchy and reject them entirely.

Feminisms are historically and geographically situated and hence context specific. Concepts such as equality, for instance, that were privileged during the Enlightenment, can be reclaimed to serve postmodern feminist ends. Rita Felski finds in "The Doxa of Difference" that critiquing the notion of equality implies "an expanded, more adequate notion of equality that is genuinely open to diversity" (16). Lila Abu-Lughod in *Remaking Women* speaks of the difficulty of attempting to be skeptical of modernity's progressive claims of emancipation and to be critical of its social and cultural operations and yet to be appreciative of the forms of energy that modernity might have enabled for women (12). There are certainly good reasons for feminists to redefine rather than to reject concepts such as equality.

Modern, antimodern, and postmodern feminist perspectives are neither linear historical periods nor clearly distinct categories. They overlap, interact, and manifest themselves in different ways at different historical moments and in different geographical locations. Postmodern feminism does not necessarily follow from modern feminism or antimodern feminism in a linear or spatial progression. Examining the struggle to achieve feminist goals in non-Western contexts makes evident the pertinence of as well as some limitations of the perspectives I have developed here beyond the context of European and Anglo-American feminisms.[1]

Thus far I have described modernism in European and Anglo-American contexts, focusing on the scientific revolution as it developed in Europe in the late-seventeenth and eighteenth centuries and took on new forms in the nineteenth and twentieth centuries as it evolved in Europe, England, and America. The influence of modernism, though, has been worldwide because Western and non-Western cultures intersect in complex ways. Most obviously, it has taken the form of colonialism—of political domination by Europeans over indigenous peoples—and of capitalism—of economic domination by developed countries over less developed countries. As Susan Stanford Friedman points out in *Mappings*, however, representations of European cultures as dominating non-Western cultures are too simple. She finds that conquest and colonialism have been and are still worldwide phenomena, and she questions the metanarrative of "the unidirectional hegemony in which white/western people (always already) dominate people of color/nonwestern people" (6). Leila Ahmed in *Women and Gender in Islam* speaks of the discourses within Arab societies as being enmeshed in the discourses of the West and "thoroughly implicated" in the history of colonialism (243). It is too easy to cast Western cultures as the colonizers and non-Western ones as the colonized. Western cultures and non-Western cultures are heterogeneous and not clearly distinct. Also, non-Western cultures have, at times, themselves been complicit in processes of colonialism.

The inevitable intersection of Western and non-Western cultures as a result of colonialism is illustrated by Oyeronke Oyewumi's unsuccessful attempt to claim, in his response essay "De-confounding Gender: Feminist Theorizing and Western Culture, a Comment on Hawkesworth's 'Confounding Gender'," that a belief that gender is a universal category is contradicted by the example of African Yorba culture. Oyewumi criticizes Hawkesworth's essay for assuming that gender is a universal category and sees it as the expression of her situation as a feminist from the United States. He argues, further, that Hawkesworth's belief in gender as a universal category is rooted in a kind of biological determinism despite a stated commitment to social construction. Oyewumi claims that gender is absent from Yorba culture as evidenced by the fact that there are neither concepts/words connoting son, daughter, brother, or sister nor any corresponding social roles (1053). In Yorba culture, according to Oyewumi, seniority is defined by age rather than gender (1053), and there are no categories of *man* and *woman* (1054). He explains in a footnote, however, that he uses the past tense because, through sustained contact with the West in a colonial relationship, "there now exist increasingly in Yorubaland Western gender categories, coexisting and commingling with the indigenous" (1054, n 6). The footnote undercuts Oyewumi's claim that there are cultures in which gender plays no role in the social construction of reality. He has clearly not provided an example of a culture in which, at present, gender plays no role, though he is certainly correct that it plays different roles in different cultures.[2]

Denunciations of modernism by equating it with Western imperialism and colonialism often fail to take into consideration the complexity of the various modernisms as they have arisen in various locations or the complexity of relationships between Western and non-Western cultures. The association of Western modernism with political repression is widespread and is exemplified by Foucault's critique of the Enlightenment in *Discipline and Punish,* which I discussed in chapter 1. European modernism, however, in addition to giving rise to colonialism, racism, and imperialism, also gave rise to Enlightenment feminism as well as Marxism, perspectives that have resulted in worldwide liberation movements. If modernism has enabled colonialism, imperialism, and inequality, it has also enabled the development of struggles for equality for women, for minorities, for the working class, and for the poor in colonized countries. If it has resulted in the creation of disciplinary punishment, it has also enabled the development of knowledge that has contributed models of freedom and liberation.

Outright rejection of modernism, therefore, amounts to a rejection of liberatory ideologies as well as repressive ones. Trinh T. Minh-ha, a writer and filmmaker who teaches at an American university but who was born and raised in Vietnam, makes clear in *Woman, Native, Other* the dangers of blanket repudiations of modernism. She is sympathetic to Foucault's critique of disciplinary knowledge and recognizes the dangers of imposing Euro-American criteria of equality and of representing Third World women as a coherent cultural subject and source of scientific knowledge (106). For Trinh, however, the challenge is to define feminism within the context of the ethnic culture and in so doing create a new version of it. While she recognizes that reversion to tradition is counterproductive, a conservative move, she also thinks that feminists need not repudiate history entirely but can re-write it thereby discovering the "buried treasures of women's unknown heritage" (84).

Certainly, uncritical acceptance of Western feminist approaches to the problems of non-Western women is unacceptable. If non-Western traditions are completely repudiated and Western ones embraced enthusiastically, hierarchies of domination are likely to be reinforced rather than mitigated. At the same time, total rejection of modernism is problematic for feminists in non-Western countries because extricating feminism from modernism means extricating feminism from commitments to equality. What is needed is a third way—new conceptualizations of feminism within indigenous contexts and new hybrids. It is postmodern feminism, I suggest, that enables the development of such hybrids. Shahnaz Khan, drawing on the work of Homi Bhabha, calls for such a conception of hybridization in her essay, "Muslim Women: Negotiations in the Third Space." In her ethnographic study of two Muslim women who emigrated to Canada, she concludes by emphasizing that Muslim identity is neither monolithic nor homogeneous and that Muslim culture is a multiple, shifting, and contradictory site (492). Muslim culture has found its way to Western countries such as Canada but has been altered in the process. Following are three perspectives on the situation of non-Western women: a modernist, Western one; an antimodernist, indigenous one; and several postmodern hybrids.

A Modern Feminist Perspective

A news story from the *New York Times* focusing on the plight of poor women in Islamic Morocco who are raped and then ostracized for bearing illegitimate children is a good example of the limitations of the first approach, the imposition of Western feminist perspectives in non-Western contexts. The story, "After the Rape, a Lifetime of Shame. It's Morocco," by Marlise Simons that appeared in the Monday, 1 February 1999 web edition, describes the situation of Moroccan women who are shunned and forced into a life of shame and poverty after they are raped and bear illegitimate children. According to Simons, such women are considered outcasts in conservative, Islamic society. Pregnant girls, even when they are very young or have been raped, are commonly rejected by their families, threatened with death, and provided no support by the government or religious charities. Abortion is forbidden and unavailable to anyone other than the rich and educated. Simons explains that women in general are treated as inferior under Morocco's Qur'anic law. They are legal minors, inherit less than their brothers, need permission from a male relative to marry, and can be repudiated by their husbands.

Simons focuses her story on the plight of Rashida, a shy twenty-three-year-old in Agadir, Morocco, who sleeps on the floor of a small, dank room inside the compound of a fish cannery where fifty other women also live. Rashida, the dark-skinned, unmarried mother of a fair-skinned, four-year-old, had been raped by the light-skinned son of the family for whom she worked as a maid. When she was found to be pregnant, Rashida, who had been sent away to become a maid at age six, was told not to return home by her father and brothers. Before finding work, she was forced to sleep in the street and beg. Simons explains that Rashida's daughter, Hiba, is her joy.

Although Moroccan officials have no statistics about single mothers or illegitimate children, according to Simons, social workers claim that the number of poor, single mothers has grown, the women and their children are ostracized, and some are forced to become beggars or prostitutes. Babies are sometimes left on the street or in parks or hospitals, and because adoption does not exist under Qur'anic law, unwanted children end up in state orphanages.

Simons's description of the situation is Western feminist in that it depends on a repudiation of Islamic law and Islamic culture, which she sees as the sole cause of the women's problems.[3] Their situation is far worse than that of their brothers, according to Simons, in that the women have far fewer legal and inheritance rights and no alternative other than to marry. In order to marry, however, they must have the permission of a male, and in marriage they can look forward to a lifetime of domination by their husbands. If a woman is raped, marriage is not a possibility. She will be shunned by her family, by the state, and by the church and will have to accept menial jobs and poor working conditions that will allow her a meager existence and no opportunities for advancement.[4]

Simons also focuses on the working conditions of the women (though she does not mention that the deplorable conditions she describes are as much a result of Western capitalism as Islamic culture). The women must sleep on the floor of the fish cannery where they work, and they are virtually owned by the company because they have no alternative than to live on its premises and can be summoned at any hour to work, depending on when the fishing fleets come in. The women workers make only five dollars a day, and they must put up with a "piercing stench" (1).

Simons points out, however, that life for Rashida and other women in her situation is not entirely grim. Despite adverse circumstances, Rashida takes delight in her daughter and will one day show her a picture of her light-skinned father. Rashida is not entirely disconnected from her past life, and her daughter represents the possibility of a brighter future. There are also references in Simons's story to attempts to improve the situation. Simons interviews a woman who operates a day care center for children of poor, single mothers that is financed by a Swiss foundation. Simons also makes reference to a legal aid center created to help women.

The modern feminist solution to the problem implied by the article is modernization and abandonment of outmoded Islamic customs and laws. The article suggests that women must be provided opportunities to become educated and have the same legal rights and the same opportunities as men within the workplace and the home. Laws must be changed so that abortion becomes legal for all women, even those who conceive out of wedlock. Educational institutions must provide information about birth control to all girls of childbearing age, and the government must provide support for unwed mothers and their children. The help of international organizations such as UNESCO, the United Nations Educational, Scientific, and Cultural Organization, an organization that is mentioned in the story, should be enlisted.

Simons's story is partial in the sense that it portrays the situation of the women victims in a sympathetic way. It is also partial, however, in that it suggests a decidedly Western perspective that is completely unsympathetic to Islamic culture. The solution of doing away with an outmoded and unfortunate Islamic culture and Westernizing its laws and traditions leaves out other causes of the problem such as capitalism, colonialism, and racism. The story says nothing, for instance, about the nature of the company that employs the women. We do not know who owns it or who profits by it. There is also the suggestion that racism is an important dimension of the problem, but it is only hinted at, not explored. The story also represents Moroccan culture in a one-dimensional way, describing it as Islamic and as subject to Qur'anic law.[5]

Moroccan society, however, is quite diverse and its history complex. A north African country bordering Algeria, Mauritania, the Atlantic Ocean, and the Mediterranean, its history includes control by powerful Berber merchants, Roman rule, a Muslim invasion, occupation by the Spanish, colonization by the French, and a struggle for independence, which was granted in 1956. Muslim culture, then, though a powerful influence, was not the only influence, and an analysis of the situation described in the article would have to take Morocco's complex past into account. It would also have to provide more specific information about race relations in the country and about the complex ways in which gender, race, and class intersect to place women such as Rashida in degrading situations. A more-nuanced discussion might focus on ways in which the women are the victims of multiple oppressions. It might focus not only on the ways in which Islamic culture oppresses women but also on the ways in which French colonization and Western capitalism were oppressive as well.

An Antimodern Feminist Perspective

A considerably different perspective is presented in Anouar Majid's "The Politics of Feminism in Islam." Majid is wary of the dangers of imposing Western feminist traditions on non-Western cultures and attempts therefore to recuperate a feminist tradition within traditional Islamic culture, though he is not entirely successful in doing so. Majid recognizes that the problems women face in Islamic societies cannot be divorced from European colonialism. For Majid, the political and economic structures that have resulted from independence from European domination have not emancipated the poor (341). He feels that nationalist elites have established Eurocentric models of government, namely nation-states (342, n. 17). For Majid, representations of Islamic culture as undemocratic and patriarchal reifies the history of Muslim culture and downplays the impact of imperialism on gender relations in Islamic countries (349).

The creation of nation-states based on a European model has resulted in secularism or the separation of church and state, which is a Western ideal (340). Majid sees a connection between secularism and imperialism in that both depend on an erosion of indigenous cultural values (341). Majid also focuses on the ways in which capitalism has contributed to the oppression of women in Islamic societies. It has created privileged intellectuals and theories that have not been sufficiently examined by Muslim feminists or Western scholars writing on feminism in the Islamic world (331). It has also created economic dependencies and eroded the self-sufficient economies that once granted autonomy to Islamic societies (343).

Majid finds that a major problem in attempting to develop Islamic feminist perspectives is the difficulty of overcoming the Western and often Orientalist biases that pervade feminist thought. These biases include a dehistoricized notion of human rights and "an implicit acceptance of the bourgeois political apparatus as a reliable mechanism for negotiating the grievances of the exploited" (339). Western feminism cannot be readily separated from hostility to Islamic culture, according to Majid. To illustrate the point, he cites the example of upper-class Islamic women who have sometimes embraced Western feminist values and in the process "condemned native customs as backward, proclaimed the superiority of the West, and uncompromisingly equated unveiling with liberation" (338).

Majid's solution is to recuperate feminist perspectives within traditional Islamic culture. He recognizes that Westernization is not the solution given its associations with Eurocentrism, imperialism, secularism, and capitalism. Instead, he argues for the need to recover an Islamic past that is "thoroughly cleansed of the residue of centuries of male-dominated interpretations" (332). It is male-manipulated interpretations of the religion of Islam, Majid argues, that are the problem. The religion of Islam does not need to act as a barrier to women's fulfillment (353). Majid calls for a redefined Islam as a defense against "the unrelenting process of Westernization" as well as the extremist practices of fundamentalists (353). He finds that there are ways for Islamic women to affirm themselves without rejecting Islamic culture. Some Islamic women, for instance, according to Majid, argue that it is premature to do away with the veil (339). Majid also finds that within Islamic culture, the boundaries of individual freedom are not determined by individual law but by divine decree (348). He suggests as a possible model Mahmoud Mohammed Taha's *The Second Message of Islam,* a work in which Taha calls for the elimination of the traditional patriarchal law and the creation of a new law based on Meccan Revelation (351). According to Majid, Taha does not revert to secular ideology but envisions reforms that would place Islamic culture at the center of reform efforts.

As Suad Joseph makes evident in her comment on the essay, though, Majid does not spell out very clearly or very fully just how a reversion to Meccan Revelation will result in the improvement of the situation of Islamic women. Joseph is also critical of Majid's attack on secularism. For Joseph, secularism is "about tolerance of diversity, discourses of difference, and the decentering of canonical hegemonies of all sorts" (368). Ann Elizabeth Mayer in her comment on Majid's essay focuses on his attempt to defend Islamic states and Islamists against the charges that they support reactionary policies on women (370). Mayer calls Majid's approach to feminism a "pseudofeminism" (370) and suggests that he is an enthusiast for Islamization (377). She sees his essay as an attempt to discredit genuine feminists and rehabilitate political Islam (377).

Postmodern Hybrids

An approach that is considerably more accepting of Western feminism but that is nevertheless responsive to the particularities of indigenous cultures is described in Barbara Molony's "Japan's 1986 Equal Employment Opportunity Law and the Changing Discourse on Gender." Although Molony does not contextualize her discussion in quite this way, the analysis she provides illustrates an attempt to reconcile Western modernist commitments to equality in the form of equal opportunity employment with Japanese cultural traditions and attitudes toward appropriate roles for women.

Molony traces dramatic changes in the roles of Japanese women in the recent past as they have moved from housewives and mothers to women who work outside the home. She also traces legislation and policies that attempt to be responsive to these changes as well as some ways in which they fail to resolve the contradiction between motherhood and the workplace. Her analysis illustrates ways in which modern feminism with its emphasis on similarities between women and men and its goal of equality with men contradicts cultural feminism with its emphasis on differences between women and men and its goal of valorizing women's traditional roles. Molony contextualizes the problem in terms of the equality and difference debate within feminist scholarship and activism in the United States (274, n. 7).

As Molony's title suggests, she focuses on Japan's 1986 Equal Employment Opportunity Law. The law was the result, according to Molony, of pressure to conform to international standards (282, n. 20). It calls for employers to "make efforts" to give women equal opportunity in recruitment, hiring, assignment, and promotion (286). The law was opposed by feminists when it was a bill, however, and is still criticized for not providing adequate "motherhood protection." The law provides maternity leave for only six weeks before birth and eight weeks after (289). While on leave, women workers are to receive sixty percent of their regular wages (eighty percent for workers in the public sector and one hundred percent for government workers), though many women employed by small companies or working part-time receive nothing (289). The law also limits the amount of overtime women may work (290).

According to Molony, the law is in some ways an erosion of motherhood protection that had previously been in place. Prior to the enactment of the law, Japanese women had been provided automatic menstruation leave (289). The law has also created an unfortunate implicit and sometimes explicit two-track system whereby single women are able to become managers whereas women with families are not. According to a study that Molony cites, in 1988 women were just 1.2 percent of all managers in Japan's large firms (292). An advantage of the "mommy track," though, is that women can leave the office at 5:00 P.M., take breaks and legally granted leaves of absence, and be exempt from transfers (293).

Molony's essay traces the emergence of feminist initiatives and responses that attempt to reconcile modernist commitments to equality and nondiscrimination with traditional women's roles as wives and as mothers. The story she tells is hardly one of triumph and unqualified success. The Equal Employment Opportunity Law is far from ideal and has created as many problems as it has solved. Molony concludes that women on the "mommy track" are no better off than before (297). She also concludes that merit is usually defined as adherence to male job requirements (298). The analysis Molony provides nevertheless chronicles struggles to reconcile cultural feminist commitments to valuing and maintaining women's traditional roles and values with modern feminist commitments to equality, nondiscrimination, and a place in the traditionally male world of work.

Molony's essay makes clear that modernist commitments to equality take different forms in different cultural contexts. The essay also makes clear, however, the importance of critiquing modernist projects. In the context of equal opportunity employment legislation in Japan, a struggle for equality is not enough. It is also important and necessary to struggle for the protection of the rights of mothers, and this struggle necessitates that women be constructed not as the equals of men but as different from them. Equal rights without recognition of difference would leave women, especially potential and actual mothers, in vulnerable positions.

Zakia Pathak and Saswati Sengupta in "Between Academy and Street: A Story of Resisting Women" describe and enact a somewhat different hybrid strategy. Their own discourse is multiple, complex, and an interesting blend of Western and non-Western forms. Pathak and Sengupta juxtapose narrative—their own, that of a student whose diary plays a central role in the essay, and a description of an audiocassette textualization of the myth of the Hindu goddess Durga—with poststructuralist analysis. In an appendix, they also provide extracts from books by four scholars of Indian culture.

A central concern is the relationship between Western feminism and traditional culture, in this case the culture of India. Pathak and Sengupta are critical of traditional culture, which they associate with the Hindu political right, for imposing limiting roles on women. They describe the "true" Hindu woman as physically chaste, a virgin before marriage, physically faithful during marriage, religious, and a devoted wife and mother (546). This social construction of gender, which they see as going on "quietly and continuously in myriad ways" (546), is reinforced by the Hindu religion and culture. They speak of "rightest codes of dress and speech" (558). They do not idealize Western traditions or liberal approaches to the emancipation of women, however, and they recognize that political movements of the left or right are riddled with contradictions of class, caste, and gender (559). They also see that the objectivist, academic discourse of the student diary they quote is just as limiting for women as Hindu religious traditions (548).

Pathak and Sengupta suggest that a solution to the complex problems described in the essay is engagement between feminism and traditional culture. Feminism, they observe, cannot compete with rightest inventions of traditions unless it accepts those traditions by accepting the traditional culture's source texts, both written and oral: "It would be more politically productive to insinuate resistance within this rightest tradition of the 'true' Hindu woman instead of repudiating it and inventing a 'modern' tradition to counterpose it" (550). They demonstrate how this might be done by describing a Bengali hymn that declares female energy to be the autonomous force behind the world (566). They see the hymn as constructing a new creation myth in which "the original creative impulse, autonomous agency, and speech are claimed for the female," and their recuperation of the hymn enables a creation myth that emphasizes the struggle between dominant and dominated (567).

The essays discussed above illustrate different ways in which feminism might move beyond modernism in non-Western contexts. They suggest that Western modernism cannot simply be embraced uncritically because doing so can easily become another form of domination. Rather, modern feminism needs to be integrated into the context of traditional culture and transformed in the process. The modernist commitment to equality between women and men needs to be recontextualized in traditional contexts. Moving beyond modernism, then, does not necessarily involve repudiating modernist goals. It can involve attempting to refigure them in new situations. It does not necessitate eliminating commitments to equality, objectivity, democracy, and disciplinarity but might involve ensuring that they serve progressive ends, what Gayatri Spivak speaks of as arresting the "disciplinary currency . . . by keeping our eye on the double (multiple and irregular) movement of the local *and* the overall" (75). The local, that is, the indigenous, is not embraced uncritically nor is a universalized commitment to equality for women. Rather, local and global intersect to create new feminist forms, hybrids that are postmodern rather than modern or antimodern.

This reading of global feminisms suggests the usefulness of the reconfigurations I have outlined in addressing a current problem within feminist studies— the difficulties of enacting feminist goals in non-Western contexts. In the remainder of the book I make clearer, especially within the context of English studies, the distinction I am making between antimodern perspectives that oppose modernist ones and postmodern perspectives that critique them and explore more fully the complex relationship between modernism and postmodernism. Non-fictional works by Virginia Woolf, Adrienne Rich, and Alice Walker are in some ways antimodern feminist in their rejection of patriarchal institutions and their delineation of the characteristics of women's culture. Woolf, Rich, and Walker worked within modernist contexts but resisted them, often by opposing them.

Woolf elevated the status of the common reader and the common writer and identified a female literary tradition. Rich resisted patriarchal culture considerably more dramatically, embracing an openly lesbian lifestyle and calling for radical changes in familial and educational structures. Walker, too, rejected the role the traditional-family structure imposes on women by divorcing her husband and developing alternative child-care arrangements for her daughter. Her radical womanist perspective takes race as well as gender into consideration in the exploration of women's culture. If Rich describes in detail the damaging effects of traditional conceptions of motherhood, Walker focuses on African American women's culture as an alternative to modernist patriarchal culture.

PART TWO: *Opposing Modernisms*

3

Woolf's (Anti)Modern Reading

[I]t is inevitable that Woolf's views on reading should partake of the same ambivalences which haunt her meditations on human relationships, and indeed which demand a continually mobile response from the readers of her own fictions.
　　　　　　　　　　　—Kate Flint, "Reading Uncommonly:
　　　　　　　　　　　Virginia Woolf and the Practice of Reading"

Current attempts to think about the ways in which modern aesthetic strategies differ from those of post-modernism are, in general, productive and illuminating. Yet Virginia Woolf is one writer who frustrates this binary by writing across it. May she continue to confound, through the complex character of her writing, our attempts at such classifications.
　　　　　　　　　　　—Michele Barrett, "Virginia Woolf Meets Michel Foucault"

As I suggested in the introduction, although twentieth-century modernism is often seen as an aesthetic movement identified with the late-nineteenth and early-twentieth centuries encompassing both objectivist and subjectivist tendencies, it is useful to associate it with Western Enlightenment commitments to science, objectivity, individual rights, and rationality as distinct from commitments to spirituality, subjectivity, and individuality associated with Romanticism. If late-nineteenth- and twentieth-century modernism is contextualized in relation to the Western Enlightenment, then manifestations of Romantic tendencies in twentieth-century literature and art are usefully described as antimodern. My position challenges assumptions that inform much scholarship in both literary studies and art history and enables a connection between literary modernism and modernism as it is usually spoken of in fields such as philosophy and history. In the following discussion of Woolf's representations of the reading process, I use modernism in this way.

Woolf's perspective on reading is a curious blend of the modern and the antimodern.[1] She writes about reading as do her male modernist peers as a matter of uncovering textual meaning but alters their approach by insisting that emotion is an important part of the process. As a radical feminist, however, she is critical of traditional approaches to knowledge, to literature, and to reading and is well aware of the dangers that such approaches pose for the woman reader.

As a cultural feminist, she privileges the reading of the common reader over the professional reader and emphasizes that women have a distinct literary tradition.

In her work on reading and in her actual reading, Woolf draws on seemingly conflicting traditions, a female-inflected version of modernism as well as radical and cultural feminisms. She respects professional literary critics but is wary of professional reviewers and identifies strongly with outsiders who have not had the advantages of an education. Woolf's approach to reading is both respectful of certain canonical critics and critical of canonical reading. Radical and cultural feminisms provided Woolf a critical, egalitarian, and ethical perspective. At the same time, she recognizes the value of reading traditions developed over centuries by professional critics. She sees reading both as an important professional endeavor as well as a source of pleasure for nonprofessionals. It is not enough to say that Woolf merely modified the perspectives of her male counterparts on the activity of reading. She did so, but she also directly challenged those perspectives in radical ways and in so doing created an opening for a more highly politicized conception of reading, one in which the reader's gender and active role are crucial.

Woolf was preoccupied with the theme of reading, reflecting on her own reading practices in her essays and on the activity in general. In some ways Woolf's modern perspectives on reading contradict her radical- and cultural-feminist perspectives in that modernism tends to be objectivist and radical- and cultural-feminism subjectivist. Brenda R. Silver in her introduction to *Virginia Woolf's Reading Notebooks,* in discussing Woolf's reading habits and attitudes toward reading as expressed in the notebooks Woolf kept as preparation for her critical essays, finds that Woolf read with a divided consciousness.

> Woolf's vision of herself as reader and inheritor, however, was from the beginning a dual one. If, on the one hand, she felt herself part of the long line of writers and readers whose minds had joined through the centuries to produce her cultural heritage, she recognized, on the other, the peripheral role women have played in the creation and transmission of that heritage. (5)

I suggest in this chapter that these contradictions play themselves out in her actual reading practices because she read both as a professional, reading with the intent of publishing, and a nonprofessional, reading for her own pleasure. I then illustrate Woolf's dual allegiance to both modernism and antimodernism, to professional reading and common reading, by discussing her essay "Phases of Fiction" and the reading strategies she employed as she prepared to write the essay. Her reading notebooks reveal that she read both as a common reader and as a professional reader. A nuanced examination of Woolf's views on reading and of her own reading practices makes evident her complex relationship to modernism and to feminism. It also makes evident the complexities of these movements[2] and contributes to an understanding of the history of reading, a topic in which there is growing interest.[3]

Modern and antimodern approaches to reading differ substantially. The relationship between eighteenth- and nineteenth-century literary realism and modern Enlightenment rationality is well established within literary scholarship. If texts are seen as reflections of social reality, then they are relatively transparent media and relatively accurate mimetic representations. Reading from a realist perspective becomes a process of engaging a text in order to discover what it has to say about external reality. Readers are seen as uncovering textual meaning that resides within the text and as engaging in a process that is the same for all readers and hence uninfluenced by factors such as gender, race, and class. Twentieth-century modernism adds considerable complexity to the process because the text ceases to be a transparent medium, and readers cease to be mere discoverers of textual meaning but complex psychological beings whose reading processes can greatly influence the meaning-making process. Within a modern context, reading still tends to be universalized and described as the same for all readers regardless of their cultural situations, however.[4]

Antimodern approaches to reading such as those informed by radical and cultural feminisms differ from modern ones in that they deal directly with the politics of reading and with the situation of the woman reader. As I suggest in the introduction and in chapter 1, radical and cultural feminisms tend to be antimodern in orientation. Radical feminism identifies patriarchy or rule by men as the primary cause of women's oppression and associates traditional institutional structures and knowledges with patriarchal domination. Radical feminists oppose modern commitments to scientific and technological innovation and to professionalization because they see them as directly related to male domination and the oppression of women. According to radical feminists, women will be liberated only when such structures and knowledges are overthrown. Radical feminist approaches to reading relate the traditional literary canon with patriarchy and emphasize that women must defend against the alienating effects of canonical reading.

Cultural feminism focuses on women's common culture and on women as a group having characteristics distinct from men's. It tends to portray women's culture in positive terms, seeing it as an alternative to men's culture, which is associated with aggression, acquisitiveness, and violence. Cultural feminist approaches to reading call into question the traditional hierarchy whereby professional reading is valued more highly than nonprofessional reading, distinguish between women's and men's approaches to reading, and call for appreciative readings of women's texts and critical readings of men's texts.

I will demonstrate, then, that Woolf's approach to reading is modern in that she often portrays reading as a matter of recuperating relatively stable and determinate textual meaning but that, unlike many of her male counterparts, she emphasizes the importance of emotion in the reading process. When describing reading from a modern perspective, she tends to universalize, ignoring differences in reading practices that result from gender, race, class, and other factors. Her modernism was no doubt a result of her own situation as a professional writer and critic appreciative of the literary tradition and concerned that texts, including her own, not be misread. As I will also demonstrate, though, Woolf's approach to reading is also antimodern in that as a radical and cultural feminist, she sees reading as a political activity directly related to women's exclusion from traditional, patriarchal institutions including literary institutions. In discussing the activity of reading, therefore, she is often critical of professional readers and reading and ennobles the common reader, the nonprofessional woman reader who does not share the privilege afforded males and who reads outside patriarchal institutions for her own pleasure. In addition, Woolf sees that women need to read women's literature appreciatively and identifies a female literary tradition.

Modern Reading

Modern approaches to reading tend to be formalist and to emphasize the importance of the literary tradition in the reading of individual works. They also tend to be universalist and foundational in their conception of readers and reading. Readers are not differentiated in terms of their gender or cultural, historical, or racial situation. Formalists also emphasize the stability and determinacy of meaning.[5] The relationship between varieties of twentieth-century formalism and the Enlightenment is complicated. Although it is difficult to generalize about a complex and disparate movement, at the very least, formalism insists on the importance of the artistic medium, representing it as foundational, and disallows conceptions of the relationship between reader and text that ignore the textual artifact. If art is primarily form, it can be examined objectively and is itself an object. Often, too, formalism factors in perception, thus complicating the process. A result can be experimentation with point of view. Perception, however, tends to be seen as a process that is the same regardless of the perceiver's political situation.

Woolf makes reference to modern formalism of the Bloomsbury[6] variety in her biography of Roger Fry when she quotes a letter from Fry to G. L. Dickinson in which he says, "I want to find out what the function of content is, and am developing a theory which you will hate very much, viz. that it is merely directive of form and that all the essential aesthetic quality has to do with pure form. . . . the emotions of music and pure painting are really free abstract and universal" (*Roger Fry* 183). In Fry's version of formalism, content or the representational nature of literature or art is not negated but subordinated to form, which is associated with a work's aesthetic quality. In the passage referred to above, Fry says, "As poetry becomes more intense the content is entirely remade by the form and has no separate value at all" (*Roger Fry* 183). Formalism, for Fry at least, enables a synthesis of content and form but does not eliminate content or the mimetic nature of literature or art.

Percy Lubbock's *The Craft of Fiction,* a work to which Woolf refers in her essays, illustrates well what a formalist approach to reading can entail. Lubbock makes clear in the first sentence of the book that reading is a complicated process and that discovering textual meaning is not easy: "To grasp the shadowy and fantasmal form of a book, to hold it fast, to turn it over and survey it at leisure—that is the effort of a critic of books, and it is perpetually defeated" (1). For formalists such as Lubbock, books are difficult to grasp because reading is an experience involving memory and impressions gathered in a moment of time. The form of a book may be whole and unified, but individuals are capable of experiencing and retaining only part of that form because of the limitations of their memories.

Lubbock calls the reader's limitations a "disability" (3) and recommends that in order to overcome it, readers attempt to detach themselves from the text they are reading. He says, "So far from losing ourselves in the world of the novel, we must hold it away from us, see it all in detachment, and use the whole of it to make the image we seek, the book itself" (6). Readers must attempt to identify the form of a novel because "a literal transcript of life is plainly impossible" (10). A "really scientific account" (11) of the structure of the simplest book would not be possible because the memory of readers is not infallible. It is nevertheless necessary to attempt to "read aright . . . to get into touch with the book as nearly as may be" (13).

Another dimension of modern approaches to reading is an emphasis on the importance of the literary tradition. T. S. Eliot speaks in "What is a Classic," for instance, of maintaining an "unconscious balance" between tradition, "the collective personality . . . realized in the literature of the past," and the "originality of the living generation" (58).[7] In "Tradition and the Individual Talent," he says, "No poet, no artist of any art, has his complete meaning alone. His significance, his appreciation is the appreciation of his relation to the dead poets and artists" (72).[8] Eliot's perspective is clearly objectivist in his emphasis on depersonalization and on the relationship between depersonalized art and science (73). Eliot does not exclude emotion from consideration in discussing the reader's experience of a poem, but he insists on the difference between art and event and speaks of emotion as being "transmuted" (75). He says, "Poetry is not a turning loose of emotion, but an escape from emotion; it is not the expression of personality, but escape from personality" (76). The tradition Eliot speaks of is collectivized and universalized just as Fry and Lubbock universalize form.[9]

The modern emphasis on the stability and determinacy of meaning is exemplified by I. A. Richards's *Practical Criticism.* Richards focuses on misunderstanding, the ways in which a reader "garbles the sense, distorts the feelings, mistakes the tone and disregards the intention" (177). He demonstrates the point by examining in detail the "errors" in the reading protocols of student readers who were asked to respond to poems that had been stripped of contextual cues including title and author. He speaks of meanings in terms of intentions and of readers' distortions of intentions: "The rapidity with which many readers leap to a conviction as to a poem's general intention, and the ease with which this assumption can distort their reading, is one of the most interesting features in the protocols" (197). Richards does not ignore emotion but sees that sense and feeling are closely linked and that both can be distorted by readers insensitive to a work's intentions.

Woolf's Modern Reading

I suggest, then, that Woolf's approach to reading is modern rather than radical or cultural feminist when she modifies androcentric approaches to reading rather than rejecting them entirely and when she makes clear her respect for professional critics and the traditional canon. She makes a distinction, for instance, between professional critics such as Samuel Johnson, John Dryden, Samuel Taylor Coleridge, and Matthew Arnold, and reviewers who lacked their cultivated sensibilities. She says in "How It Strikes a Contemporary" that public critics "scan the horizon; see the past in relation to the future; and so prepare the way for masterpieces to come" (246). Such professional critics become a centralizing influence by keeping the main principles of literature closely in view, and they are especially helpful in assessing the value of works from the past and in determining how literature is developing (238). Great critics, if they are not themselves great poets, are "bred from the profusion of the age" (239). Critics may disagree in their assessments of contemporary works, but they agree in their assessment of works from the past (236).

Woolf also demonstrates modern rather than radical or cultural antimodern tendencies when she modifies rather than opposes formalist approaches to reading such as that of Percy Lubbock. Like Lubbock, she sometimes sees the text as an object whose meaning must be discovered. The goal of the reader is to attempt to achieve impartiality in the process of uncovering textual meaning. Texts have objective meaning in some varieties of formalism, but readers, because of their limitations, are unable to grasp that meaning completely or accurately. To Lubbock's cognitive description of reading, though, she adds the dimension of emotion.

Like Lubbock, she recognizes that readers cannot possibly grasp the full meaning of a work at any one time. She says in "On Not Knowing Greek," for instance, that the truth of a text is "various" (34) because it can only be partially understood in a single reading.

> And so, as you read on across the broad pages with as many slips and somnolences as you like, the illusion rises and holds you of banks slipping by on either side, of glades opening out, of white towers revealed, of gilt domes and ivory minarets. It is, indeed, an atmosphere not only soft and fine, but rich, too, with more than one can grasp at any single reading. ("Reading" 164)

Woolf often sees, as does Lubbock, that textual meaning is relatively stable but cannot be grasped fully because of the limitations of readers, and more than one reading is often required to comprehend a text. As a number of feminist literary scholars have demonstrated, however, Woolf's modernism differs in important ways from that of many of her male counterparts. Bonnie Kime Scott, for instance, explains that modernists such as Woolf, Djuna Barnes, and Rebecca West question the universality assumed by male modernists. They attend to the specificities of female experience and see that experience as positive rather than negative. Scott introduces her discussion of the modernism of Woolf, West, and Barnes by acknowledging that they were attached to "the canonized masters" but promised "different terms of attachment and a modernist weave of their own" (xxii).

One way in which Woolf's modernism differs from that of her male counterparts is her emphasis on reading as an emotional as well as an intellectual process. In "On Re-Reading Novels," Woolf repudiates the new critical belief in the literary text as a static "form." In discussing Lubbock's *The Craft of Fiction,* she says that his conception of a textual object erects an unnecessary barrier between reader and text. He has created an "alien substance." For her, form is not an object but an emotion: "The 'book itself' is not form which you see, but emotion which you feel, and the more intense the writer's feeling the more exact without slip or chink its expression in words" (160). Authors and readers connect on an emotional level, and this is achieved through the activity of the reader. Readers create order in their encounters with the different parts of a text by "feeling their right relations to each other" (160).

Woolf's conception of reading as both an emotional and cognitive process and as a process of discovering textual meaning is illustrated in her discussion in "On Re-Reading Novels" of how a reader processes a short story by Flaubert:

> The title [of Flaubert's "Un Coeur Simple"] gives us our bearings, and the first words direct our attention to Madame Aubain's faithful servant Félicité. And now the impressions begin to arrive. Madame's character; the look of her house; Félicité's appearance; her love affair with Theodore; Madame's children; her visitors; the angry bull. We accept them, but we do not use them. We lay them aside in reserve. Our attention flickers this way and that, from one to another. Still the impressions accumulate, and still, almost ignoring their individual quality, we read on noting the pity, the irony, hastily observing certain relations and contrasts, but stressing nothing; always awaiting the final signal. Suddenly we have it. The mistress and the maid are turning over the dead child's clothes. A sudden intensity of phrase, something which for good reasons or for bad we feel to be emphatic, startles us into a flash of understanding. We see now why the story was written. Later in the same way we are roused by a sentence with a very different intention. Again we have the same conviction that we know why the story was written. And then it is finished. All the observations which we have put aside now come out and range themselves according to the directions we have received. Some are relevant; others we can find no place for. On a second reading we are able to use our observations from the start, and

they are much more precise; but they are still controlled by these moments of understanding. (159–60)

Woolf's reader would seem to be a woman reader who can empathize with the situations of the women characters in the passage. Her language stresses, however, that textual details are directing the cognitive and emotional response of the reader. She also speaks of sentences having intentions. In the passage, the text seems considerably more active than the reader, who simply allows the impressions to accumulate. Her description bears some resemblance to Wolfgang Iser's "consistency-building" (*Act of Reading* 16), attempting to formulate a consistent pattern of meaning from the myriad impressions encountered as textual details are processed, though Iser's reader seems to be considerably more active than Woolf's. She finds that amidst the confusion of encountering textual details there are "moments of understanding" ("On Re-Reading Novels" 160) and that these moments accumulate and arrange themselves according to the directions we have received from the text. A second reading will be more productive in that we will have the benefit of previous observations from the text. In Woolf's account, the reader is responding to textual cues that have been arranged to communicate meaning. She is clearly optimistic that persistence will yield a satisfying interpretation.[10]

Woolf's conception of the nature of reading also differs from Iser's in that she sees the reading process as originating in an emotional response to a text. Unlike Louise Rosenblatt, whom I discuss in chapter 5, David Bleich, and Lynn Pearce, all of whom emphasize the importance of emotion in the reading process, Iser's account of the reading process ignores the emotional dimension of reading. Woolf says in "On Re-Reading Novels," "Both in writing and in reading it is the emotion that must come first" (161). Emotion is only the first step, however. "We must go on to test it and riddle it with questions. . . . Is there not something beyond emotion, something which though it is inspired by emotion, tranquilizes it, orders it, composes it?" (161).

Given Woolf's emphasis on emotion, it might seem that her perspective is Romantic and subjective.[11] When she speaks of the reading process, though, she often emphasizes that readers are responding to textual cues rather than projecting onto texts their own subjective and idiosyncratic responses. The text for her is often the active agent, the reader more passive. Like many of her male, modernist contemporaries, she often represents reading as involving the definite intentions of authors that are realized when competent readers read their work and sees that meaning is largely determinate. Readers have a responsibility to attempt to be true to the author's intended meaning and cannot simply construct meaning on the basis their own predilections. Woolf observes in her essay "Reading" that it is possible to "over-interpret," "misinterpret," and read into texts (177) and that readers must attempt to communicate with an author, to remain faithful to an intended effect. She was, after all, a writer bent on communicating with an audience—one especially sensitive to the dangers of misinterpretation. In "On

Not Knowing Greek," she speaks of the possibility of "reading wrongly," of reading into Greek poetry "not what they have but what we lack" (36). In "The Russian Point of View," she observes that inexperienced readers may be unable to experience the harmony of great works and may find that an author such as Tchekhov is "rambling disconnectedly" (180) whereas in fact he "struck now this note, now that with intention, in order to complete his meaning" (180–81). Reading Tchekhov necessitates a very "daring and alert sense of literature to make us hear the tune" (180), but the reader who has not developed such a sense may do Tchekhov's work an injustice. She warns in her essay "Addison" that readers may treat works as if they were collectors' items, "broken jars of undeniable age but doubtful beauty, to be stood in a cabinet behind glass doors," (101) and they may treat writers such as Addison with condescension.

Woolf sees that the guidance of the text is often visual.

> From the first page we feel our minds trained upon a point which becomes more and more perceptible as the book proceeds and the writer brings his conception out of darkness. At last the whole is exposed to view. And then, when the book is finished, we seem to see (it is strange how visual the impression is) something girding it about like the firm road of Defoe's storytelling; or we see it shaped and symmetrical with dome and column complete, like *Pride and Prejudice* and *Emma*. ("Phases of Fiction" 143)

A characteristic of masterpieces is that the author

> inflicts his own perspective upon us so severely that as often as not we suffer agonies—our vanity is injured because our own order is upset; we are afraid because the old supports are being wrenched from us; and we are bored—for what pleasure or amusement can be plucked from a brand new idea? Yet from anger, fear, and boredom a rare and lasting delight is sometimes born. ("Robinson Crusoe" 44–45)

Woolf was no doubt drawn to a modern perspective because she was herself a professional who wanted to be understood. To an extent, she embraced a form of objectivist modernism that has positivistic overtones in its emphasis on meaning residing within the text and on the reader's passive role in recovering it. Her objectivism, though, was modified by her insistence that reading is not simply a cognitive activity but has emotional dimensions as well.

Woolf's Radical and Cultural Feminist Reading

Although Woolf's approach to reading is, at times, modern in its emphasis on the text's control of readers, the reader's obligation to read a text correctly, and the value of professional reading, it is at other times radical feminist in its critique of the traditional canon and of traditional ways of reading, associating both with patriarchy.[12] Professions are seen as male-dominated and alienating for women. If women, nonprofessional readers for the most part, are to survive oppressive structures, they must find separate spaces where they can find protection against the damaging tendencies of the professions.

In emphasizing Woolf's radical feminism, I do not preclude consideration of Woolf's socialist tendencies or her internationalism. Her radical feminism is usually combined with other tendencies. Jane Marcus argues convincingly in *Art and Anger,* for instance, that Woolf's intellectual position is that of a "committed and active socialist, pacifist, and feminist" (68). Susan Stanford Friedman in *Mappings* finds that for Woolf, the local is co-complicit with the national and international (118). Friedman asks that we see Woolf's work as ethnographies of travelling in which systems of power outside the home perpetually destabilize the home (120). Friedman uses the example of *To the Lighthouse,* with its location on the Isle of Skye, to make the point that for Woolf, Britain, like all nations, "has its own centers and peripheries, its history of internal conquest and colonization, its 'foreigners' and 'others'" (120).

Woolf's radical feminism is especially pronounced in *A Room of One's Own* and *Three Guineas.* In both, Woolf denounces patriarchal institutions and explores ways in which women can defend against them. In *A Room of One's Own,* Woolf focuses directly on the activity of reading, especially in her critiques of male-dominated universities, which excluded women, and the male-dominated literary canon. She speaks of libraries that house books written by men and of the situation of women who were often poor and excluded from writing and literature because of the responsibilities of childrearing. If women are to counter the effects of patriarchy within the literary realm, they must create a countertradition by thinking back through their mothers (79). They must also have a room of their own and money to be productive.

In *Three Guineas* the emphasis on reading is less direct. Woolf sees that patriarchy results in warfare and oppressive political and economic power, and warfare results from the need of educated men to demonstrate their superiority over others. Education does not teach people to hate force but to use it. Success in a profession results in professionals losing their senses and their sight (72). She also speaks of the sciences as being gendered male and "infected" by patriarchy (139). If women are to help prevent war, they need to create a "Society of Outsiders" who will seek freedom, equality, and peace but have different traditions and values than those of men (113).

Woolf sees that the professions have been implicated in the oppression of women and that they perpetuate oppression through their systematic exclusions and distortions. To maintain their own integrity, women need to remain outside or on the margins of patriarchal institutions. They will need a room of their own and a modest amount of money in order to liberate themselves from oppressive circumstances, but ambitions greater than these would certainly be corrupting.

Woolf's conception of reading has radical-feminist tendencies in that she is critical of professional reviewers who typify for her approaches to reading that can destroy writers. Most of the professional readers in Woolf's age were male reviewers whom she despised because they had a powerful effect on the reputation of an author but had not developed the critical abilities of a great critic. She explains in her essay "Reviewing" that in the nineteenth century, the distinction between critics and reviewers became more pronounced. Critics such as Coleridge and Arnold were professionally responsible, taking "their time and their space" in their writing (128), whereas reviewers became less and less responsible. Their reviews were often anonymous and written hurriedly, without reflection. As a writer sensitive to the damage a reviewer could inflict, Woolf did not disguise her contempt for these incorruptible policemen of literary texts whose assessments can lead to a "desiccation of living tissues of literature into a network of little bones" ("How It Strikes a Contemporary" 239).

Woolf distinguishes between those who love learning and those who love reading. The former are professionals who read for a purpose and search "through books to discover some particular grain of truth" (24). Common readers, in contrast, read purely and disinterestedly and must check their desire for learning, their temptation to read systematically in order to become a specialist or an authority ("Hours in a Library" 24). Readers have their own purpose and function. And though the readers' activity is bound to be limited, personal, and erratic, their language neither universal nor learned as is the critic's, their ignorance gives them an advantage. Readers are less dependent on fixed labels and settled hierarchies ("Phases of Fiction" 94). Readers are not rushed and so do not make premature judgments. A reviewer, in contrast, often leads a pressured life and is "driven by force of circumstances and some human vanity to hide those hesitations which beset him as he reads, to smooth all traces of that crablike and crooked path by which he has reached what he chooses to call a 'conclusion'" ("An Essay in Criticism" 86).

If modern conceptions of reading focus on the ways in which texts control readers' responses, radical-feminist ones see that texts can dominate and harm readers. Readers can be overpowered by texts just as women can be overpowered by domineering males. In "A Friend of Johnson," for instance, she says, "A great book, like a great nature, may have disastrous effects upon other people. It robs them of their character and substitutes its own" (187). In "Notes on an Elizabethan Play," she speaks of the power that a body of literature has to impose itself.

> Literature will not suffer itself to be read passively, but takes us and reads us, flouts our preconceptions; questions principles which we had got into the habit of taking for granted, and, in fact, splits us into two parts as we read, making us, even as we enjoy, yield our ground or stick to our guns. (49)

Because nonprofessional readers can become overpowered by texts, Woolf encourages them to read with independence and not to bow to recognized authority. In "How Should One Read a Book?" she urges readers, "Take no advice, to follow your own instincts, to use your own reason, to come to your own conclusions" (234). Readers need to be free to evaluate works on their own terms, to discover their own approaches to the texts they encounter.

> To admit authorities, however heavily furred and gowned, into our libraries and let them tell us how to read, what to read, what value to place upon what we read, is to destroy the spirit of freedom which is the breath of those sanctuaries. Everywhere else we may be bound by laws and conventions—there we have none. ("How Should One Read a Book?" 234)

Readers can also defend themselves by choosing the texts they read carefully, because great writers attempt to control the power they have over readers. Although great writers could use their power to excite human sympathy, they modify this reaction by erecting barriers between reader and text so that readers do not slip easily into a familiar world. The masterpiece guides without becoming overwhelming.

Woolf's approach to reading is also cultural feminist in that she focuses on common readers, nonprofessional readers who read for their own pleasure, on the ways in which women should read other women's works, and on women's literary traditions.[13] Woolf's common reader, often a woman reader, is a nonprofessional reader who reads for her own pleasure rather than for her own professional advancement. In defining herself as a common reader rather than a professional critic, Woolf was aligning herself with her less-privileged sisters many of whom were no doubt her actual readers, individuals outside the elite circles of educated males who wrote books and prepared critical reviews of other books. Such readers, she argued, had a degree of power in the sense that their opinions had an effect on the reputations of writers.

> It is unlikely that we shall be able, even after a lifetime of reading, to make any valuable contribution to its criticism. We must remain readers; we shall not put on the further glory that belongs to those rare beings who are critics. But still we have our responsibilities as readers and even our importance. The standards we raise and the judgments we pass steal into the air and become part of the atmosphere which writers breathe as they work. An influence is created which tells upon them if it never finds its way into print. And that influence, if it were well instructed, vigorous and individual and sincere, might be of great value now when criticism is necessarily in abeyance. ("How Should One Read a Book?" 244)

Common readers are bound to writers in intimate ways, the writer dependent on the reader. Readers may at times seem more powerful than the delicate and fragile writers, but they are nevertheless a vulnerable class, often female, and in need of support and advice. They will no doubt feel themselves inferior to the professional critic and thus may lack confidence: "So the crude trumpet blasts of critical opinion blow loud and shrill and we, humble readers that we are, bow our submissive heads" ("An Essay in Criticism" 86).

Common readers have a special obligation to women writers. In chapter 5 of *A Room of One's Own,* Woolf imagines a common reader, her narrator, encountering a novel, *Life's Adventures,* written by a woman writer, Mary Carmichael. The narrator is a nonprofessional reader browsing in the library looking for no particular book and allowing the situation to dictate what she will read. She pulls Carmichael's *Life's Adventures* from the shelf at random; other novels would have done as well. The book is Carmichael's first book, but it is actually a volume in a long series or tradition, in this case a women's tradition: "For books continue each other, in spite of our habit of judging them separately" (84). Books are not discrete works. A single woman writer is a descendant of other women writers and inherits their characteristics and restrictions.

The narrator begins the reading process itself by taking up a pencil and a notebook, lest she glide into a torpid slumber. She is going to read actively. Although her initial impression is somewhat negative, she restrains herself from forming a firm opinion. She is determined to "do her duty" by her as a reader (85). We learn that the narrator is self-consciously aware of the audience for whom she is describing her reading process—they are other women. This becomes crucially important because she needs to feel that her listeners will not censor her comments, will not be unsympathetic to her observation that Carmichael's sentence, "Chloe liked Olivia," represents a profound shift in the subject matter of novels in modern times. A woman writer has noticed that sometimes women do like women. A woman writer has described women from a woman's perspective.

The narrator becomes appreciative of Carmichael's style, referring to it as "highly developed" and "infinitely intricate." She observes that women are difficult to evaluate because measures of evaluation have been developed by men to evaluate men's achievements. There is no "mark on the wall" to measure women's achievements. She develops this idea further, commenting that it would be a pity if women wrote like men and concluding that education ought to bring out and fortify the differences rather than the similarities between men and women (91). Women should chronicle women's achievements, the obscure lives that have been ignored by men's narratives (93), but also the vanities of men because men cannot see their weaknesses themselves (94).

Final judgment is withheld, though, until the narrator has read more of the work. The real test is whether Carmichael can demonstrate that she has looked into the depths of her material, has brought the reader to a summit, and presented to her a majestic vision beneath (97). The narrator decides that Carmichael has at least made the attempt. Considering that she was no genius, was an unknown woman writing her first novel without sufficient time or money, she did not do badly (98). What she needs is a room of her own, money, and another hundred years' time (98).

Woolf's suggestions in the chapter are analogous in some ways to recommendations discussed in essays such as "How Should One Read a Book?" though here her recommendations are gender inflected. She suggests in the chapter that it is important for women readers to read women's texts appreciatively, even those by obscure authors. Once a text has been selected, the woman reader should place the woman's text within a larger context and should see it as belonging to a long tradition of women's writing. Although it is difficult to withhold judgment of a work, the woman reader should attempt to do so when she is reading another woman's work. She should read the work appreciatively, looking for its strengths and defending against the inevitable reservations that come to mind as one reads. In contrast, the woman reader should read men's texts critically, deliberately attempting to identify manifestations of men's "vanities" (*Room of One's Own* 94). Her approach is similar to the one Patrocinio P. Schweickart takes in "Reading Ourselves." Schweickart recommends that feminist readers read women writers in a caring way, defending them against possible misreadings and placing their work within the context of their lived lives. In contrast, feminist readers should take control of their reading of androcentric texts by becoming self-consciously aware of the ways in which those texts are alienating (51).

Assertive Reading

Woolf develops her radical-feminist and cultural-feminist approaches to reading by exploring ways in which common readers should read lest they be overwhelmed by powerful texts. She suggests in "How Should One Read a Book?" that the reading of nonprofessional readers should involve both sympathy and judgment. Readers must allow texts to speak for themselves; they must submit to them. On the other hand, readers cannot allow themselves to be dominated by texts or by the opinions of established critics, and so readers must also judge the works they read. Reading, then, is a lifelong process that involves cultivation of an informed sensibility that allows the reader to respond actively to texts without being consumed by them. The common reader must learn to read responsively and assertively without losing her own identity in the process.

As the title of "How Should One Read a Book?" suggests, the essay focuses on how common readers should go about reading and thus crystallizes Woolf's thinking on what the reading process should be for the nonprofessional reader, the woman reader. The essay is therefore cultural feminist in its assumptions even if it is not overtly so. The title, Woolf reminds us, is a question rather than an assertion. Woolf does not want to prescribe how all readers should read. Hers is advice and no more, helpful suggestions from one common reader to another, from one equal to another. Women readers should not follow prescriptions rigidly, because the most important quality they need to develop is independence and the freedom to explore on their own (234). Freedom, though, necessitates control and selection. Libraries are places of "multitudinous chaos" (235) that must be ordered in some way.

The first step is to banish all preconceptions. The reader should try to become the author, to become a "fellow-worker" and "accomplice." Initially, the mind must be opened as widely as possible, and criticism and reservations should be suspended. Woolf calls for empathy on the part of the reader and goes so far as to suggest that the reader become a writer and attempt to recreate a scene as a writer would in order to appreciate the difficulty inherent in the task and the "mastery" of great writers such as Daniel Defoe, Jane Austen, and Thomas Hardy. These great writers are capable of creating consistent visions of reality, of uniting the "thousand conflicting impressions" (236) that constitute our daily experience. Their works, therefore, demand fineness of perception and boldness of imagination on the part of the reader (236).

Not all books, however, are masterpieces. Most works are less demanding and are read in a different way for a different purpose. They provide information about how other people live their lives; they satisfy our curiosity, but they can also be read as a way of refreshing and exercising our creative powers. The reader can complete the half-truths that such works contain. She is free to stop reading and contemplate life beyond the library. The reader will no doubt return, though, to more demanding reading, to poetry, for instance, because "rubbish-reading" is not, finally, very satisfying. It provides us with mere facts rather than interpretations (239).

If the first stage in the process Woolf describes is to acquire a posture of openness to the text in order to understand it, the second stage involves judgment. We will not fully appreciate a work, not fully enjoy it, until we have compared it to other works. This second stage necessitates allowing for the "dust of reading to settle" and for the conflict and questioning to die down (242). The reader should set the text aside, do other things, and allow the book to return to the mind's eye as a whole. Apparently without conscious control or intent, details of the work will fit themselves into a pattern.

In this second stage, however, the reader is no longer the friend of the author but rather a judge. "And just as we cannot be too sympathetic as friends, so as judges we cannot be too severe," for books that waste our time and sympathy are "criminals" and "the most insidious enemies of society, corrupters, defilers" (242). Books are judged by comparing them with the greatest of their kind. The reader, then, must be well read and must have formed refined judgments of literary masterpieces.

This second stage is more difficult than the first because it necessitates that the reader read without the book before her, and the second stage is successfully accomplished only if the reader has read widely and well. It involves "imagination, insight, and learning" (243). Preparation for this stage is a lifelong process and primarily involves cultivation of our feelings and of the "nerve of sensation" (242) that sends shocks through us. In time, the reader can train her taste and submit it to control. The result is an ability not only to judge particular books but also to generalize about common characteristics of books. We can create "rules" that allow for greater powers of discrimination and thus greater pleasure. These "rules" are constantly changing, though, as new texts are encountered and judged (244).

Only after the reader has gone through this extensive process should the common reader, that is, the woman reader, turn to critics such as Coleridge, Dryden, and Johnson. At this stage in the process, their judgments are often surprisingly relevant. They "light up and solidify the vague ideas that have been tumbling in the misty depths of our minds. But they are only able to help us if we come to them laden with questions and suggestions won honestly in the course of our own reading." They can do nothing for us if "we herd ourselves under their authority and lie down like sheep in the shade of a hedge" (244). We can only understand their judgments when they come in conflict with our own and vanquish them (244).

This training of the taste of the common reader is important because it can have social value. The quality of writing will improve if the opinion of common readers has as much influence on writers as the "erratic gunfire" of reviewers in the "shooting gallery" of professional criticism (245). Ultimately, however, we read because we want to, because it gives us pleasure. Reading does not need to be justified on any other grounds. It is fulfilling in itself. In "How Should One Read a Book?" Woolf does not suggest that the process should vary in accordance with the nature of the text under consideration. Elsewhere in her writings, however, and in her own reading practices, it often appears that the sympathetic stage, which involves emotion, is protracted and the judgment stage diminished or eliminated completely in the reading of women's texts. The process is reversed in the reading of men's texts.[14]

Woolf as Both Common and Professional Reader

Woolf provides us a useful illustration of how the process she recommends in "How Should One Read a Book" actually works in her essay "Phases of Fiction." Her extensive discussions of common reading are in some ways contradicted by her own reading practices, though, in that she was both a nonprofessional reader and a professional one.[15] The notebooks she used as she prepared the essay suggest that in some ways Woolf read as a common reader, reading for her own pleasure, and that she sometimes read women's novels differently from men's novels. They also reveal, however, that Woolf also read as a professional reader with very specific goals because she was often preparing a work that she hoped would be published.

Woolf tells us that her intention in writing "Phases of Fiction" is to "record the impressions made upon the mind by reading a certain number of novels in succession" (93). She is recording the extended process of a common reader who is reading neither historically nor critically but randomly, ignoring chronology and canonical status. This reader selects books to read on the basis of personal taste rather than received opinion. Unlike critics or historians who speak a universal language and bring to their reading extensive knowledge of an author's biography and reputation, the common reader confronts the writer directly, is unhampered by predispositions, and hence is more likely to find the center of a work and to read creatively, actively.

The essay records Woolf's considered impressions after reading approximately twenty-five novels and five short stories in an attempt to classify them and to identify their common and distinguishing features. The categories she arrived at are as follows: the Truth-Tellers (Defoe, Norris, Maupassant, Trollope, and Swift); the Romantics (Scott, Stevenson, and Radcliffe); the Character-Mongers and Comedians (Dickens, Austen, and Eliot); the Psychologists (James, Proust, and Dostoyevsky); the Satirists and Fantastics (Peacock and Sterne); and the Poets (Meredith, Hardy, Emily Brontë, and Melville).

The style of the essay conveys the impression of informality and spontaneity, the language is fresh and conversational, and the transitions between sections seem to arise naturally. Woolf has captured the sensation of the mind in the process of making judgments and synthesizing material in an unfettered way. We are made to feel that Woolf as reader is at the second stage in the process described above—she has read her material, and now she is attempting to make sense of it, to arrive at critical assessments, and to distill what she has read.

The reading notebooks that Woolf kept as she prepared "Phases of Fiction" indicate that in some ways she did adhere to her prescriptions of how common readers should read as she prepared for this essay. For the most part, the comments in the notebooks are observations or descriptions of portions of the texts rather than judgments on them. The observations are brief, fragmented, spontaneous, and sometimes punctuated by longer discussions occasioned, apparently, by moments of understanding.

The notebooks also make evident that Woolf proceeded through a book fairly quickly, pausing now and then to jot down whatever came to mind, usually indicating in the margin the specific page that prompted the reflection, as common readers might. These pauses were not too frequent, nor are the entries themselves extensive. Often they were phrases rather than complete sentences, and they were clearly intended only for Woolf herself. She often used abbreviations and frequently omitted conjunctions, verbs, and punctuation. The entries vary in length. The notes for Thomas Love Peacock's *Crotchet's Castle,* for instance, are only a page long. Here, Woolf paused six times at irregular intervals to make brief observations about the novel (14, B.15). The notes on Laurence Sterne's *Tristram Shandy,* in contrast, are ten pages long, and Woolf paused thirty-four times to make observations, again at irregular intervals (14, B.16). The entries are occasionally direct quotes from the text or questions that perplexed her. They are seldom plot summaries. More often, they are comments on action, on characters, or on the craft of the writer, or they are comparisons with other texts or authors.

Woolf also seems to have read the women's novels more sympathetically than the men's as would a cultural feminist. The entry on George Eliot's *Silas Marner,* for instance, is appreciative and even handed. She begins the entry with the observation, after reading through page 5 of the novel:

> [A]t once the author's reflections and deduction begin—men in general—to them pain and mishap present a far wider range of possibilities than gladness and enjoyment—the generalizing—the melancholy. Very characteristic and "I" is at once a person—never in J.[ane] A.[usten]. (14, B.11)

These observations exemplify phase one of the two-phase reading process Woolf recommends in "How to Read a Book." She is beginning to form an impression of the novel and to generalize about it. These impressions and generalizations may prove useful in writing the actual essay. Woolf develops more fully the comparison between Austen and Eliot in "Phases of Fiction" and specifically mentions the intervention of the *I* in *Silas Marner* (118). Later, in the notebook entry, Woolf observes, "Every fact is commented upon, used to illustrate something. . . . A large part of our pleasure is that this is old mellow—picturesque. These are very simple—any complexity comes from G.[eorge] E.[liot]'s own reflections" (14, B.11). Woolf's notes on Austen's *Pride and Prejudice* are also appreciative. She mentions Austen's sense of "real" life and of minute traces of character ("Jane Austen" 46, B.18).

Her entries on work by two male writers, George Meredith and Sterne, however, are different. She is quite critical of Meredith's *Richard Feverel* right from the start, observing, "M.[eredith] doesn't write plain narrative at all well—sketchy, jerky" ("Richard Feverel" 46, B.5). She observes after 91 pages of Meredith's *Beauchamp's Career,* "A dialogue of incredible soppishness," and says after 186 pages, "Given up at Vol. I because of the incredible long windedness" (46, B.6). She suspends her harsh judgment of Sterne's *Sentimental Journey,* though, until after she has completed the work. She concludes that "the effect of the whole is rather too monstrous—all done in the same kindly mood—unlike T.[ristram] S.[handy]" ("Sen¹ Journey" 46, B.14).

Woolf clearly read as a woman reader, a common reader, as she proceeded through the novels in preparation for "Phases of Fiction, but there is also considerable evidence in the notebooks that Woolf read the books she discusses as a professional would, for a definite purpose, in this case to write what was to have been a book about reading novels. *Phases of Fiction* was announced as forthcoming by the Hogarth Press in 1927 but was not completed until 1929 when it appeared in essay form in *Bookman* in April, May, and June of 1929. Woolf clearly read somewhat systematically in preparation for the essay. In notebook 14, for instance, which includes entries made between 1927 and 1929, she makes evident that she was working from a tentative plan for the essay. She observes about Jane

Austen's *Northanger Abbey,* "The whole character is given in dialogue. It shrinks up the vapours amazingly" ("Northanger Abbey" 14, B.4). Then she digresses somewhat: "This however does make one wish for more psychology: therefore the ps: chapter should come next: then the stylists. then the poets" (14 B.4). At the conclusion of this notebook, Woolf makes some general observations that are clearly preparation for the essay. She observes that one identifies oneself much more completely with Proust than with Defoe (14 B.23), an observation that finds its way into "Phases of Fiction."

Another indication that she read methodically is that the apparent order in which she read the novels does bear some resemblance to the order in which she discusses them in "Phases of Fiction." In Notebook 14, for instance, the entries are arranged as follows: Radcliffe's *Mysteries of Udolpho,* Austen's *Northanger Abbey,* Dickens's *Bleak House,* Eliot's *Silas Marner,* James's *What Maisie Knew,* Proust's *The Guermantes Way,* Dostoyevsky's *The Possessed,* Peacock's *Crotchet's Castle,* Sterne's *Tristram Shandy,* and Melville's *Moby-Dick.* She treats these authors in roughly this sequence in the essay itself. She did not select the texts she read and the order in which she read them on the basis of impulse alone as would a common reader. She clearly had reasons for reading what she did, and she read with this purpose in mind. She was reading systematically, somewhat hurriedly, it would seem, in order to complete a project. She was testing hypotheses, trying to work through a vague plan as she proceeded through the texts. This plan she refined and altered considerably as she proceeded.

Woolf's reading processes illustrate her commitments to both nonprofessional reading and professional reading, to modernism and antimodernism. If she was a radical and cultural feminist and hence antimodern in her insistence that reading is associated with androcentric traditions and in her focus on the reading of common readers who read for their personal ends, she was modern in her purposefulness, in her emphasis on the importance of reading with accuracy, and in her appreciation for the literary canon and for professional critics.[16] Her advice on how a book should be read was aimed at the common reader, but she was herself, very often, a professional reader reading for very specific purposes and intent on earning a living, establishing a reputation, and competing with her male counterparts for respect within literary circles. As a professional critic, she published over five hundred critical articles in the most important forums for literary discussion of her day. She was both a common reader and a professional writer and critic, both an outsider and an insider. It mattered to her a great deal how common readers and reviewers read because she was a writer who wanted desperately to be understood and appreciated.

The radical and cultural feminisms nascent in Woolf's work are developed more fully in the work of Adrienne Rich and Alice Walker, whom I discuss in chapter 4. Like Woolf, they challenge patriarchal institutions and structures. Unlike Woolf, however, who had to suppress and repress the contradictions that troubled her in many areas including sexual orientation and marriage, Rich and Walker developed alternative lifestyles and more fully developed feminist perspectives. Their opposition to modernism was considerably more hard-hitting and considerably more direct.

4

Rich and Walker on Writing and Mothering: Radical/Cultural Feminist and Womanist Perspectives

> I do not mind being my mother's daughter, I like it even. I like the attention, the way the people who love my mother's writing dote on me and make me feel like I am special, too. Standing by my mother's elbow at the end of the long line of people, I make myself available to them and drink in all of their adoration. They want to touch my mother, but mostly they want to look at me, to search my face for signs of her. Do I write? What do I want to be when I am grown up? Am I proud of my mama?
> —Rebecca Walker, *Black, White, and Jewish: Autobiography of a Shifting Self*

*A*drienne Rich, like Virginia Woolf, needed to free herself of the influence of her successful father, who was a teacher and researcher in the Department of Pathology at the Johns Hopkins Medical School, and hence to free herself of modern approaches to the family and to education. She also had to come to terms with the Jewish heritage her father attempted to deny. In contrast, Alice Walker, the African American daughter of a Georgia sharecropper, grew up considerably farther removed from modern educational institutions. Both Rich and Walker nevertheless obtained college degrees and had to deal with the challenges and contradictions of attempting to integrate a professional life of writing with the traditional role of motherhood, but they did so in different ways. Rich's writing occurred largely after she had raised her three sons, and the impossibilities of mothering in a heterosexist, patriarchal culture became an important focus of her radical-feminist critique. Walker was better able to integrate writing and mothering, perhaps because she had only one child, though her struggle was sometimes accompanied by depression.

In this chapter, I explore the theme of writing and mothering in the essays of Rich and Walker, arguing that both had strong antimodern-feminist tendencies, though Rich's perspective is primarily radical feminist, Walker's primarily what she calls a womanist perspective, a form of cultural feminism. Both, however, move in the direction of postmodern perspectives as they attempt to deal with the complexities of the approaches they embrace. Suzanne Clark in *Sentimental Modernism* speaks of Walker as a postmodernist writer. She sees *The Color Purple* as a "rewriting of nineteenth-century slave narratives, but also of sentimental love narratives and the epistolary mode" (182). Neither Rich nor Walker was dogmatic in discussions of the oppressions of women and blacks. Rich found ways to break out of the essentializing logics of radical feminism, Walker out of the essentializing logics of cultural feminism. Rich came to recognize the importance of differences within the category woman and Walker the importance of inclusive discussions of oppression. Finally, then, they are both helpful in providing a richly nuanced view of the relationship between writing and mothering. As both Rich and Walker illustrate, the woman writer who is also a mother can choose the role of intellectual or researcher and thus report on the situation of those who would otherwise have no opportunity to speak. Ultimately, both Rich and Walker move beyond the limitations of their gender and their culture and of modern attitudes toward the family and education and provide an expansive view of what it means to mother and what it means to write. Before discussing Rich and Walker, however, I will provide a brief overview of some feminist approaches to writing and mothering.

Feminist Perspectives on Writing and Mothering

Modern, antimodern, and postmodern feminist perspectives on writing and mothering differ in important ways. Modern feminist perspectives elevate the activity of writing above the activity of mothering, privileging men's projects over ones that have been traditionally reserved for women and calling for relief from the onerous task of raising children so that women can get on with the most important work, contributing to public life. Antimodern feminist ones either emphasize the damaging effects patriarchal culture has had on mothering in the case of radical feminism or emphasize the importance of women's work and mothering in the case of cultural feminism. Postmodern feminist perspectives on writing and mothering attempt to find ways of enabling women to deal with the contradictions and complexities of the two activities.

Mary Wollstonecraft's *A Vindication of the Rights of Woman,* which I discuss in chapter 1 in the context of liberal feminism, exemplifies the modern feminist approach. Wollstonecraft argues that women would be better mothers if they were allowed to become rational creatures and free citizens.

> As the rearing of children—that is, the laying a foundation of sound health both of body and mind in the rising generation—has justly been insisted on as the peculiar destination of woman, the ignorance that incapacitates them must be contrary to the order of things. (280)

According to Wollstonecraft, women would be able to pursue a "plan of conduct" if there were an interval between the birth of each child. Their children should not prevent them from reading literature, studying science, or practicing one of the arts (282). Presumably, too, their children would not prevent them from writing.

Simone de Beauvoir's modern perspective, which I also discuss in chapter 1, reflects the influences of twentieth-century movements such as socialism and existentialism.[1] Her approach to writing and mothering is similar to Wollstonecraft's, however, in that she, too, lauds scientific approaches to mothering and sees that women need to undertake projects that lead to self-actualization rather than immanence (604). Certainly writing is one of these projects. In *The Second Sex,* Beauvoir focuses on the negative aspects of mothering, claiming that infants in our culture are almost always born to discontented women who are sexually frigid or unsatisfied, socially inferior to men, and with little independent grasp on the world or the future (484). She begins her chapter "The Mother" in *The Second Sex* with a discussion of the value of scientific approaches to contraception and with a defense of abortion. Beauvoir emphasizes that there is no maternal "instinct." The mother's attitude depends on her total situation and her reaction to it (482). Because women often find themselves in positions of servitude and humiliation, it is unlikely that they will be successful mothers or that their offspring will thrive. Beauvoir finds the contradiction between contempt for women and respect for mothers an "extravagant fraudulence" (494). Like Wollstonecraft, Beauvoir feels that women need to participate in the economic, political, and social life of the times if they are to be effective mothers (495).

Radical feminists place greater emphasis on the ways in which traditional women's roles have been damaging to mothers, preventing them from achieving selfhood. Tillie Olsen in *Silences* speaks of "the unnatural thwarting of what struggles to come into being, but cannot" (6). She compares silences to other unnatural occurrences: "When the seed strikes the stone; the soil will not sustain; the spring that is false; the time is drought or blight or infestation; the frost comes premature" (6). Olsen writes of her own silences and of the twenty years she bore and reared her children and worked outside the home when the simplest circumstances for creation did not exist. Nevertheless, the hope of writing was "the air I breathed" (19).

> Bliss of movement. A full extended family life; the world of my job (transcriber in a dairy-equipment company); and the writing, which I was somehow able to carry around within me through work, through home. Time on the bus, even when I had to stand, was enough; the stolen moments at work, enough; the deep night hours for as long as I could stay awake, after the kids were in bed, after the household tasks were done, sometimes during. . . .
>
> In such snatches of time I wrote what I did in those years, but there came a time when this triple life was no longer possible. The fifteen hours of daily realities became too much distraction for the writing. I lost craziness of endurance. What might have been, I don't know; but I applied for, and was given, eight months' writing time.

> There was still full family life, all the household responsibilities, but I did not have to hold an eight-hour job. I had continuity, three full days, sometimes more—and it was in those months I made the mysterious turn and became a writing writer. (19–20)

Radical feminist Azizah Al-Hibri in "Reproduction, Mothering, and the Origins of Patriarchy" attempts to explain why women have traditionally been relegated to the traditional roles Olsen speaks of. Al-Hibri argues that because males were threatened by women's reproductive power, they minimized the importance of reproduction and maximized the importance of production; "both male technology and patriarchy are based on the male's feeling of inadequacy and mortality vis-à-vis the female" (87). Writing is no doubt one of these technologies. If the institution of motherhood is to be transformed, according to radical feminists, patriarchy must be overthrown.

Cultural feminists, in contrast, focus on the positive aspects of mothering, sometimes seeing that mothering enhances writing. Alicia Ostriker in *Writing Like a Woman,* for instance, thinks that motherhood is an advantage for a woman writer because it puts her in immediate and inescapable contact with the sources of life, death, beauty, growth, and corruption (130). Mothering can become a woman writer's subject, one relatively unexplored yet rich in social and political implications, according to Ostriker, as writers such as Adrienne Rich, Dorothy Dinnerstein, Olsen, Phyllis Chesler, and Nancy Chodorow have demonstrated (131). Like Ostriker, Mary Catherine Bateson in *Composing a Life* speaks of writing and mothering in positive terms, describing the lives of women who were able to successfully integrate mothering with writing and other professional activities. She distinguishes between physical energy, which is finite and must be conserved, and "energy" or vitality, which is psychological. An activity that affects vitality is not directly competitive or subtractive from other activities but may enhance them (170). To Bateson, mothering is clearly such an activity.

Cultural feminist Sara Ruddick in *Maternal Thinking* argues that to be a mother is to meet three demands for preservation, growth, and social acceptability through works of preservative love, nurturance, and training (17). For Ruddick, maternal thought involves developing intellectual capacities, making judgments, assuming metaphysical attitudes, and affirming values (24). Maternal thought, then, should complement and enable other kinds of thought. Carol Gilligan in *In a Different Voice* promotes the relationality and connectedness of women's approaches to moral reasoning, and the *Women's Ways of Knowing* collective, Mary Field Belenky, Blythe McVicker Clinchy, Nancy Rule Goldberger, and Jill Mattuck Tarule, values connected knowing and cooperative learning.

Alice Adams's "Maternal Bonds: Recent Literature on Mothering" provides an overview of feminist work on mothering, most of which has a cultural orientation. Adams finds that themes of separating and connecting are central, as they have been in the past, to recent works on mothering, but the focus has shifted from the mother-child relationship to the relationship of mothers to society as a whole (415). Mothers have brought about profound social and economic changes that outstrip the interpretive power of representations of motherhood (427). Mothering, it would seem, is more powerful than male-dominated activities such as writing.

Feminist compositionists sometimes approach writing and mothering from a cultural-feminist perspective as well. Elisabeth Daeumer and Sandra Runzo in "Transforming the Composition Classroom," for instance, begin their essay by making a connection between the work of teachers and the work of mothers (45). Donnalee Rubin in *Gender Influences: Reading Student Texts* argues that teachers, male and female alike, who employ conferencing and a process-based pedagogy follow maternal patterns of behavior (58). Mothering is held up as an ideal, a model for all relationships that involve nurturing.

Postmodern feminists, however, tend to be critical of the celebratory mode of some cultural feminists. Ellen Ross in "New Thoughts on 'the Oldest Vocation': Mothers and Motherhood in Recent Feminist Scholarship," for instance, criticizes Ruddick's *Maternal Thinking* for failing to emphasize that mothering also involves unending hard work, trouble, and sorrow. Ross finds that more recent work on mothering establishes more realistic contours of motherhood that can start to heal "our mass mother-blaming psychosis" and reorient public policies and debates on numerous issues in which women and their children figure (399). Janice Hays in "Intellectual Parenting and a Developmental Feminist Pedagogy of Writing" deliberately uses "parental" in place of "maternal" in order to "avoid the dichotomizing gender-role attributes that the term *maternal* inevitably evokes" (161).

The perspective on mothering expressed in *Black Feminist Thought* by Patricia Hill Collins is postmodern in that she avoids essentialized conceptions of mothering. She defends black mothers against charges of failing to discipline their children, of emasculating their sons, of defeminizing their daughters, and of retarding their children's academic achievement (115), but she also writes against equally damaging representations held by black men that black mothers are superstrong, arguing that such images fail to acknowledge the real costs of mothering to African American women (116). Collins recognizes that there are "othermothers" as well as bloodmothers. Much of black women's status in African American communities, according to Collins, stems not only from actions as mothers in black family networks but from contributions as community othermothers (132).

Julia Kristeva's perspective in "Stabat Mater" is also postmodern in that she sees that a fantasy of motherhood has overshadowed the real experience of mothering and that feminism needs to create new representations of femininity and of motherhood. Some feminist groups, though, according to Kristeva, unfortunately reject motherhood entirely or accept, consciously or not, traditional representations of motherhood (161). Kristeva attempts to begin creating an alternative feminist discourse in the interpellations she provides in the essay. She tries to capture the experience of childbirth in language: "Let a body venture at last out of its shelter, take a chance with meaning under a veil of words" (162). Her attempt results in powerful meanings.

> Shiver of the eyelashes, imperceptible twitch of the eyebrows, quiv-
> ering skin, anxious reflections, seeking, knowing, casting their
> knowledge aside in the face of my non-knowledge: fleeting irony of
> childhood gentleness that awakens to meaning, surpasses it, goes past
> it, causes me to soar in music, in dance. (173)

Kristeva speaks of the process of creating a new discourse on mothering, one that she hopes will provide both women and men with a new ethics encompassing both reproduction and death. She also speaks of motherhood not having a discourse (184) and of the often reactionary role of mothers in the service of male domi-nating power (183). As the stories of Walker's and Rich's experiences in the next section will demonstrate, the actual fact of mothering has always been the site of contradictory tensions between social expectations and individual realities.[2]

Rich's Radical and Cultural Feminisms

Adrienne Rich had considerable obstacles to overcome in her attempt to be both a writer and a mother. She was a traditional housewife in the 1950s and had primary responsibility for raising three boys. Her radical feminist perspective on mothering in *Of Woman Born* was a direct result of her considerable frustrations, especially her inability to write while she was mothering. In *Of Women Born,* she writes of her inability at once to realize her ambition to write poetry and to mother her three children. When asked why she never wrote poetry about her children, she answered that poetry was where she lived as no one's mother, where she ex-isted as herself (12). Rich says in *Of Woman Born* that she wrote in her diary in August of 1958:

> I have to acknowledge to myself that I would not have chosen to have
> more children, that I was beginning to look to a time, not too far
> off, when I should again be free, no longer so physically tired, pur-
> suing a more or less intellectual and creative life. . . . The only way
> I can develop now is through much harder, more continuous, con-
> nected work than my present life makes possible. Another child
> means postponing this for some years longer—and years at my age
> are significant, not to be tossed lightly away. (9)

In *Of Woman Born,* Rich sees the domination of males and of the father out-side and inside the home as the cause of women's problems and as damaging the institution of motherhood. Men have power within society; women perpetuate that power through the conservative activity of mothering children (45). Like other radical feminists, Rich sees matriarchy as an alternative to patriarchy. In a matriarchal society, female creative power is pervasive, and women have organic authority, in contrast to patriarchy, where men dominate and control (43). Patriarchy is associated with science, with control, with power, and with traditional forms of writing reserved for men such as academic scholarship; matriarchy, in contrast, is associated with nature, with magic, and is best exemplified by the organic connection between mother and child (43). Rich sees that the institution of motherhood as we know it needs to be destroyed, and the mother's battle for her child needs to become the common human battle (286). Mothering needs to be central rather than peripheral to other human projects.[3] Rich's perspective shifts toward a postmodern feminist one, however, especially in her 1984 essay, "Notes Toward a Politics of Location" and in work written subsequently in that she begins to question the binary logic of radical feminism.

Rich is a radical feminist in that she focuses on the institutional structures that impede the development of women's capacities, including the capacity to write. The language she uses in her discussions of writing and mothering is the language common to radical feminism with its emphasis on patriarchy or rule of the fathers. She suggests that patriarchy must be replaced by women-centered approaches to the teaching of writing. Her perspective is also radical feminist in that she emphasizes that women must remain outside traditional institutions if they are to maintain their own integrity and resist domination. Unlike cultural feminists who tend to idealize women's traditional roles, especially mothering, Rich focuses largely on ways in which patriarchal institutions have made satisfying mothering and writing impossibilities.

In her essay "The Antifeminist Woman," Rich defines patriarchy as any kind of group organization in which males hold dominant power and determine what part females shall and shall not play (78). Patriarchal rule is directly linked, according to Rich, to compulsory heterosexuality, which she refers to in "Compulsory Heterosexuality and Lesbian Existence" as a "beachhead of male dominance" (28).[4] In the essay, Rich is critical of cultural feminists such as Dorothy Dinnerstein, Jean Baker Miller, Nancy Chodorow, and others who seem to think that shared parenting is the solution to the inequality between the sexes. Rich feels that men could undertake childcare on a large scale without radically altering the balance of male power in a male-identified society. What is needed, according to Rich, is a radical change in the sexual politics of our present social order so as to eliminate men's control over women's bodies in the form of rape, unpaid production within marriage, sexual harassment, pornography, isolation of women from education, the taboo against lesbianism, and other forms of oppression.

Rich's focus on patriarchy no doubt was motivated, in part, by her complex relationship with her father. Her essay "Split at the Root" is an attempt to "claim" her Jewish father and to confront her ambivalence toward her own identity as a Jew. Clearly, she identified most strongly with her gentile mother, the white Southern Protestant. Her father's Jewishness was repressed, denied, and certainly a result of his having become successful within white, middle-class society. At the time of her birth, he was a young teacher and researcher in the department of pathology at the Johns Hopkins Medical School, one of the few Jews to attend or teach at that institution (177). She speaks of his dissociating himself from Jews who were not middle class and not well educated. He was himself, then, anti-Semitic in some ways, a dictatorial patriarch who demanded absolute loyalty, absolute submission to his will (188). Rich's exploration of her relationship to her father taught her "a great deal about patriarchy, in particular how the 'special' woman, the favored daughter, is controlled and rewarded" (188).[5]

Like Woolf, Rich sees universities as embodiments of patriarchal authority and certainly as places inimical to mothering and to the development of women's writing abilities, a radical-feminist perspective. In "Toward a Woman-Centered University," Rich says that the style of the university is identical to the style of a society invested in military and economic aggression. Universities are dominated by a masculine ideal, a race of men against one another. The disciplines represented within universities obscure or devalue the history and experience of women as a group. According to Rich, outside of women's studies, we live with textbooks, research studies, scholarly sources, and lectures that treat women as a subspecies, mentioned only as peripheral to the history of men. In disciplines where women are considered, they are perceived as the objects rather than the originators of inquiry (135). What traditional university education obscures, according to Rich, is that civilization has been built on the bodies and services of women, services such as mothering that are unacknowledged, unpaid, and unprotected in the main (135). Rich says that, like the history of slave revolts, the history of women's resistance to domination awaits discovery by the offspring of the dominated.

Like Woolf's, one manifestation of Rich's radical feminism is recognition of male domination of universities. She sees the university as a hierarchy with a small cluster of highly paid and prestigious persons, chiefly men, at the top whose careers entail the services of a very large base of ill-paid or unpaid persons, chiefly women—wives, research assistants, secretaries, teaching assistants, cleaning women, waitresses in the faculty club, lower-echelon administrators, and women students who are used in various ways to gratify the ego. The system divides women from each other. Each woman in the university is defined by her relationship to the men in power instead of her relationship to other women up and down the scale (136–37). Rich's solutions to the problems of patriarchal education are also radical feminist in that she emphasizes the need for women to come together to oppose patriarchal culture and to develop ways of teaching that are nurturing rather than alienating. She calls for the elimination of compulsory heterosexuality and the transformation of our social institutions, including educational institutions.

Many of her solutions, though, have a cultural-feminist cast. She says that universities need to be restructured so as to allow women to connect with one another and to become a presence at all levels. This will necessitate an excellent network of childcare. It will also necessitate the involvement of staff and community members in part-time study. According to Rich, the university should also become responsive to the visible community within which it exists—the neighborhood, the city, the rural county, its true environment. As a research institution, the university should organize its resources around problems specific to its community—adult literacy; public health; safer, cheaper, and simpler birth control; drug addiction; communication education; pediatrics; the sociology and psychology of aging and death; the history and problems of women and those of people in nonwhite, non-middle-class cultures; urban (or rural) adolescence; public architecture; child development; urban engineering; folk medicine; psychology; architecture; economics; and the economics of the small farmer ("Toward a Woman-Centered University" 152–53).

Both the content and the style of university education need to be changed in order to empower women, according to Rich. Women need a reorganization of knowledge, of perspectives, and of analytical tools that can help them know their foremothers, evaluate present historical, political, and personal situations, and take themselves seriously as agents in the creation of a more-balanced culture. She sees that a radical reinventing of subject, lines of inquiry, and method will be required. She suggests that it is perhaps in the domain that has proved least hospitable or attractive to women—theoretical science—that the impact of feminist and of women-centered culture will have the most revolutionary impact.

Rich sees that there will need to be a breakdown of traditional departments and disciplines, of that fragmentation of knowledge that weakens thought and permits the secure ignorance of the specialist to protect him from responsibility for the applications of his theories. A women-centered curriculum would not allow quantitative methods and technical reason to continue to become means for the reduction of human lives and specialization to continue to be used as an escape from wholeness (143). Teaching styles would be more dialogic, more exploratory, and less given to pseudo-objectivity than traditional ones. The underlying mode of the feminist teaching style is thus by nature antihierarchical (145).

The teaching of composition would become cultural feminist. In "Teaching Language in Open Admissions," Rich describes herself as someone for whom language has implied freedom and who is trying to aid others to free themselves through the written word. She sees that people come into the freedom of language through reading, before writing, and that their reading suggests to them different possible modes of being (63). She recognizes, however, that language and literature are often used against certain students to keep them in their place, to mystify, to bully, and to make them feel powerless. We therefore need to revise our notion of what a classic text is. We need to select more carefully the texts that we give our students to read.

Rich also speaks of the importance of establishing trust in the writing classroom. As a writer, Rich says she needs to believe there is someone willing to collaborate subjectively by reading her work sympathetically. Teachers need to develop within the classroom a working situation in which trust becomes a reality, where the students are writing with the belief in their own validity, and reading with the belief that what they read has validity for them. She hesitates to provide specific suggestions, however, because she thinks each situation is different. Descriptions of strategies, exercises, and reading and writing topics that have been successful in one context may not be successful in another context. More than anything else, a teacher must have a fundamental belief in the students. This involves realistically assessing where the student is while never losing sight of where she or he can be.

Rich sees that students can be taught the capabilities of language to change reality. She wants her students to find language and those abilities that accompany language—reflection, criticism, renaming, and creation—to use language as a tool and weapon for the transformation of our educational institutions. In our teaching, according to Rich, we need to be acutely conscious of the kind of tool we want our students to have available, to understand how it has been used against them, and to do all we can to ensure that language will not someday be used by them to keep others silent and powerless (68).

Rich's radical- and cultural-feminist attitudes toward the teaching of writing are no doubt a result of her experience as a teacher of composition. In the late 1960s, she taught in the basic-writing program at City University of New York under the direction of the late Mina Shaughnessy. "Teaching Language in Open Admissions," which first appeared in *Harvard English Studies* in 1973 and was later reprinted in *On Lies, Secrets, and Silence,* recounts Rich's experience as a teacher of writing. Other essays published in *On Lies, Secrets, and Silence* and in *Blood, Bread, and Poetry* deal directly or indirectly with reading, writing, and teaching.

In "Blood, Bread, and Poetry: The Location of the Poet," published in 1984, Rich speaks of writing as a continuing process, one that is directly related to the writer's everyday life and situation in history. She describes her own evolution as a writer, a long process of attempting to locate herself and her identity as a woman. Although she began writing poetry in college in the late 1940s and early 1950s, she did not begin to find her own voice until the early 1960s as her political consciousness developed, and mothering ceased to be a burden. Her teaching at City University enhanced her political awareness, and she began to see the dynamic between poetry as language and poetry as a kind of action, "probing, burning, stripping, placing itself in dialogue with others out beyond the individual self" (181).

In the essay, Rich says that her poetry began to become powerful when she was able to write as a woman. It would seem, then, that she was able to write only when she was freed of the constraints of mothering but that her writing also necessitated reflection on her identity as a woman including the activity of mothering.

> To write directly and overtly as a woman, out of a woman's body
> and experience, to take women's existence seriously as theme and
> source for art, was something I had been hungering to do, needing
> to do, all my writing life. It placed me nakedly face to face with both
> terror and anger; it did indeed *imply the breakdown of the world as I*

had always known it, the end of safety, to paraphrase Baldwin again [Rich's emphasis]. But it released tremendous energy in me, as in many other women, to have that way of writing affirmed and validated in a growing political community. I felt for the first time the closing of the gap between poet and woman. (182)

The kind of poetry she says she was able to begin to write was a part of a long conversation with her elders and with the future. The artist writing in this way draws on a tradition in which political struggle and spiritual continuity are meshed (187).

In "When We Dead Awaken: Writing as Re-Vision," Rich speaks of the freedom of mind that is necessary to create poetry. For a poem to coalesce, there has to be an imaginative transformation of reality, a certain freedom of mind, to "enter the currents of your thoughts like a glider pilot, knowing that your motion can be sustained, that the buoyancy of your attention will not be suddenly snatched away" (43). She sees that women trying to fulfill traditional female functions in a traditional way are in direct conflict with the subversive function of the imagination (43). Rich says that the awakening of consciousness is not like the crossing of a frontier—one step and you are in another country. Much women's poetry has been a cry of pain, of victimization, and has been charged with anger (48).

Rich exhibits a cultural-feminist perspective, then, in emphasizing that women need to learn to write as women, to take the theme of women's existence seriously as theme and source for their writing. The process of getting in touch with her experience as a woman is a difficult one, however, necessitating decades of political involvement. Clearly, Rich's formal education did little to foster an awareness of her identity as a woman. Her training in literature and in language led in the opposite direction, toward a conception of language as aesthetic object, as self-contained artifact: "It was a rare teacher of literature at Harvard who referred to the world beyond the text" ("Blood, Bread, and Poetry" 172).

Learning to write as a woman is also radical feminist in that it necessitates that the woman maintain an outsider's consciousness, an outsider's view, a perspective that resembles Woolf's "Society of Outsiders" in *Three Guineas.* In "What Does a Woman Need to Know?" Rich says that one of the dangers of a privileged education for women is that women may lose the eye of the outsider and come to believe that those patterns hold for humanity, for the universal. Women can become tokens and can take on the perspective of those who oppress them. The tools to do independent research, to evaluate data, to criticize, and to express discoveries in language and visual form should not be exchanged for a knowledge of the unprivileged or the knowledge that women have historically been viewed and still are viewed as existing in the service of men (4).

Rich also sees that women critics and reviewers need to develop a clear sense of their own political and cultural identity and to locate themselves honestly in relation to the works they attempt to criticize. In "Toward a More Feminist Criticism," she calls for a kind of feminist criticism that implies continuous and conscious accountability to the lives of women. For white feminists, this involves deliberately trying to unlearn the norm of universal whiteness. It also means trying to unlearn the norm of universal heterosexuality. This goal of inclusiveness goes far beyond merely ritualistically taking on a chapter or a paragraph or a footnote alluding to women of color and/or lesbians. Rich reiterates in the essay that feminist critics must move beyond an infatuation with language and must focus attention on action. Language needs to be critiqued as well as revered. Critics also need to be committed to readers and should write so as to appeal to a diverse readership, to the women readers Woolf speaks of (91).

Women writers, then, need to become engaged in an extended process of discovery, one that is lifelong, and that puts them in touch with their own experience as women through connection with other women, including women of color and lesbians. In order to maintain contact with women less privileged than themselves, white, middle-class women need to remain outsiders to the established order, refusing the position of token women, refusing co-optation. They need to learn to become critical of the dominant tradition, with its infatuation with language, and to speak in their writing to a wide audience rather than a select few.

As I have suggested, Rich's identification of patriarchy as the cause of women's oppression and as the solution the creation of separate women-centered institutions and forms of expression is, like many of Woolf's perspectives, both radical feminist and cultural feminist in orientation. The final essay in *Blood, Bread, and Poetry,* "Notes Toward a Politics of Location," however, represents a shift in Rich's perspective from a radical and cultural feminist to postmodern feminist in that here she questions essentialized and dichotomized conceptions of gender.[6] She speaks initially in the essay of her radical feminism and of the concerns that arose out of it including the politics of orgasm, rape, incest, abortion, birth control, forcible sterilization, prostitution, marital sex, sexual liberation, prescriptive heterosexuality, and lesbianism (212–13). She also speaks, however, of postmodern themes such as the limitations of theory (213) and of the contingent nature of truth (214). She also recognizes the limitations of an inclusive paradigm that represents all women and the importance of situating or locating women's speech (214). She regrets that much of what we usually think of as politics rests on "a longing for certainty" (216). She also speaks not of a single form of oppression but of "a tangle of oppressions" (218). She recognizes that there are differences among women that necessitate a more-nuanced approach to examinations of the oppression of women.

> Words that should possess a depth and breadth of allusions—words like socialism, communism, democracy, collectivism—are stripped of their historical roots, the many faces of the struggles for social justice and independence reduced to an ambition to dominate the world.
>
> Is there a connection between this state of mind—the Cold War mentality, the attribution of all our problems to an external enemy— and a form of feminism so focused on male evil and female victim-

ization that it, too, allows for no differences among women, men, places, times, cultures, conditions, classes, movements? Living in the climate of an enormous either/or, we absorb some of it unless we actively take heed. (221)

Rich's critique here of forms of feminism that are dichotomous, that are rooted in either/or thinking, and that do not allow for differences within the category woman have a postmodern cast. She seems to be questioning the premises of radical and feminisms to which she had previously been committed. In the essay she also recognizes that feminism is too often Eurocentric and sees that the intellectual roots of feminism are actually analyses of African American experience articulated by Sojourner Truth, W. E. B. DuBois, Ida B. Wells-Barnett, C. L. R. James, Malcolm X, Lorraine Hansberry, and Fannie Lou Hamer. Rich asks who is the *we* feminists speak of? She no longer seems to be comfortable with the assumption that women's oppression is primarily a result of a single cause— rule by men—and to have become aware of the difficulty of generalizing about women (231).

Rich's shift from a radical and cultural feminist to a postmodern feminist no doubt resulted from changes within feminism and within her personal life. Radical and cultural feminisms during the late 1970s and early 1980s were coming under increasing attack for their exclusive concern with the problems of white, middle-class feminists, and Rich was no doubt sensitive to the criticisms. She had also greatly expanded her own social network, and her relationship with Michelle Cliff, a black novelist, no doubt gave her new insights into the problem of racism in the United States. Her reflections on her Jewish heritage certainly also contributed to an expanded conception of the intersections of gender, race, ethnicity, and social class. She says in the foreword to *Blood, Bread, and Poetry,* "The woman who seeks the experiential grounding of identity politics realizes that as Jew, white, woman, lesbian, middle-class, she herself has a complex identity." She also acknowledges, "For women in whose experience—and in whose theory, therefore—sex, race, and class converge as points of exploitation, there is no 'primary oppression' or 'contradiction,' and it is not patriarchy alone that must be comprehended and dismantled" (xii). By the mid-1980s, radical feminism was perhaps no longer possible, at least for Rich.

Walker's Womanism

Alice Walker's background was considerably different from Rich's. She was the daughter of a black sharecropper rather than a white college professor, and her feminism reflects her considerably different situation. If Rich's father was a powerful and often oppressive presence, Walker's was considerably less so. She speaks in her essay "Father" of her father always being sick as a result of being overweight and having high blood pressure and diabetes (13). If Rich's experiences resulted in the development of both radical and cultural feminist perspectives, the approach Alice Walker takes in her essays tends to be cultural feminist. She demonstrates an appreciation for the important role that women played in the agrarian society in which she was raised. Walker tells us in *In Search of Our Mothers' Gardens* that hers is a "womanist" perspective. She defines *womanist* as "a black feminist or feminist of color" and as characterized by "outrageous, audacious, courageous or *willful* behavior." Womanists, though, are not concerned exclusively with women. Rather, they are committed "to survival and wholeness of entire people, male *and* female." They are not separatists but universalists (xi). Walker's womanist perspective is closer to a cultural-feminist one than a radical-feminist one in that she devotes considerable attention to identifying black women's traditions and appreciating black women's traditional roles. She speaks of the heritage she derived from her mother of a love of beauty and a respect for strength, a heritage that manifested itself in her mother's garden. In "Looking for Zora," she talks of her need to seek out foremothers such as Zora Neale Hurston as a way of connecting with a tradition of African American women writers. If Louise M. Rosenblatt's connection with Hurston was a tenuous one despite the coincidences of their biographies, as I will explain in chapter 5, Walker made deliberate attempts to seek Hurston out and to reclaim her as an important African American writer.

Walker's cultural feminism as evidenced in her essays does not depend on sharp divisions between male and female culture as do many feminist versions of cultural feminism that are inattentive to racial issues, however. Her explanation that womanism is not separatist but, rather, universalist, suggests that she does not exclude black men from consideration. What is less clear is whether universal includes whites. When it does not seem to, womanism tends toward cultural feminism in its emphasis on a single culture, in this case black women's culture.[7] Womanism, however, also seems at times to have radical tendencies in that Walker writes not only about women's special talents and traditions but also about racism, poverty, and illiteracy. She is acutely aware of the oppression of blacks and of black women because she was raised amidst poverty and deprivation.[8]

Walker's novels and short stories often focus on radical-feminist themes such as the domination of women by men, but her essays tend to emphasize the positive aspects of black women's culture or of black culture generally. Some critics, however, emphasize the cultural-feminist themes in Walker's novels. In speaking of Jane Lazarre's *The Mother Knot* and Alice Walker's *The Color Purple,* for instance, Maureen Reddy says, "Readers of these novels are taught to think like mothers—to accept *process* as the underlying structural principle—and goal— of both art and life" (228). E. Ellen Barker in "Creating Generations: The Relationship Between Celie and Shug in Alice Walker's *The Color Purple*" speaks of Walker calling upon the influence of her maternal ancestor, her mother, and her literary ancestor, Zora Neale Hurston, as the collective models for Shug Avery (56). Perhaps her perspective on writing and mothering has a more positive valence than Rich's because Walker was better able to successfully integrate writing and mothering. Walker speaks in "One Child of One's Own" of the birth of her daughter, Rebecca, as an incomparable gift of seeing the world at quite a different angle than before (369). One's child can help allay fears and thereby help develop a writer's confidence (382). Walker does mention in "Recording the Seasons," however, that at times she finds motherhood to be onerous and a threat to her writing (224). It disrupts the habits of a lifetime—easy mobility, wandering, and daydreams (224). She says in "A Writer Because of, Not in Spite of, Her Children" that she needs an absolutely quiet and private place to work (69).[9] Mothering for Walker sometimes takes the form of teaching, and she sees that black artists, in general, have a responsibility for assuming the role of the "remedial reading teacher" (134). Her experience with illiteracy is close to home. She writes, for instance, of how reading and writing were at one time punishable crimes for black people (234) and of how reading and writing were not part of the lives of either her mother or her father.[10]

If Walker's womanism has a cultural-feminist emphasis, it nevertheless differs in significant ways from cultural-feminist works that do not take race into consideration. For instance, she writes in "One Child of One's Own" of Patricia Meyer Spacks's exclusion of blacks from her study of the female imagination, seeing Spacks as exemplary of a form of academic feminist criticism that deals exclusively with the experience of white, middle-class women (372). She says in her 1972 convocation talk at Sarah Lawrence, "Ignorance, arrogance, and racism have bloomed as Superior Knowledge in all too many universities" ("A Talk" 36).

Walker's writer, then, is usually the black woman writer who, for lack of models, must forge her own sense of how to write. She speaks in "Saving the Life That is Your Own: The Importance of Models in the Artist's Life" of Toni Morrison writing the kinds of books she wants to read, that is, the kind that have not previously been written. Walker also speaks of the models she has relied on in her writing, the works of writers such as Hurston, Olsen, Woolf, Jean Toomer, Colette, and Anaïs Nin (13) and her mother's oral stories.

Hurston becomes an especially powerful foremother, quite obviously because she is a Southern, black woman.[11] Hurston's story is ultimately a tragic one, the story of a talented woman who died in ill health, poverty, and obscurity. Her last days were spent in a welfare home, and her burial was paid for by "subscription" (Walker, "Looking for Zora" 87). Walker in "Looking for Zora" describes her difficulty in locating Hurston's unmarked grave in a cemetery in Florida. Hurston's is a story of racial and gender oppression that is in many ways bleaker than that of her white, middle-class counterparts such as Woolf and Sylvia Plath. Walker relates that Hurston was an orphan at nine, a runaway at fourteen, a maid and manicurist before she was twenty (90–91) who nevertheless managed to become a novelist, an anthropologist, and one of the literati associated with the Harlem Renaissance. In her lifetime, however, according to Walker, her work received little other than misleading, deliberately belittling, inaccurate, and generally irresponsible attacks by almost everyone (86).

Walker portrays Hurston's life and work as characterized by racial health, through a sense of black people as complete, complex, "undiminished" human beings. Walker says Hurston was portraying not simply an adequate culture but a superior one (84). She speaks of Hurston growing up in a community of black people who had enormous self-respect and an ability to govern themselves (85). Walker says that not many black people in America have come from a self-contained, all-black community where loyalty and unity are taken for granted, a place where black pride is nothing new (100). Walker, the young writer riddled with self-doubt, decides that she will vindicate Hurston, to fight for Hurston and her work, "for what I knew was good and must not be lost to us" (87).

The young, black woman writer, then, must attempt to establish a tradition, must connect herself with other black women writers and foremothers, and must defend them against unfair readings and learn from them so that they, too, may acquire a voice. Walker also makes it clear, however, that her models need not be literary ones. In "Coretta King: Revisited," she describes her visit with Coretta King, a visit that resulted in Walker's discovery that Martin and Coretta King gave the South to black people and reduced the North to an option (157). The visit connected her more intimately with her Southern heritage. The two women did not see eye to eye on every issue. King is not the feminist Walker is and places the goal of the liberation of all blacks above the goal of the liberation of women. Their conversation on the topic of women's issues was nevertheless productive. King made an observation with which Walker agreed:

> Women, in general, are not a part of the corruption of the past, so they can give a kind of leadership, a new image for mankind. But if they are going to be bitter or vindictive they are not going to be able to do this. But they're capable of tremendous compassion, love, and forgiveness, which, if they use it, can make this a better world. When you think of what some black women have gone through, and then look at how beautiful they still are! It is incredible that they still believe in the values of the race, that they have retained a love of justice, and that they can still feel the deepest compassion, not only for themselves but for anybody who is oppressed; this is a kind of miracle, something we have that we must preserve. (King qtd. in Walker, "Coretta King" 153)

As a way of describing the women's tradition of which she was a part, Walker describes her mother and grandmothers as artists whose forms of expression were outside reading and writing. They expressed themselves through their oral stories and in art forms such as quilting and gardening. Walker says that so many of the stories that she writes are her mother's stories. Walker's female forebears were women who were often driven to "numb and bleeding madness by the springs of creativity in them for which there was no release" ("In Search" 233). They were creators who lived lives of spiritual waste because they had no adequate outlet for their spirituality, which is the basis for art (233). The strains of enduring their unused and unwanted talents drove them insane. She compares the life of eighteenth-century African American writer Phillis Wheatley to that of Woolf. Not only did Wheatley not have a room of her own or money, she was a slave who didn't even own herself (235).

Walker's adult life, in contrast, is one of relative privilege. She has become a successful writer, was educated at a prestigious women's college that is primarily devoted to the education of white, middle-class women, Sarah Lawrence, and has become economically comfortable. Clearly, however, she sometimes shares part of the heritage she describes in "In Search of Our Mothers' Gardens"— numbing despair. She speaks in "From an Interview" of her poetry emerging after periods of depression. Her poems are her way of celebrating with the world that she did not commit suicide the evening before. Her essays, short stories, and novels arise out of feelings of happiness or from feelings that are neither happy nor sad; her poems, even the happy ones, emerge from an accumulation of sadness (249). Walker speaks of exploring the "oppressions, the insanities, the loyalties, and the triumphs of black women" (250).

Walker may also have been drawn to cultural forms of feminism because the men in her life in her formative years were not especially powerful or threatening. Walker's father was poor and unsuccessful, a man "exploited by the rural middle-class rich." When she was a child, she thought that her father's poverty was a result of his own peculiar failing (213). Her own acculturation into middle-class society after she went off to college brought an end to their "always tenuous relationship." She found it painful to expose her thoughts in language to "this brilliant man—great at mathematics, unbeatable at story telling, but unschooled beyond the primary grades. . . . This separation, which neither of us wanted, is what poverty engenders. It is what injustice means" (216).

Her essay, "Beauty: When the Other Dancer Is the Self," however, suggests that her father did socialize her to an extent into destructive feminine behaviors and patterns of thought. Like Rich, Walker was her father's favorite daughter for a time, no doubt because she was "the prettiest." Her position of privilege ends, though, when an older brother deliberately shoots her in the eye with a BB gun with the result that a "hideous cataract" develops on her eye. She ceases to be the "cute" little girl, and for six years, she "does not raise her head" (387). Only when the cataract is surgically removed does she regain her self-confidence. The males in Walker's life in her formative years, then, did have an adverse effect on her. She was socialized into compulsory heterosexuality by her father and victimized by her brothers.

But as I indicated above, Walker's womanism allows for the possibility of alignment between black women and black men. She speaks very positively, for instance, of Martin Luther King, Jr., seeing him as role model for her despite his womanizing. She sometimes insists, however, that the problems black women face are different from the problems black men face, and so she sometimes emphasizes difference. In her essay, "A Letter to the Editor of *Ms.,*" for instance, she says, "it was 'different' being Frederick Douglass than being Harriet Tubman—or Sojourner Truth, who only 'looked like a man,' but bore children and saw them sold into slavery" (275). In the essay, she affirms her identification with lesbians and explores what she calls "colorism" within black culture, the tendency to privilege light blacks over black blacks. She says that colorism, like colonialism, sexism, and racism "impedes us" ("If the Present Looks Like the Past" 291). The problem of the twenty-first century will still be the problem of the color line including "the relations between the darker and the lighter people of the same races, and of the women who represent both dark and light within each race" (311). She sees black women writers as being in an especially good position to "present a fuller picture of the multiplicity of oppression—and of struggle" (311).

In a later essay, "Gifts of Power," she speaks of the desirability of womanist women to be concerned with all black people—their fathers, brothers, and sons—no matter how they feel about them as males. For her, *womanist* connotes connectedness to the entire community and the world rather than separatism: "[T]he main problem with Lesbos . . . is not . . . that it was inhabited by Greek women whose servants . . . were probably stolen from Egypt, but that it (Lesbos) is an island" (81).

Walker's perspective, then, though primarily cultural feminist in its emphasis on black culture, especially black women's culture, moves in the direction of a postmodern one when she recognizes the need for a larger perspective that includes whites as well as blacks, men as well as women. She speaks, for instance, of the complex relationships between African Americans and American indigenous peoples in "My Big Brother Bill," of African Americans and Chinese peoples in "A Thousand Words," and of whites and blacks in "In the Closet of the Soul." She says in "In the Closet of the Soul," "We are black, yes, but we are 'white,' too, and we are red. To attempt to function as only one, when you are really two or three, leads, I believe, to psychic illness: 'white' people have shown us the madness of that" (82).

Walker sees the black writer as inheriting as a natural right a sense of community ("The Black Writer" 17), and this community clearly includes whites as well. In "Beyond the Peacock," she writes she would never be satisfied with a segregated literature (43). Each writer "writes the missing parts to the other writer's story. And the whole story is what I'm after" (49). Blindness about other human beings is equivalent to death for a writer (19). Walker also departs from a cultural perspective when she speaks of the importance of white feminists in her development, citing Woolf as an influence, especially her essay *A Room of One's Own.* The title of Walker's essay "One Child of One's Own" echoes one of Woolf's titles, and in "Zora Neale Hurston: A Cautionary Tale and a Partisan View," Walker says, "Without money of one's own in a capitalist society, there is no such thing as independence" (90). Walker also takes seriously Woolf's observation that "we think back through our mothers if we are women" (*A Room of One's Own* 79).[12]

Walker seems also to move beyond the relativism of some cultural-feminist perspectives. She sees the writer as having a responsibility to attempt to tell the truth, to capture lived experience as accurately as possible. She says in "The Unglamorous but Worthwhile Duties of the Black Revolutionary Artist, or of the Black Writer Who Simply Works and Writes,"

> The strength of the artist is his courage to look at every old thing with fresh eyes and his ability to re-create, as true to life as possible, that great middle ground of people (137). . . . There must be an awareness of what is Bull and what is Truth, what is practical and what is designed ultimately to paralyze our talents. (133)

For Walker, it is possible to distinguish between Bull and Truth, and the writer has an obligation to write the truth. For Walker, writing is a political act that has consequences in the world: "It is, in the end, the saving of lives that we writers are about" ("The Black Writer" 14).

Rich and Walker, nearly a generation apart, found different ways to be mothers and writers. Rich has done most of her writing after she raised her three children. Becoming a serious writer was possible for her only after she left her marriage of seventeen years and embraced feminism and lesbianism. Walker left her marriage when her daughter was eight and found a way to integrate being a single parent with writing. Both are success stories, if bleak ones at times, in that they are both well-known and respected writers who have had lucrative careers. The example of Hurston serves as a reminder, however, that writing does not always result in sufficient income to support oneself. Trying to balance an academic career and mothering is very difficult as graduate student Leslie Yoder's "Resisting the Assignment" makes clear. Yoder includes a journal entry:

> I'm broke, paying over $500 a month on child care just to cover the hours I'm on campus. After over two years of haggling, the campus child care center has finally admitted that I will never get in on a subsidized basis unless I quit my job and go on welfare or have more babies. (287)

She also includes scenarios of the situations of women in different contexts trying to integrate mothering and writing, all of whom conclude, "I am going insane!" (286). Attempting to integrate writing and mothering does not always work.

The turn toward postmodern-feminist perspectives in the later essays of both Rich and Walker marks the emergence of postmodern feminism within the field of literary studies as a whole and anticipates this shift within rhetoric and composition. Unlike antimodern-feminist perspectives, which tend toward binary representations of relationships between men and women and toward opposition to modern thinking and practices, postmodern ones critique modernism without rejecting it completely. Discussions of Rosenblatt's transactional approach to literature, an approach that enables the development of postmodern perspectives on reading and writing; the emergence of postmodern feminist perspectives within the field of rhetoric and composition; and postmodern feminist perspectives on the teaching of both reading and writing, make clearer the distinction I am making between antimodern and postmodern feminisms, the blurred boundaries between them, and the different ways in which they move beyond modernism. In the next chapter, I argue that although Rosenblatt's work, like John Dewey's, is modern in its unquestioning acceptance of the sciences and the social sciences, her transactional approach to reading, which is indebted to Deweyan pragmatism, anticipates postmodern, nonfoundational approaches. Her work therefore illustrates ways in which modern assumptions and values begin to give way to alternatives that directly challenge those assumptions and values. Rosenblatt writes on the cusp of an important shift in ways of understanding how people use language.

PART THREE: *Critiquing Modernisms*

5

Pragmatic Reading and Beyond: Rosenblatt and Feminism

> *Pragmatism* 4. Philos. The doctrine that the whole "meaning" of a conception expresses itself in practical consequences, either in the shape of conduct to be recommended, or of experiences to be expected, if the conception be true (W. James); or, the method of testing the value of any assertion that claims to be true, by its consequences, i.e., by its practical bearing upon human interests and purposes.
>
> —F. C. S. Schiller, "Pragmatism"

*L*ouise M. Rosenblatt's work is modern in her attempts to describe language processes in a general way and to develop models that apply across categories. She uses the singular rather than the plural in the title of her theoretical statement, *The Reader, the Text, the Poem,* and when she addresses feminist concerns, her perspective is primarily liberal-feminist in orientation. The individuals she mentions most frequently as influencing her work are male, Anglo-American pragmatists[1] such as John Dewey, Arthur Bentley, William James, Charles Sanders Peirce,[2] and Franz Boas. Furthermore, her commitment to modern anthropology becomes evident when contrasted with that of African American writer Zora Neale Hurston who, like Rosenblatt, studied with Boas at Barnard. I will suggest, however, that in developing an approach to reading that is in some ways nonfoundational, in distinguishing between aesthetic reading and efferent reading, and in emphasizing the emotional components of reading, Rosenblatt moves beyond modern conceptions of reading. Contrasting Rosenblatt's perspective with that of Wolfgang Iser makes clear the nature of her resistance.[3] I will also suggest that her concept of aesthetic reading is useful to contextualize in relation to radical, cultural, and multicultural feminisms, and her emphasis on fluid transactions between readers and texts bears some resemblance to a postmodern-feminist conception of reading. Steven Mailloux in "The Turns of Reader-Response Criticism" calls Rosenblatt a neopragmatist and emphasizes her antifoundationalism. I am suggesting that Rosenblatt's orientation is primarily pragmatist but that in some ways she anticipates postmodernism and neopragmatism.

Rosenblatt and Hurston

Rosenblatt's modernism is evident in her uncritical acceptance of the sciences and the social sciences in general and of anthropology in particular, a perspective that differs from that of Hurston who became increasingly disillusioned with both. The two women are interesting to compare because they both studied at Barnard College in the 1920s with Franz Boas, and both had interests in anthropology and literature.[4] Rosenblatt and Hurston did not meet at Barnard, though they missed each other by only a matter of months; Rosenblatt graduated from Barnard in the spring of 1925, and Hurston enrolled in the fall of 1925, graduating in 1928 (Hurston, *Dust Tracks* 169). They met only once, at a party some years later.[5] Because Hurston was African American, she had fewer opportunities for professional advancement than did Rosenblatt. As Hurston struggled to survive as a collector of folklore and a writer, she distanced herself from anthropology and from the academy.

Although Rosenblatt and Hurston had similar training and similar interests as undergraduates, their careers took radically different directions. Rosenblatt became a successful academic who focuses especially on the reading and the teaching of literature, though traces of her scientific training can be found in her defense of the sciences and the social sciences in *Literature as Exploration* and in her insistence on the interconnectedness of aesthetic and efferent reading in *The Reader, the Text, the Poem*. Hurston began her career enthusiastically embracing academic approaches to folklore but ultimately rejected them.[6] No doubt as a result of her race, her situation outside the academy, and her need to support herself through her writing, she shifted her attention from systemic collection of folklore to popularizing the folklore she collected through the writing of fiction and dramatic productions.[7]

Rosenblatt took a course given by Boas when she was a sophomore at Barnard College in 1922 ("Retrospect" 98). Her roommate at Barnard, Margaret Mead, certainly influenced her, and Rosenblatt later studied anthropology on the graduate level with Boas at Columbia. In "Epilogue: Against Dualisms," she discusses her undergraduate work with Boas and Ruth Benedict and her graduate-level work in ethnology and linguistics in the Department of Anthropology at Columbia, indicating that she focused on linguistics and studied Native American languages Kwakiutl and Maidu (179). A significant factor in her decision to study literature rather than anthropology, however, was her parents' opposition to her travelling extensively. As a compromise, she decided to study literature in France.[8] She was a woman intent on obtaining a professional position at a time when it was by no means expected that women would do so. There were pressures, however, to enter a field such as literature more traditionally open to women.

There is ample evidence that Hurston began her career committed to the scientific investigation of African American culture. While still an undergraduate, she began doing field work for Boas in Harlem (Wall 1016). In 1928, Boas arranged for her to go south and collect Negro folklore (Hurston, *Dust Tracks*

171). She speaks of Boas in her autobiography, *Dust Tracks on the Road,* as the greatest anthropologist alive because of his insatiable hunger for knowledge and "genius for pure objectivity" (174). She also speaks of his wanting "facts, not guesses" (170). She concludes the chapter on research by speculating that if science ever gets to the bottom of voodoo in Haiti and Africa, "it will be found that some important medical secrets, still unknown to medical science, give it its power, rather than the gestures of ceremony" (205).

Hurston, however, became increasingly disillusioned with academic scholarship. *Mules and Men,* the result of her extensive anthropological fieldwork, was originally published by a popular press rather than an academic press. As Robert Hemenway makes clear in his biography of Hurston, as she moved away from the academy, she began to see the literary and personal dimensions of folklore and to become increasingly critical of its scientific dimensions. Her failed attempt to begin a Ph.D. in anthropology at Columbia under the direction of Boas in 1934 makes evident her increasing discomfort with traditional academic training. Hemenway includes a letter from Hurston to the Rosenwald Foundation, the sponsor of her graduate work, in his biography.

> The major problem in my field as I see it is, the collection of Negro folk material in as thorough a manner as possible, as soon as possible. In order for the collection to [be] exhaustive, it must be done by individuals feeling the materials as well as seeing it objectively. In order to feel it and appreciate the nuances one must be of the group. In order to see it objectively one must have great preparation, that is if [one is] to be able to analyze, to evaluate what is before one.
>
> In my humble opinion, it is almost useless to collect material to lie upon the shelves of scientific societies. It should be used for the purpose to which it is best suited. The Negro material is eminently suited to drama and music. In fact it *is* drama and music and the world and America in particular needs what this folk material holds. (207)

Hurston may have been trained to be an objective scientist, but her experiences in the field and her success as a writer of fiction and as a producer of dramatizations of the folklore she collected changed her perspective on the academy and made work on the Ph.D. an impossibility. Hemenway states, "After 1935 she had relatively little interest in the formalities of the academic method" (212).

Rosenblatt's acceptance of the academy was no doubt a result of her situation as an academic and the continuing influence throughout her career of individuals who embraced scientific approaches to knowledge such as Dewey and Peirce. If Rosenblatt had her frustrations as an academic, being ignored by the literary establishment until quite recently, for instance, the academy and the profession of English studies have nevertheless been kind to her. Hurston, in contrast, did not have the security afforded by an academic position and increasingly saw the academy as rigid and stultifying. Rosenblatt, however, did not remain entirely faithful to her male mentors, Anglo-American pragmatists such as Dewey, but altered their perspectives in important ways.

Rosenblatt's Pragmatism

Rosenblatt's perspectives on reading have a modern cast in their emphasis on the value of scientific knowledge and their commitment to cultural pluralism and cultural unity. She emphasizes individual choice, has implicit faith in Western culture and the scientific enterprise, and rejects poststructuralist approaches to language. Her transactional approach to reading, however, in some ways anticipates a postmodern conception of language.

Rosenblatt's modernism in many ways parallels Dewey's.[9] He explains in *Democracy and Education* that the method of knowing he advances in the book can be called pragmatic. By this he means that knowing is seen in relationship to activity that purposely modifies the environment: "Knowledge as an act is bringing some of our dispositions to consciousness with a view to straightening out a perplexity, by conceiving the connection between ourselves and the world in which we live" (344). Dewey makes clear that his perspective differs from scholasticism, sensationalism, rationalism, idealism, realism, empiricism, and transcendentalism (339).[10]

Dewey is clearly committed to a scientific approach to learning. In *Democracy and Education,* he speaks of science as "a name for knowledge in its most characteristic form" (188). In discussing the natural tendency to blame failure on untoward fate rather than error or incomplete inquiry into conditions, he says that science "represents the safeguard of the race against these natural propensities and the evils which flow from them" (189). He sees learning as involving assimilating into their experience the ideas and facts communicated by those who have had more experience, thus gaining "scientific insight in the materials and laws involved" (193).[11]

Dewey's modernism is also evident in his commitment to political liberalism in *Liberalism and Social Action.* He makes clear, however, that his version of liberalism differs in important ways from the liberalism of John Locke with its emphasis on the institutions of governments to "protect the rights that belong to individuals prior to political organization of social relations" (4). Lockeian liberalism was replaced by a form of liberalism associated with Adam Smith in which political concerns are subordinated to economic ones. In this view, "the convergence of a multitude of individual efforts are put at the disposal of men collectively, of society" (8). Dewey then traces the development of nineteenth-century liberalism from the utilitarianism of Bentham to the reaction against the industrialization of England on the part of Romantics such as Coleridge, Wordsworth, Carlyle, and Ruskin (21). He sees John Stuart Mill as valiantly attempting to reconcile the laissez-faire liberalism he was born into with the emphasis on the values of poetry, of enduring historic institutions, and of the inner life as portrayed by the Romantics (23).[12] Dewey's liberalism, in contrast, is "radical" in that it recognizes the need for thoroughgoing changes in the set-up of institutions and corresponding activity to bring the changes to pass (62). He sees a socialized economy as the means of free individual development (90). He calls for a "courageous democratic liberalism" reenforced by the scientific method and "experimental intelligence" and warns against a reversion to "savagery" (92).[13]

Like Dewey, Rosenblatt has considerable faith in scientific approaches to teaching and the study of literature. She says in *Literature as Exploration* that it is important for undergraduate and graduate programs to provide time for "building up a sound acquaintance with at least the general aspects of current scientific thought on psychological and social problems" (23). Such background is necessary to the study of literature, because Rosenblatt sees literature as both aesthetic and social (23), and these elements are indistinguishable within a literary text. She speaks of the personal value of literature being its "objective presentation" of problems (41). This process of "objectification" can lead to a clarification of the values of the reader (41). In addition to learning about literary forms, students need to learn about life (53).

In *Literature as Exploration,* Rosenblatt argues that teachers of literature need to be aware of work in the social sciences in order to "arouse in the student a desire for social understanding" (132). Teachers have a responsibility, according to Rosenblatt, to continually add to their knowledge of the behavioral sciences in addition to their knowledge of the field of literature (133). She goes on to say that it is not science but the way that it has been misused that should be opposed (134).

> More and more evidence is accruing to demonstrate that science, properly exploited, may eventually so reduce time devoted to work that the entire population will have the leisure and the energy for the rich imaginative life that literature and the arts offer. (134)

She insists, "Scientific knowledge is essentially a cooperative product" (138).

Rosenblatt indicates in "Looking Back and Looking Forward," an interview with Mary Maguire published in 1995, that she was influenced by Dewey's conception of "cultural pluralism" (160), a modern approach to multiculturalism given its emphasis on unity, the individual, and the need for a common language. She says, "Cultural pluralism accepts the existence of differences, but within a common—hence pluralistic—culture. 'American' includes all the intermingled ethnic strains" (160). She feels that there is too much emphasis on diversity rather than commonality (160) and that greater emphasis needs to be placed on the "value of the individual without reference to race, or creed, or gender, or religion and nationality" (157). She feels strongly that English teachers need to make sure that our students have a "common language" (158). In a democratic society, according to Rosenblatt, there should be "diversity within unity" (164).

In "Whitman's *Democratic Vistas* and the New 'Ethnicity,'" Rosenblatt also emphasizes a modern concept, the need for unity. She speaks of Whitman's reminding us of the need to participate in "the common life of humanity" and warns against "aggressive withdrawal into groups" (201). She finds that for Whitman, the individual is more than "his ethnic label" and must be free to make choices, seek out friends, and "enter freely into other associations, other groups" (200). She takes a strong stand against separatism, arguing against the idea that only blacks can produce or understand literature dealing with blacks (201) and makes reference to Horace Kallen's "cultural pluralism" in which the image of the melting pot is replaced by the image of the orchestra. According to Rosenblatt, Kallen "affirms the positive role of the various cultural or ethnic groups while stressing the primary importance of the individual" (203).

The individuals Rosenblatt lists as influencing her in the preface to *The Reader, the Text, the Poem* also make evident her modern roots. She mentions Boas and Benedict, with whom she studied at Columbia University, and William James, C. S. Peirce, George Santayana, and Dewey (xi). She also mentions being influenced by psycholinguistics, sociolinguistics, and semiology, and by Sigmund Freud, Alfred North Whitehead, Bertrand Russell, Ludwig Wittgenstein, and the Gestaltists (xiv-xv).[14] She concludes the interview with Maguire referred to above by emphasizing modern concepts such as reasonableness and the quest for certainty.[15] Speaking of "the reasonableness of seeking humane, democratic solutions," she says, "I feel it important to stress confidence in tentative pragmatic solutions to the quest for certainty both in interpretation and in the world" (172).[16]

Despite Rosenblatt's strong modern orientation, her transactional approach to reading in some ways anticipates a postmodern one, though one with a decidedly Anglo-American cast. In seeing reading as a relationship between a reader and a text and in repudiating the text orientation of New Critical perspectives, she prepares the way for nonfoundational approaches to language influenced by the pragmatism of Dewey, Arthur Bentley, Charles Sanders Peirce, William James, and others. She quotes Bentley's discussion of the relationship between the organism and environment in his "The Fiction of 'Retinal Image,'" published in *Inquiry into Inquiries.*

> For further study we differentiate between organism and environment, taking them in mutual interaction. We do not, however, take the organism and environment as if we could know about them separately in advance of our special inquiry, but we take their interaction itself as subject matter of study. We name this *transaction* to differentiate it from interaction. We inspect the thing-seen not as the operation of an organism upon an environment nor as the operation of an environment upon organism, but as itself an event. (qtd. in *The Reader, the Text, the Poem* 17)

Rosenblatt also observes that early on in his career, Dewey rejected the simple stimulus-response model and emphasized the ways in which the living organism selects from its environment the stimuli to which it will respond (17). In

Rosenblatt's transactional approach to reading, the relation between reader and text is not linear: "It is a situation, an event at a particular time and place in which each element conditions the other" (16).

In a subsequent essay, "Viewpoints: Transaction Versus Interaction—A Terminological Rescue Operation," Rosenblatt explains that Dewey shifted from the term "interaction" to "transaction" in 1949 because he felt that the term "interaction" suggested a mechanical rather than an organic process (99). She sees that "interaction" suggests a processing model, one that is dualistic and linear (100). For her, reading is an event in time involving a particular individual and a particular text that come together in a dynamic process "in which all elements take on their character as part of the organically-interrelated situation" (100). She explains that both cognitive and affective aspects of consciousness are activated in the transaction with verbal signs (101). In what she calls "efferent reading" (24), the reader focuses on public meaning; in aesthetic reading, on the lived activity of reading.

The language Rosenblatt uses in "Viewpoints" suggests a turn toward postmodernism. She speaks of replacing a paradigm based on Newtonian physics and Cartesian dualism with an Einsteinian paradigm in which the acts of observation are seen to alter the states of the particles observed (97–98). In the interview with Karolides, she speaks of "we postmodernists" (165). She consistently distinguishes her perspective from that of deconstructionists and poststructuralists, though, finding the latter espousing "extreme relativism" ("Retrospect" 106) and repeats this concern in "Theory and Practice" (163). She explains that whereas poststructuralists sees the individual as caught in "the prison house" of language and culture, she emphasizes that cultural conventions are individually internalized (106). Whereas "cultural" critics often have a negative attitude toward Western culture, Rosenblatt aims to develop "a discriminating attitude of mind, a readiness to question and to reject anachronistic or unjust assumptions, but a willingness to build on what is sound in our culture" (106). Rosenblatt's readers make active choices, deciding if they will read efferently or aesthetically, thereby controlling the effect of the text on themselves. Furthermore, through pedagogical approaches that encourage their active engagement with texts, Rosenblatt's readers can be helped to "develop criteria based on democratic assumptions about the freedom and well-being of individual human beings" ("Retrospect" 107). Her readers definitely have agency, are definitely individuals, and are definitely in control of their lives. Rosenblatt's readers are also able to defend their reading against charges of relativism and can contribute to the creation of or maintenance of democratic values and therefore have a salutary effect on their environments.

Beyond Pragmatism

Although Rosenblatt's transactional reading owes a considerable debt to Anglo-American pragmatism, in important ways she moves beyond it. She acknowledges, for instance, that there is a difference between efferent and aesthetic reading, at times privileging the latter, and emphasizes the importance of emotion in the reading transaction. Rosenblatt finds that scientific and literary texts alike can be read either aesthetically or efferently, thereby blurring the boundaries between the scientific and the aesthetic. She says of nonaesthetic reading in *The Reader, the Text, the Poem*, "The reader's attention is focused primarily on what will remain as the residue *after* the reading—the information to be acquired, the logical solution to a problem, the actions to be carried out" (23). In aesthetic reading, in contrast, "the reader's primary concern is with what happens *during* the actual reading event" (24). The reader's attention is "centered directly on what he is living through during his relationship with that particular text" (25).

Rosenblatt illustrates that the same text can be read either efferently or aesthetically (25) by describing how manipulation of mathematical symbols can be either efferent or aesthetic. It is primarily the attitude of the reader that makes the difference, not the nature of the material being read. Literature can be read efferently, scientific texts aesthetically. She recognizes, however, that it is more likely that literary works will be read aesthetically and scientific ones efferently because how an individual decides to read depends, to an extent at least, on the nature of the text being read. Differences between artistic and scientific texts are not determined by differences in the texts alone. There is no such thing as "poetic" diction, according to Rosenblatt, just as no other aspect of the text is an "essential and differentiating sign of poetry" (34).

Rosenblatt frequently emphasizes the ways in which aesthetic and efferent reading complement one another, no doubt a result of her commitment to modern conceptions of reading. By the end of "On the Aesthetic as the Basic Model of the Reading Process," published in 1981, for instance, she returns to the position she takes in *The Reader, the Text, the Poem*: "The transactional model incorporates both the aesthetic and the efferent stances as equally fundamental alternatives" (30). In "Looking Back and Looking Forward," she says, "I think it's just as important for us to understand a piece of writing about economics as to have had experience in sensing and analyzing literary, aesthetic experiences" (170).

At times, however, she departs from this perspective, suggesting that aesthetic reading is preferable to efferent reading. In "On the Aesthetic as the Basic Model of the Reading Process," in addition to emphasizing that there should be a balance between aesthetic and efferent reading as discussed above, she also says that emphasizing the aesthetic dimensions of reading serves to counteract "the present obsession with the efferent. . . . If it were necessary to choose, I would indeed opt for the aesthetic" (30).[17] In "The Transactional Theory of Reading and Writing," she speaks of the "overemphasis on the efferent in our schools" (1084). In "Theory and Practice," she says, "My first impulse is to welcome what seems to be a pendulum-swing effort to do justice to the aesthetic" (167).

She also recognizes that reading has an important emotional dimension in addition to a cognitive one. She says in *The Reader, the Text, the Poem*, "The mark of the reader's aesthetic activity is precisely that he does not respond to either of these elements separately but, rather, fuses the cognitive and the emotive" (46). In "Looking Back and Looking Forward," she makes a related point that there are aesthetic dimensions to nonliterary experience: "In order to read the nonliterary, you have to be sensitive to the aesthetic aspects of the nonliterary experience just as much as you may have to be sensitive to and evaluate the logical, or rational, or factual implications of your literary experience" (170).

Rosenblatt and Iser

The extent to which Rosenblatt provides alternatives to modern approaches to reading becomes clear when her perspective is contrasted with that of Iser. Rosenblatt and Iser are ideally suited for a detailed comparison because their positions are similar in so many ways. *The Reader, the Text, the Poem* and Iser's *The Act of Reading* were both published in 1978. Both books emphasize the importance of the reader in the act of interpreting a literary text, though both recognize that the text also plays a significant role in the interpretive process. Both eschew the extreme subjective position that eliminates the possibility of distinguishing between valid and invalid interpretations.

Iser, however, embodies an approach to reading that is primarily concerned with issues of what Patrocinio P. Schweickart in "Reading Ourselves: Toward a Feminist Theory of Reading" calls control and partition—how to distinguish the contribution of the author/text from the contribution of the reader. Schweickart suggests that such an approach is androcentric and that an alternative model would focus not on control or partition but on managing the contradictory implications of the desire for relationship and the desire for intimacy. The problematic is defined by the drive to "connect" rather than to "get it right" (55).

Rosenblatt's work exemplifies this alternative approach and as such is considerably more gynocentric. Everything she writes has an implicit or explicit pedagogical motive. Students must be taught to connect with the texts they are introduced to. They must learn to experience and appreciate literature before they learn to analyze it. For Rosenblatt, literature is a powerful tool in the socialization process. Students learn about life, about themselves, by experiencing literary events, but too often, according to Rosenblatt, classroom literary instruction has the opposite effect. Students are introduced to literary texts as if the texts were structures to be dismantled rather than experiences to be relived. Students are taught that literary texts are objects rather than subjects. Traditional instruction in literature has an alienating rather than a healing effect.

Rosenblatt and Iser also use different terms to describe the act of reading.[18] As we have seen, for Rosenblatt, reading is a "transaction" between reader and text, whereas Iser sees it as an "interaction." Rosenblatt rejects the term "interaction" because she sees it as dualistic and implying "separate, self-contained, and already defined entities acting on one another—in the manner . . . of billiard balls colliding" (17). For her, transaction designates an ongoing process in which the elements or factors are aspects of a total situation, each conditioned by and conditioning the other (17). The metaphor is an organic one and emphasizes merging and loss of separate identity. She sees the model as an "ecological" one in which "sharp demarcation between objective and subjective becomes irrelevant" (18).

Iser's conception of interaction sometimes sounds much like Rosenblatt's conception of transaction, certainly because he, too, was influenced by the work of John Dewey. At one point, for instance, Iser speaks of past feelings, views, and values being "made to merge" with the new experience (132). Dewey is only a minor influence on Iser's work, though, and more often Iser employs the more mechanistic language of the German phenomenologists. Readers and texts more often appear to be separate entities that do not lose their separate identities. Later in *The Act of Reading*, for instance, he says, "Reading is an activity that is guided by the text; this must be processed by the reader, who is then, in turn, affected by what he has processed. . . . The two partners are far easier to analyze than is the event that takes place between them" (163). There is little sense that the "two partners" lose their separate identities and merge. Later in the same section, he discusses "contingency" as a constituent of interaction and speaks of the "behavioral plans" of the two partners as being "separately conceived" (164). And because the two partners never really lose their separate identities, one partner can control the other. Ultimately, for Iser, texts control readers. Readers play an active role in the interaction by allowing themselves to be stimulated by the text and by responding appropriately to the textual cues that are provided. Iser says that the constitutive activity on the part of the reader "is given a specific structure by the blanks and the negations arising out of the text, and this structure controls the process of interaction" (179). Texts, which are composed of "blanks" and "negations," control readers' responses through structures that are created in the act of reading. Presumably, these structures stimulate interpretations that are the same for all readers. We are back to issues of control and partition and a long way from the language of merging stimulated by a discussion of Dewey's work.

Rosenblatt's emphasis on the event and on the ecology of the act of reading, allows for a consideration of the importance of context in the literary transaction. The concept is really only latent in her work—the title, after all, does not include the word *context*, but she does observe that the situation within which reading takes place has an effect on the "poem" that is evoked. Her position allows, then, for a consideration of historical, social, and political factors that affect the literary transaction.

Iser, in contrast, says very little in *The Act of Reading* about the situation within which reading takes place. He is primarily interested in characteristics of texts that structure responses. The phenomenological processes that a reader undergoes—responding to images, filling in blanks and gaps, "wandering" from one perspective to another, and consistency-building—are largely reactive ones, responses that are triggered by a text. There is little discussion in *The Act of Reading* of the context within which reading takes place.[19]

Rosenblatt's position is different, too, in that she places her discussion within the context of practical concerns. She begins *The Reader, the Text, the Poem* with a discussion of student response statements, and her purpose in writing the book at all seems to be to improve classroom pedagogy. Rosenblatt wants to empower student readers, to disrupt the traditional hierarchy whereby critics and teachers have greater interpretive authority than nonprofessional readers. Iser reinforces established hierarchies. He is interested in how professional critics read texts and does not concern himself at all with the concerns of developing readers or with the problem of misreading or misinterpretation. He does not need to take up the problem of validity of interpretation because he assumes that his reader is competent, trained, and able to respond appropriately to the signals within the text. Iser's reader is a kind of ideal reader—perhaps Iser himself.

Rosenblatt emphasizes that reading is an emotional as well as an intellectual experience. She discusses the effect that literature can have on the development of emotional maturity of adolescents in *Literature as Exploration* (1976 ed. 42) and argues that literature offers us an emotional outlet (36, 74). In *The Reader, the Text, the Poem,* she emphasizes that aesthetic reading involves emotional involvement in the text, a fusion of the cognitive and the emotive (46). Rosenblatt's reader is an individual who feels as well as thinks and who has emotional as well as intellectual needs. Iser says very little about the emotional dimensions of reading and describes an activity that seems to be almost entirely cognitive. In a discussion of the "emotive theory" of psychoanalysts such as Norman Holland and Simon Lesser, for instance, he transforms emotion into cognition. He sees that Holland's approach is little different from the eighteenth-century concept of *beau désordre,* "which indicated the aesthetic pleasure derived from a temporary disturbance of order accompanied by the expectation that in some unforeseeable way order would be restored" (*Act of Reading* 44). For Iser, reading involves the restoration of order after a temporary disturbance, and order is restored through the cognitive activity of consistency building.

Rosenblatt's Feminism

Because Rosenblatt emphasizes the value of aesthetic reading and the emotional dimensions of reading, it is not surprising that she has some sympathies for feminism. In the preface to the fifth edition of *Literature as Exploration,* for instance, she suggests that she is a feminist. In speaking of her use of the generic *he* in the book, she says,

> For various reasons, the format of this book remains essentially the same as in earlier editions. A reminder of when the book first appeared is the generic *he,* then taken for granted, no matter how feminist, as in this case, the writer might be. To remedy this would have required a total rewriting. I must simply assume that my readers are sufficiently free of old patriarchal attitudes to keep in mind my statement at the beginning of chapter 2, in which I point out that "the

reader" is a fiction, that there is no generic reader, that each reader is unique, bringing to the transaction an individual ethnic, social, and psychological history. Gender, of course, is a part of that uniqueness. (xix)

I first heard a version of this portion of the preface when Rosenblatt called some years ago to get some feedback on it. My initial reaction, as I recall, was to suggest that all generic *he*s be eliminated. This, obviously, was neither practical nor appropriate. Virginia Woolf and Simone de Beauvoir, after all, use the generic *he*.[20]

Rosenblatt's feminism is not pronounced in either *Literature as Exploration* or *The Reader, the Text, the Poem.* She does not emphasize that gender is an important component of the reading transaction, and most of the theorists cited or the authors discussed in both books are male. In the bibliography appended to *Literature as Exploration,* for instance, there are ninety items listed, only seven of which are by women. Of the 173 individual references in the index to *The Reader, the Text, the Poem,* only eight are women. When Rosenblatt speaks of literature, she usually seems to be referring to work written by white males with an occasional reference to George Eliot, Jane Austen, Emily Brontë, or Virginia Woolf or to Richard Wright or Ralph Ellison. In the interview with Mary Maguire mentioned previously, Rosenblatt discusses some of the limitations of excessive concentration on one issue characteristic of New Criticism, Marxism, poststructuralism, postmodernism, and feminism (164–65) and calls for a multiplicity of approaches to the literary experience (165).

When Rosenblatt does make reference to feminist concerns, those concerns are primarily modern feminist. *Literature as Exploration,* for instance, contains numerous references to women's subordination to men and explicit or implicit suggestions that both women and men need to develop an awareness of the changing status of women in society. In the chapter, "Some Basic Social Concepts," she makes the point that "the individual will be liberated from blind subservience to the norms of his group, not by throwing overboard all standards, but by seeing them in relation to the whole complex of attitudes and values into which they fit." She illustrates the point by saying it was not enough for women to resent the norms set up by the Victorian image of the submissive, self-effacing female. Women had to learn in what ways this image was linked with economic dependence and the habits of mind derived from acceptance of political and intellectual authoritarianism (*Literature as Exploration* 1976 ed. 152).

Later in the same chapter, she discusses the impact of emotionally rooted attitudes on behavior in moments of indecision. She illustrates the point by discussing the hypothetical situation of a young man who has become familiar, in history and sociology courses, with modern ideas concerning women's potential equality with man. He becomes convinced of the desirability of the new ideal of marriage as a partnership and a mutual give-and-take. But Rosenblatt says, "The success with which he carries out his program for a modern marriage, however, will largely depend on the degree to which these intellectual convictions have been translated into emotional attitudes and have displaced the old automatic sets" (178).

In the chapter "Personality" in *Literature,* Rosenblatt makes the point that old patterns of behavior can be surmounted only because conditions have so changed that there is a pressing need for a new adjustment. The new image will probably need to be reinforced by constant repetition over a long period of time. She uses as an example the image of the emancipated woman that appears in literature at least beginning from the time of Percy Bysshe Shelley and Mary Wollstonecraft. It was not until early in the twentieth century, however, that the image was translated into the practical lives of an appreciable number of women (*Literature as Exploration* 1976 ed. 198). Later in the chapter she makes the point that literary images are not always liberating ones but are sometimes irrelevant to actual life. She suggests, for instance, that literature can sometimes be held responsible for instilling in women emotional obstacles to their sincere ambition to be independent emotionally and intellectually: "Throughout their entire experience with literature, they have been led to identify themselves most often with the older image of woman as temperamentally, as well as economically, subordinate and dependent" (*Literature as Exploration* 1976 ed. 221).

There are fewer discussions of women's issues in *The Reader, the Text, the Poem,* though the ones that do appear also tend to be modern feminist in orientation. At one point, for instance, in a discussion of the limitations of professional critics, scholars, and teachers, Rosenblatt observes that ordinary readers may bring to the text experiences, awarenesses, and needs that have been ignored in traditional criticism. She illustrates the point by explaining that women are finding their own voices as writers and critics. She rejects the idea, however, that only women can speak about women in literature: "The aim should be to widen the range of critical voices—not to reject the contributions of the professional students of literature but to strengthen the affinities between them and ordinary readers" (143). Some of the examples Rosenblatt uses in *The Reader, the Text, the Poem* are woman oriented. She illustrates efferent reading, for instance, by citing the example of the mother whose child has swallowed a poisonous liquid and who frantically reads the label on the bottle to discover the antidote to be administered (24). Rosenblatt is clearly deeply committed to women's equality in the home and in the workplace.

In "Whitman's *Democratic Vistas,*" she speaks of Whitman's concern about "the political participation of women" and to their "present egalitarian demands" (189–90).

> Throughout Whitman's concern for the individual, he again and again makes clear his view that men cannot become whole until women too are given the opportunity and the impetus to live wholly from their own centers, and to fulfill themselves not only through a nobler motherhood but also through all the roles of work and thought and creativity open to men. (190)

She finds that Whitman sees that "individual men or women are to be liberated from old irrelevant images, in order to live freely and fully and nobly from their own centers" (191). She also finds that Whitman calls for "women's equality in politics, work, and intellectual life" (192).

If Rosenblatt's feminism is primarily modern feminist, her conception of aesthetic reading would nevertheless no doubt be of use in the development of radical- and cultural-feminist perspectives on reading. Aesthetic reading would be especially useful to cultural feminists as they attempt to identify the characteristics of women's reading. Patrocinio P. Schweickart in "Reading Ourselves" argues that women must learn to read texts by men and women differently. The feminist reader of a male text must defend against it, resist it, and sit in judgment of it. Feminist readers of a female text, in contrast, should speak as a witness in defense of the women writer. Schweickart says, "The feminist reader takes the part of the woman writer against patriarchal misreadings that trivialize or distort her work" (46) According to Schweickart, feminist readers should also construe the work not as an object but as the manifestation of the subjectivity of the absent author, another woman (47).

If readers need to learn to read women's texts sympathetically, Rosenblatt's aesthetic reading provides a useful model. Readers can serve as witnesses in defense of women writers by suspending judgment initially, attempting to relive the experience conveyed in the work, and partaking of the reading event fully. Here the reader also suspends analytical skills and all knowledge of literary categories. The reader attempts to merge with the work of women writers and to become it. Such a strategy would be especially useful in attempting to teach male student readers to read women's writing appreciatively and to suspend judgment of it. It is similar to the sympathetic reading Woolf recommends in "How Should One Read a Book?" discussed in chapter 3.

Unlike many radical- and cultural-feminist literary critics, however, Rosenblatt assumes that all works are liberatory. The problem with our educational practices, according to Rosenblatt, is that students are being taught to read incorrectly and are not being encouraged to enjoy literature or to partake of its therapeutic powers. If they were encouraged to read literature within the context of social scientific knowledge and to read it aesthetically, they would learn from it and build better lives on the basis of it. Radical- and cultural-feminist literary criticism, however, demonstrates that this is not always the case. Too often the experience of reading canonical male texts is counterproductive, even dangerous. Students do not only need to learn to merge with texts and to partake of their wisdom. They also need to learn to defend against them and to recognize when their messages are threats to their own sense of self as Judith Fetterley makes clear in *The Resisting Reader.*

If Rosenblatt's feminist perspective is primarily a modern feminist one and if her concept of aesthetic reading would be useful in the development of radical and cultural approaches to reading, contextualizing perspective and concept in relation to postmodern feminism is also useful, as she herself seems to be aware.

> It's ironic, in a way, that I share with other postmodern theorists the understanding that there are no absolute answers, that there are conflicts of interest and power, yet I do not share their tendency to overemphasize uncertainty, to approach the society and even the text with skepticism and pessimism. ("Looking Back and Looking Forward" 172)

Her perspective, with its positive valence, is usefully compared to that of Linda Alcoff's positionality. Like Rosenblatt, Alcoff is dissatisfied with poststructuralist feminism with its attack on the authenticity of the subject and of the essential identity of the individual. In "Cultural Feminism Versus Post-Structuralism: The Identity Crisis in Feminist Theory," Alcoff argues that for French feminists strongly influenced by Lacan, Derrida, and Foucault, the subject is not a locus of authorial intentions or natural attributes or even a privileged, separate consciousness. Individual practices and experiences are entirely social in origin. Alcoff objects to the seeming erasure of any room for maneuver by the individual within the social discourse or set of institutions. She argues that gender is not a point to start from, not a given, but a construct, formalizable in a nonarbitrary way through a matrix of habits, practices, and discourses (431). She also finds it both possible and desirable to construe a gendered subjectivity in relation to concrete habits, practices, and discourses while recognizing the fluidity of these (431). According to Alcoff, the way to avert the tendency to produce general, universal, or essential accounts of gendered subjectivity is to emphasize its historical dimension, and the way to avert the tendency to negate the possibility of identity at all is to recognize that one's identity is always a construction yet also a necessary point of departure (432). Alcoff finds it useful to see the concept *woman* as defined by the external context within which a woman is situated (433). Alcoff's positionalist view translates into a conception of reading in which there is no transcendental category of "woman reader" just as there is no transcendental category of "woman's text." All reading is gendered reading and can be analyzed as such, but we can only do so in terms of transactions, contexts, processes, and positions. The gender of the reader, a myriad of experiences, attitudes, ideas, memories, and feelings before the reading event, is reconstructed in the act of reading. The reader becomes a woman as the text is encountered. That becoming can take multiple forms, though. If the text is one that should be resisted, becoming can mean either alienation or active resistance. If the text is one that should be embraced, becoming can mean either passivity or active acceptance. What we need to do is to teach male and female students effective reading practices and effective ways of constructing gender in the process of reading. A good way to begin is to make them aware of the specificities of the processes they presently employ.

Rosenblatt's transactional view of the reading process bears some resemblance to Alcoff's positionalist view. Rosenblatt emphasizes that reading is an event in time that subsumes the individual participants so that they are no longer recognizable as individual entities. She also emphasizes that reading is an active process, one in which meaning is constructed rather than simply discovered. Rosenblatt's rejection of the extremes of objectivity of the New Criticism and the subjectivity of certain forms of reader-response criticism is similar to Alcoff's rejection of the extremes of cultural feminism and French feminism. Meaning, for Rosenblatt, does not reside in the text as it does for the New Critics and sometimes for Woolf, nor does it reside in the reader as it does for reader-response critics such as David Bleich but in the transactional process that is the result of the merging of reader and text. The term *reader,* then, is a shifting category and is best defined in relation to reading events and motives for reading.

However, the feminist theory of reading suggested by Rosenblatt's transactional model and Alcoff's positionalist model allows for considerably more agency on the part of the reader than would one based on a postmodern-feminist one strongly influenced by continental intellectual traditions. For instance, Judith Butler speaks of performativity as

> a reiteration of norms which precede, constrain, and exceed the performer and in that sense cannot be taken as the fabrication of the performer's "will" or "choice"; further, what is "performed" works to conceal, if not to disavow, what remains opaque, unconscious, unperformable. (*Bodies That Matter* 234)

Reading as performativity would be a resignification of a text and an appropriation of and a redeployment of its categories in the creation of an oppositional discourse. Butler stresses, however, that performativity necessarily involves being implicated in that which one opposes, "a difficult labor of forging a future from resources inevitably impure" (241).

Rosenblatt's feminism is primarily modern in its emphasis on equality with men and the elimination of discriminatory practices although her concept of aesthetic reading is useful in the development of cultural-feminist approaches to reading. In addition, her transactionalism bears some resemblance to the positionality of Alcoff and thus in some ways anticipates postmodern-feminist approaches. Rosenblatt is also important to feminism because she has become a remarkable role model. She is a strong, successful professional woman whose career has spanned three-quarters of a century. She has been able to find a balance between family and career.[21] She is also a woman of remarkable accomplishment and has received numerous awards.[22] She chaired a department, won a distinguished-teaching award, bore and raised a child, wrote three books (one of which, *Literature as Exploration,* is in its fifth edition), published numerous articles, and is still making professional contributions in her late nineties. Hers is a story well worth telling.

In the next chapter, I make the point that postmodern-feminist perspectives emerged within the field of rhetoric and composition only after the appearance of transactional or interactional perspectives that challenged foundational and binary approaches to language. There is a direct link, therefore, between Rosenblatt's transactionalism and a number of perspectives within rhetoric and composition that provide alternatives to modern tendencies such as formalism and structuralism. If Rosenblatt is not herself a postmodernist, in some ways her work enables the development of postmodern and postmodern-feminist perspectives on reading and writing.

6

Toward Postmodern-Feminist Rhetoric and Composition

[W]e should investigate ways of giving an identity to the sciences, to religions, and to political policies and of situating ourselves in relation to them as subjects in our own right.

—Luce Irigaray, *je,tu,nous: Toward a Culture of Difference*

Clearly, differentiation between strong and weak, powerful and powerless, has been a central defining aspect of gender globally, carrying with it the assumption that men should have greater authority than women, and should rule over them. As significant and important as this fact is, it should not obscure the reality that women can and do participate in politics of domination, as perpetrators as well as victims—that we dominate, that we are dominated.

—bell hooks, *Talking Back*

In philosophy, a commitment to one or more of the following lays one open to the charge of scientism.
  a) The sciences are more important than the arts for an understanding of the world in which we live, or, even, all we need to understand it.
  b) Only a scientific methodology is intellectually acceptable. Therefore, if the arts are to be a genuine part of human knowledge they must adopt it.
  c) Philosophical problems are scientific problems and should only be dealt with as such.

—Paul Noordhof, "Scientism"

Positivism. 1. A system of philosophy elaborated by Auguste Comte from 1830 onwards, which recognizes only positive facts and observable phenomena, with the objective relations of these and the laws that determine them, abandoning all inquiry into causes or ultimate origins, as belonging to the theological and metaphysical stages of thought, held to be now superseded.

—*OED*

*I*n this chapter, I focus on obstacles to the development of postmodern-feminist perspectives within the field of rhetoric and composition, discuss a transitional commitment to transactionalism and interactionalism influenced by individuals such as Louise Rosenblatt that anticipated postmodern approaches to reading, writing, and teaching, and suggest that the field is now moving toward postmodern-feminist perspectives as it attempts to overcome the limitations of its scientistic heritage. In struggling for legitimacy within the academy from its beginnings in the mid-twentieth century, a dominant tendency within the field has been identification with modern science and repudiation of nonscientific approaches to the study of writing. As the field has matured, however, it has attempted to develop alternatives to positivistic research models by attending to the political and cultural dimensions of reading, writing, and teaching. The field's belated embrace of feminism and its struggles for legitimacy within the academy make it a valuable site for exploring ways in which modern, antimodern, and postmodern tendencies play themselves out in disciplinary and interdisciplinary arenas. I will discuss the field's complex situation, some limitations of representations of rhetoric and composition as a feminized field, especially their tendency to ignore the field's "masculinization." I will then describe the field's early identification with the sciences and explain this identification through a discussion of feminist conceptions of the alienating process of "masculinization," especially in relation to rhetoric and composition's perennial adversary, literary studies. Finally, I will discuss the field's movement beyond scientism and positivism toward postmodern feminism.

Feminization or Masculinization?

Rhetoric and composition is a hybrid of several fields including rhetoric, composition studies, and technical communication. Rhetoric has a long history and ancient origins, composition studies is considerably more recent, focusing especially on the teaching of writing at the college level, and technical communication focuses primarily on writing in nonacademic settings. Although non-Western and feminist rhetorical traditions have recently been charted, histories of rhetoric typically focus on an androcentric tradition that includes discussion of Greek, Roman, Medieval, Renaissance, Enlightenment, modern, and postmodern traditions. Composition studies emerged in 1949 with the creation of the Conference on College Composition and Communication (CCCC), a division of the National Council of Teachers of English. Primarily pedagogical in orientation, composition studies is interdisciplinary, drawing on a number of fields including rhetoric, anthropology, linguistics, literary theory, psychology, education, cultural studies, and aesthetics. Composition studies is related to technical communication in complex ways. Technical communication is both a subfield, in that much work in technical communication is undertaken within the CCCC and within composition journals, as well as a separate field in that it also has its own journals, organizations, conferences, and traditions. Combining rhetoric and composition studies makes clear that the fields are related in important ways; other reasons to combine them are that rhetoric has had an especially strong influence on the development of composition studies and that the fields have often been aligned politically. Obscured by such a joining are the considerable differences between the two fields and the divisions within them. As I have already indicated, composition studies often encompasses technical communication. Rhetoric can also be divided into two subfields of rhetorical history and theory and of speech communication—two subfields with quite different institutional histories. There are, nevertheless, ways in which the designation *rhetoric and composition* accurately describes a hybrid field. The journal *Rhetoric Review,* for instance, is as likely to contain articles on composition studies as it is on historical or theoretical rhetoric, and a number of scholars work actively in both areas.

As I explain in chapter 7, important in understanding the recent history of rhetoric and composition is its frequent situation within English departments and its conflict with the field that is often dominant within English departments, literary studies. Compositionists such as Susan Miller in *Textual Carnivals,* John Schilb in *Between the Lines,* and numerous others (e.g. Bullock and Trimbur; Berlin *Rhetorics, Poetics, and Cultures*) have pointed out that literary studies is considerably more powerful within English studies than rhetoric and composition. Within English departments, they argue, compositionists are frequently outnumbered by literature specialists, and compositionists often hold positions that ensure their marginality. If they are non–tenure-track, they are often part-time, temporary teachers of first-year English, or if they are tenure-track, they are administrators of relatively low-status programs such as first-year English or technical writing. Despite the increasing status of rhetoric and composition within the academy in recent years, there does not seem to have been a major shift in the balance of power within English departments. Technical communication is frequently even more marginalized than rhetoric and composition. Rhetoric and composition, then, is a particularly rich site for exploring the impact of feminism within the academy.

Compositionists such as Susan Miller, Sue Ellen Holbrook, Theresa Enos, and others have provided very useful accounts of rhetoric and composition's feminine attributes and marginal status within the academy and within English studies[1] as a result of its being composed largely of women, many of whom teach part-time and have heavy teaching loads. Miller in *Textual Carnivals* describes compositionists as victims and uses the metaphor of the sad woman in the basement, an allusion to Gilbert and Gubar's *The Madwoman in the Attic.* Miller's book is a portrayal of the field's struggle for legitimacy within the academy and especially of its subjugation by its most threatening adversary, the field of literary studies.[2] This struggle has been recounted in articles and books such as *The Politics of Writing Instruction* edited by Richard Bullock and John Trimbur and *Rhetorics, Poetics, and Cultures* by James A. Berlin.[3]

The concept of feminization is powerful because it suggests that feminist analyses of the situation of women can be usefully applied analogously to academic fields. If women can be abused and undervalued, fields of study can be as well. A limitation of the feminization metaphor, however, is that it can tend toward essentialized and oversimplified conceptions of gender. Compositionists are seen primarily as victims even though they are gaining power within the academy through large grants, large programs in first-year English, technical writing, writing-across-the-curriculum, the development of writing centers and computing centers, and graduate programs that are successfully placing students. Also, many compositionists who have gained administrative experience developing composition programs are now moving into positions of power and authority within university bureaucracies.

Another limitation of the feminization metaphor is that it suggests that the field is a unified one, though this is hardly the case. Compositionists occupy positions of varying status within the academy and often have very different teaching, research, or service roles so conflicts and power struggles among compositionists—sometimes among women and feminist compositionists—are inevitable. The battle in which Linda Brodkey struggled against Maxine Hairston and John Ruszkiewicz over the composition curriculum at the University of Texas at Austin was played out in a national arena.[4] Discussions among colleagues at composition conferences suggest that such intragroup struggles and tensions are widespread. In the early phases of the field's development, the situation of having a common adversary, literature specialists, may have united compositionists. As the field has matured, however, it has tended to fragment.

If compositionists have sometimes been sad women in the basement, they have also often attempted to overcome their marginalization through identification with more powerful fields. If they have been feminized, they have also sometimes been "masculinized" by attempting to increase their status by emulating the techniques, beliefs, and attitudes of fields more powerful than their own. Such emulation has been complex and has occurred on multiple sites. I will focus here on some negative consequences of identification with the sciences and social sciences on the part of empirical researchers, a form of identification I call *scientism*. Such identification has occurred as the field has struggled to gain stature within the academy and within English studies, a result of its marginalization within English departments. One consequence of scientism has been the development of positivistic approaches to language and knowledge and an inattention to the political dimensions of language. I do not mean to suggest, however, that there have been no positive consequences of identification with the sciences; scientifically oriented empirical research has contributed substantially to the field's development and growth. Also, scientism and positivism have by no means been limited to the field of rhetoric and composition. Scientistic tendencies pervade other humanistic discourses such as literary theory. The scientism and positivism of empirical researchers are but two of many tendencies identifiable as rhetoric and composition has emerged as a field and is not clearly separable from other tendencies and influences, as will become obvious when I discuss alternatives to scientism and positivism within the field.

It is tempting, in considering the marginalization of rhetoric and composition from a feminist perspective, to construct a simple, binary opposition with literary studies associated with the dominant male and rhetoric and composition with the subordinate female. As I will argue, however, such an explanation not does allow for complexity and contradiction. Literary studies, for instance, is itself marginalized within the academy, especially in relation to the sciences. Also, rhetoric and composition, because it often deals with practical rather than aesthetic concerns, is frequently in a better situation than is literary studies to align itself with powerful forces within and beyond the academy such as industry and government. A binary and hierarchical description of the relationship between the fields also overlooks the fact that there are progressive, moderate, and conservative traditions within both fields so oppositional descriptions are necessarily reductive. Finally, the two fields are concerned both with reading and writing and the production and consumption of texts. Institutional partitioning has artificially separated fields that have much in common.

Scientism and Positivism

The site of rhetoric and composition as it emerged as a discipline is well suited to a feminist analysis of the damaging effects of scientistic and positivistic tendencies on disciplinary development and to an exploration of alternative ways of achieving legitimacy within the academy. In the field's early years, research was often synonymous with scientifically oriented empirical research, and identifications with the sciences and social sciences were clear attempts to gain authority by association with more authoritative discourses. Robert J. Connors in "Composition Studies and Science" speaks of this impulse as a "yearning toward the power and success of the natural sciences" (4). As rhetoric and composition has matured, however, it has become increasingly self-reflective and self-critical and has also developed traditions that provide alternatives to scientism and positivism.

In the early years of its development, rhetoric and composition relied heavily on research models developed in the social sciences, especially psychology and education. A prevalent approach involved comparison of groups that were given different treatments. In such an approach, the researcher formulates a hypothesis, selects an experimental group and a control group, administers a treatment to the experimental group, and measures the effect of the treatment. Every attempt is made to eliminate possible contaminating effects of the researcher's intervention and to limit the number of variables being measured and controlled. The results of such experiments were often granted the authority of scientific knowledge.

Stephen M. North in *The Making of Knowledge in Composition* says that he assembled a list of well over one thousand experimental studies in rhetoric and composition conducted between 1963 and 1985 and thinks that the total number is closer to fifteen hundred—more studies than that produced by all of the other research methods in rhetoric and composition combined (142). North sees the experimentalists as having the oldest history and the largest community of researchers within rhetoric and composition (141), though he does not think they have exercised anything like a proportionate influence on the field (144).

This commitment to scientific approaches to research is evident in *Research in Written Composition* by Richard Braddock, Richard Lloyd-Jones, and Lowell Schoer. These authors make clear that they only included research that employed "scientific methods" such as controlled experimentation. They argue that research in composition has not frequently been conducted with the knowledge and care that one associates with the physical sciences, and they compare research in composition to chemical research as it emerged from the period of alchemy (5). Of the references for further research that they append to their study, all 504 are, in one form or another, experimental.

Essays by Maxine Hairston and by Linda Flower provide justifications for the field's turn toward science to gain authority and even dominance within the academy and within English departments. Hairston's "The Winds of Change" was written in the spirit of Braddock, Lloyd-Jones, and Schoer's *Research in Written Composition.* In the essay, Hairston is enthusiastic about scientific approaches to the study of writing, though her invocation of Thomas Kuhn's *The Structure of Scientific Revolutions* suggests a critical perspective on the sciences as well. She argues that the field of rhetoric and composition, at the time she was writing, was undergoing a paradigm shift from a product-oriented paradigm to a process-oriented one. Hairston attributes the emergence of an enlightened approach to the teaching of writing to research and experimentation. Empirical investigations of the composing processes of actual writers have provided the data compositionists need to understand how writing really is accomplished, she claims. Those in the vanguard of the profession, Hairston tells us, are "attentively watching the research on the composing process in order to extract some pedagogical principles from it" (78). For the first time in the history of teaching writing, Hairston says, we have specialists who are doing "controlled and directed research on writers' composing processes" (85). Even graduate assistants in traditional literary programs are getting their in-service training, according to Hairston, from rhetoric and composition specialists in their departments (87).[5]

That Hairston saw empirical research in composition as a defense against the domination of literary studies becomes clear in "Diversity, Ideology, and Teaching Writing," published ten years after "The Winds of Change." In the essay she refers to her 1985 CCCC chair's address in which she warned that the field needed to establish its psychological and intellectual independence from the literary critics if it hoped to flourish. She then proceeds to rail against the radical left who she thinks are attempting to co-opt the field (187). By 1992, however, empirical research was losing its power as a defense, and Hairston's tone changes from the spirited optimism of "The Winds of Change" to anger and frustration.

Linda Flower's "Cognition, Context, and Theory Building," though on one level an acknowledgment of the social and political dimensions of writing and hence an acceptance of approaches to language advanced by literary theorists committed to postmodernism, is ultimately an argument for the superiority of scientific approaches to research over other approaches. In this essay, Flower is indirectly responding to critics, no doubt including literary or cultural theorists within her own department, who challenge the idea that empirical research has greater authority than other forms of research.

An essay by David Shumway published several years after Flower's suggests the nature of the critique of her work that may have motivated her essay. Shumway, a colleague of Flower's at Carnegie Mellon, acknowledges in "Science, Theory, and the Politics of Empirical Studies in the English Department" that Flower is not a naive empiricist. He nevertheless finds unconvincing her claim that her work aims to build theory and finds the cognitive theory she employs self-reproducing (155). Shumway suggests that empirical studies such as those conducted by Flower and by others are arguments that have the same epistemological status as other forms of discourse and that empirical data have the same status as other forms of evidence (156). No doubt the other forms of discourse and other forms of evidence he has in mind are the interpretive investigations that he engages in.

In "Cognition, Context, and Theory Building," Flower provides a careful, well-developed defense against her challengers, though she never explicitly acknowledges who they are or what their charges are. The goal of her essay, she says, is the development of an "integrated theoretical vision" that will bring together theories that explain literacy in terms of individual cognition and those that see "social and cultural context as the motive force in literate acts" (282). Her answer is an interactive theory that will explain how context cues cognition, and how cognition, in turn, mediates and interprets the particular world that context provides (282). She calls for a "grounded vision" that can place cognition in its context while celebrating the power of cognition to change that context (284). Flower claims that cognition and context interact equally and reciprocally, so there is no need to frame the question of how they can be integrated in terms of conflict or power imbalances (287). Flower aims to eliminate rigid boundaries and artificial distinctions, values integration and synthesis, and attempts to demonstrate that intellectual traditions are not necessarily competing and agonistic. Her essay would seem to be informed by a cultural-feminist commitment to community and nurturance. As the essay proceeds, however, it becomes clear that she implicitly privileges empirical research over other forms of research.

Flower takes pains to make clear that she is not a naive positivist who believes that knowledge can be found simply by observing external reality and recording one's findings. She demonstrates she is aware that observation involves interpretation and argumentation when she says, "Within the conventions of research, however, the 'results' of a given study, especially those which merely show a correlation, are just one more piece of evidence in cumulative, communally constructed argument" (300). Although she has come a long way from the simplistic cognitive theories she was advancing in the late 1970s and early 1980s, she is finally not successful in overcoming her earlier commitments to cognitivism and positivism. For one thing, she has a limited conception of context. She says that context includes (but is apparently not limited to) other people, the past, the social present, cultural norms, available language, intertextuality, assignment giving, and collaboration (287). It would seem that context includes everything other than the individual language user. It becomes evident as the essay progresses, however, that for Flower, context means the immediate social context within which a writer is situated, the context of the classroom or of the immediate group of peers, and a social exigency (287). The historical past, the linguistic system, intertextuality, and other factors seem to drop out of the picture entirely. Although Flower admits that context can be either nurturing or oppressive (289), it becomes obvious that the individual writer she describes inhabits a relatively benign world where intentions are purposeful and fully conscious. She dismisses conceptions of context that emphasize its overdetermination and complexity and conceptions of research that insist on the situatedness and partiality of the researcher.

But for all of Flower's insistence that research is not a simple matter of gathering and reporting data in a transparent way, she continues to use language such as "Good data is assertive and intractable" (299). Such statements suggest that the researcher is a passive absorber rather than an active agent. Such a view of research is at odds with an interactional approach to language where the writer (who is also the researcher in this case) is seen as mediating contextual cues and as being a purposeful and active producer of meaning. Flower's desire to connect seemingly disparate discourses, such as cognitive and social approaches to empirical research, and to view interaction as benign and nonconflictual, certainly a utopian impulse, becomes a defense of the authority and value neutrality of the empirical researcher and, implicitly, of the superiority of the results of such research over other kinds of research. Empiricism results in authoritative truth claims because it makes use of data that accurately describe reality.[6]

Scientistic and positivistic approaches to the study of writing have often led to the development of reductive conceptions of reading and writing and limited conceptions of the role of the researcher in the research process. Rhetoric and composition professionals' longing for legitimacy and power within the academy has sometimes resulted in identifications that have had unfortunate consequences. Though valuable in providing the field, early in its development, an identity separate from that of literary studies, scientism has also provided rhetoric and composition a false sense of the significance and authority of its research results. Scientism has also begun to lose its effectiveness as a defense against postmodern literary theorists who insist that scientific truth claims are provisional and subject to change.

A commitment to scientism has at times limited the field's vision of what should be investigated. Too often, compositionists have allowed other fields to dictate to them, not recognizing the importance of having research questions and methods grow out of composition's own problems and questions. Ellen Quandahl points out in "The Anthropological Sleep of Composition" that the field has focused so exclusively on the writing student as the subject of composition that it has neglected to examine the work of reading and writing themselves (426). This neglect is no doubt a result of allowing other fields and disciplines to determine what its research questions and methods will be rather than developing its own. As Gesa E. Kirsch and Joy S. Ritchie observe in their essay "Beyond the Personal: Theorizing a Politics of Location in Composition Research," strong identifications with traditional approaches to empirical research have also resulted in our neglecting to collaborate with research subjects not only in the development of research questions and the interpretation of data at both the descriptive and interpretive but also in the writing of research reports.

One especially serious consequence of the dominance of the methods and epistemologies of the sciences and the social sciences in the field's early development has been that feminist and other approaches that provide richly contextual and politicized representations of language have been ignored until quite recently. We have not developed strategies of resistance that these approaches would encourage. The story Nancy Sommers tells in "Between the Drafts" of her identification with more-powerful male theorists, and the consequence of this identification, a muting of her own voice, powerfully demonstrates the debilitating effects of "masculinized" approaches to research. She speaks of being stuck in a way of seeing: reproducing the thoughts of others and using them as her guides (28). Feminist theory provides diverse perspectives on how this process of masculinization works. Radical feminists tend to emphasize the ways in which masculinization has been damaging to women, cultural feminists emphasize women's different ways of being in the world, whereas postmodern feminists suggest that some forms of identification with powerful males can be empowering for women.

Radical-, Cultural-, and Postmodern-Feminist Conceptions of "Masculinization"

Radical feminist Judith Fetterley in *The Resisting Reader* coined the term *immasculation* to describe the alienation experienced by women who were taught to think as men, to identify with a male point of view, and to accept as normal and legitimate a system of male cultural values, one of whose central principles is misogyny (xx). Fetterley saw *immasculation* as a better term than *emasculation* for the cultural reality of the power relations between women and men. Often, Fetterley observed, a woman "is asked to identify with a selfhood that defines itself in opposition to her; she is required to identify against herself" (xii). Fetterley urged women readers to resist domination and to become resisting readers.

Cultural feminist Tania Modelski in *Feminism Without Women* is worried about the masculinization of feminism itself, especially the tendency within postmodern feminism to place so much emphasis on the dangers of essentialized conceptions of gender that they compromise feminism's ability to bring about political change. She criticizes the emphasis on what she calls "male feminism" in such books as *Men in Feminism* edited by Alice Jardine and Paul Smith. Modelski sees that such books, insofar as they focus on the question of male feminism as a topic for men and women to engage, bring men back to center stage and divert feminists from tasks more pressing than "deciding about the appropriateness of the label 'feminist' for men" (6). Modelski also sees that these books presume a kind of heterosexual presumption and tacitly assume and promote a liberal notion of the formal equality of men and women, whose viewpoints are accorded equal weight. For Modelski, "feminism without women" can mean the triumph either of a male-feminist perspective that excludes women or of a feminist antiessentialism so radical that every use of the term *woman* is disallowed (15). Modelski concludes her book by warning that the postfeminist play with gender in which differences are elided can easily lead us back into our "pregendered" past where there was only the universal subject—man (163). Modelski's position is cultural feminist in that she thinks women and women's culture should be at the center of her investigation.

Postmodern feminist Julia Kristeva, in contrast, focuses on the complexities of identification with powerful males and explores ways in which some forms of identification can be empowering for women. She speaks in "About Chinese Women" of the namelessness of women (140) and of a tendency of monotheism, paganism, and agrarian ideologies to repress women and mothers (141). Kristeva sees that women have no access to the word or to knowledge and power (142–43). If they choose identification with the mother, they remain excluded from language and culture; if they choose identification with the father, they become an Electra, "frigid with exaltation" (152). Kristeva recommends, instead, a middle way. Paternal identification is necessary in order to have a voice in the chapter of politics and history and in order to escape a "smug polymorphism." But women need to reject the development of a "homologous" woman who is capable and virile by swimming against the tide and need to reject this by rebelling against the existing relations of production and reproduction (156).

In addition to developing perspectives on the process of masculinization, feminists have also attended specifically to the problems for women posed by the dominance of the sciences within the academy and within society. Modern feminists tend to focus on the exclusion of women from scientific work, and antimodern feminists on the damaging effects of the sciences on women or on women's different ways of doing science, whereas postmodern feminists critique the scientific enterprise as men have traditionally defined it but do not reject it entirely.

Modern-, Antimodern-, and Postmodern-Feminist Critiques of Science

Margaret W. Rossiter's *Women Scientists in America: Struggles and Strategies to 1940* is a modern-feminist exploration of the domination of the sciences by men. Rossiter refers to science as a "manly profession." She documents that the sciences in the late 1800s were attempting to establish themselves as professions and so set up gates for admissions to professional societies on the grounds that they needed to "raise standards." As a result, membership requirements were deliberately harder on women than on men (73). Rossiter concludes in her subsequent volume, *Women Scientists in America: Before Affirmative Action 1940–1972,* that during this period, most of women scientists' traditional employers—women's colleges, teachers colleges, and colleges of home economics—were no longer hiring women, largely because of a prejudice against married women, which sometimes took the form of antinepotism laws, and a fear that single women would marry (xv). By the end of the 1960s, though, women were becoming aware of their marginalization, "status of women" reports were conducted, and legislation was enacted mandating equal pay and affirmative action in the academy (xviii).

Evelyn Fox Keller's *Reflections on Gender and Science,* in contrast, is a cultural-feminist investigation of science. Whereas Rossiter was concerned with identifying the inequalities and exclusionary practices that have pervaded the sciences, Keller seeks to explore ways in which including women's experiences in investigations of science enlarges "our understanding of the history, philosophy, and sociology of science" (9). As I observe in chapter 1 in the context of Keller's study of the work of Barbara McClintock, for Keller, science can be expanded to include women's experience by examining the different ways in which women scientists go about their work and by redefining what science is so as to include women's contributions.

Sandra Harding's *Whose Science? Whose Knowledge?* differs from Keller's feminist investigation of women's role in scientific work in that it has a postmodern cast. Harding attempts to overcome the essentializing tendencies of cultural-feminist approaches, though she does think that a feminist critique of science should begin with the experiences of women. She extends inquiry into the relationship between feminism and science by including in her discussion the perspectives of feminist political philosophers, African and African American philosophers who critique Eurocentrism, African American feminists, Third World writers, and philosophers, sociologists, and historians writing in the social studies of science (viii).[7]

Postmodern-feminist critics of science also argue that beliefs in the objectivity of the scientist and the neutrality of scientific investigation serve the interests of those in positions of authority and power, usually white males, and exclude those in marginalized positions. Identification by women or by feminized fields with the sciences and social sciences, therefore, may necessitate association with discourses that ignore issues of concern to those in marginalized positions and that arise out of epistemologies antithetical to their needs and interests. Ruth Berman's "From Aristotle's Dualism to Materialist Dialectics: Feminist Transformation of Science and Society" supports this idea. Berman argues that dualist ideology pervades Western science and philosophy and serves the interests of those in positions of power. Berman is careful, however, to provide a complex view of both gender and power, acknowledging that a simple dichotomy of male/female is itself dualistic and ignores the specific details of power relationships, the contradictions within "maleness," and differences among women (241). She nevertheless sees that both Plato and Aristotle depict mind and body as split with the mind associated with a master-class, males, and the body associated with an inferior class, females. Descartes, while preserving the eternal, supernatural character of the soul, transformed the body into a machine (240). He held that rational thought is objective, and it, alone, leads to truth. The Cartesian perspective, according to Berman, conceptualizes phenomena as composed of discrete, individual, elemental units, the whole consisting of an assemblage of these separate elements. It also assumes a linear, quantitative cause-effect relationship between phenomena (235). Berman calls for a materialist dialectics that sees change as directional rather than random, as a complex, interconnected, interactive process characterized by dialectical struggle, tension, and turbulence (244).

Postmodern feminism has also contributed valuable critiques of scientific and social scientific methods and procedures, emphasizing that research methods in the sciences and the social sciences, while claiming to be objective and neutral, actually reveal a strong male bias. Postmodern feminists also point out that women are often excluded from research samples and that researchers make extraordinary claims for their research because they do not recognize or admit that their own prejudices and values affect research results. Toby Jayaratne and Abigail J. Stewart summarize some of the objections feminists have made to traditional quantitative research methods in their essay, "Quantitative and Qualitative Methods in the Social Sciences: Current Feminist Issues and Practical Strategies." Such criticism focuses on: selection of sexist and elitist research topics; the absence of research on questions of central importance to women; biased research designs, including selection of only male subjects; an exploitative relationship between researcher and the subject and within research teams; the illusion of objectivity; the simplistic and superficial nature of quantitative data; improper interpretation and overgeneralization of findings; and inadequate data dissemination and utilization (86). Jayaratne and Stewart make evident that uncritical acceptance of the epistemological underpinnings and methods of the sciences and social sciences is risky for those in marginalized positions.

A postmodern-feminist perspective on science emphasizes the situatedness and the interestedness of the researcher and hence the gendered nature of the research process. It calls into question the authority of the researcher and emphasizes that the research process is far less systematic than it is made out to be. Trinh T. Minh-ha's *Woman, Native, Other* provides a good example of a postmodern-feminist critique of anthropology. Trinh speaks of anthropology's "positivist dream" of "a neutralized language that strips off all its singularity to become nature's exact, unmisted reflection" (53). The (male) anthropologist, according to Trinh, claims objectivity and the transparency of language. Words must disappear from the field of visibility and yield ground to "pure presence" (53). What anthropology seeks, according to Trinh, is "its own elevation to the rank of Science" (57). Trinh insists, though, that work in anthropology is actually a form of intellectual *bricolage* or potpourri that may always be "re-ordered, completed, or refuted by further research" (63). She finds that in anthropological work, "The positivist yearning for transparency with respect to reality is always lurking below the surface" (64).

Beyond Scientism and Positivism

Only recently has the field of rhetoric and composition benefited from the feminist explanations of "masculinization" or feminist critiques of science discussed above because its conception research, as I have suggested, was too often positivistic and scientistic. As rhetoric and composition has matured, however, it has become increasingly aware of the limitations of such approaches to writing. Janet Emig in "Inquiry Paradigms and Writing," for instance, distinguishes between two inquiry paradigms, the positivistic and the phenomenological. For Emig, in the positivist paradigm, there is no context for the inquiry, "only the phenomenon to be examined a-contextually, with no consideration or acknowledgment of setting" (66). Emig sees that positivists believe that a "one-on-one correspondence exists or can be established between a phenomenon and an interpretation of that phenomenon" (67). For positivists, according to Emig, "meaning resides almost exclusively within a text" (68). Other empirically oriented compositionists began to recognize some limitations of the field's scientistic approaches to composition research. *Research on Composing: Points of Departure* edited by Charles R. Cooper and Lee Odell, for instance, although accepting comparison-group research as a valuable approach to the study of writing, places considerably greater emphasis on the importance of theory and cautions that research results should be seen as tentative rather than definitive.

Later overviews of empirical research in rhetoric and composition provide an increasingly critical perspective on scientific approaches to research. Lillian Bridwell and Richard Beach in *New Directions in Composition Research* speak of the "mistakes of the past" that occurred because we "grossly oversimplified the nature of written language and the processes by which humans create it" (12). They emphasize the need for a more valid and comprehensive theoretical base for research in composition and call for studies that relate writing to social, political, and psychological contexts (6). Like Cooper and Odell, they call for acknowledgment of the limitations of research methods (9).

George Hillocks, Jr.'s follow-up volume to Braddock et al.'s *Research in Written Composition* is more directly critical of experimental research. In the introduction to Hillock's volume, Richard Lloyd-Jones effectively dissociates himself from the earlier work, which he coauthored, by claiming that he is actually a "rhetorical theorist." The material he examined in 1963, he says, "forced me into empiricism" (xiv). Lloyd-Jones applauds the far more varied approach to research in Hillocks's study, which includes case studies and protocols. Also, Hillocks includes in the book an extended discussion of criticisms of experimental studies including problems with control of variables and reporting of data. By the late 1980s, scientistic composition was coming under serious attack by compositionists with political orientations but also by researchers who had begun their careers doing scientific work.

By 1988, when Janice M. Lauer and J. William Asher published their *Composition Research: Empirical Designs,* there was clearly a need to defend empirical research itself and to explain it to a community of compositionists with commitments to more ethical or humanistic approaches to scholarship. Alan Purves in his foreword speaks of the need to supplement traditions of humanistic research by social science research; Lauer and Asher in their preface are also defensive. In response to those who have reacted to empirical research either by dismissing it or by accepting its conclusions indiscriminately, they argue "that an adequate study of the complex domain of writing must be multidisciplinary, including empirical research" (ix). They call for communication among composition theorists, writing instructors, and empirical researchers and for respect for each other's efforts (ix).

Kirsch and Patricia A. Sullivan in *Methods and Methodology in Composition Research* respond to the increasing marginalization of empirical researchers by defining research broadly to include historical research and critical theory in addition to social scientific research. Theirs is a self-consciously feminist approach to research. In "Hearing Voices in English Studies," Margaret Baker Graham and Patricia Goubil-Gambrell trace the field's movement away from methodologies of the sciences and social sciences toward methodologies of the humanities by examining recent issues of *Research in the Teaching of English*. They observe that in 1978, Alan Purves, editor at the time, noted that *RTE* was publishing fewer experimental studies and more qualitative studies. By the time Judith Langer and Arthur Appleby were editors of the journal, according to Graham and Goubil-Gambrell, quantitative research was no longer the unquestioned methodology of choice in *RTE*. Graham and Goubil-Gambrell also see that Sandra Stotsky, the editor at the time their article was published, continued to shift the emphasis away from empiricism (111). Peter Mortensen and Kirsch's *Ethics and Representation in Qualitative Studies of Literacy* emphasizes the importance and increasing acceptance of qualitative research including ethnographies and case studies. They see that the ethical turn they identify has been influenced strongly by academic feminism (xxi).

Quite clearly empirical researchers within rhetoric and composition have, over the years, become increasingly aware of the dangers of uncritical acceptance of the methods of the sciences and the social sciences in the study of reading and writing. Emulation of scientific methods can lead to reductive conceptions of language and to unwarranted conclusions. Also, scientifically oriented composition research, originally embraced, in part at least, as a defense against its nemesis, literary studies, is losing its effectiveness as literary theorists influenced by postmodern critiques of Enlightenment rationality have begun to question the authority of scientific claims. Identifications intended to enhance the field's status can result, ironically, in increased vulnerability.

Transactionalism/Interactionalism

One way in which the field has resisted scientistic and positivistic approaches to the study of writing is through the development of transactional or interactional theories, approaches that are related to Rosenblatt's transactionalism discussed in the previous chapter.[8] Such approaches, if not actually postmodern, prepare the way for the development of nonfoundational conceptions of reading, writing, and teaching. In *Rhetoric and Reality* Berlin divides work in rhetoric into three categories: objective, subjective, and transactional. According to Berlin, objective rhetorics are based on positivistic epistemologies, and the dominant form is current-traditional rhetoric. The objective perspective emphasizes that the writer attempts to perceive reality with impartiality. In this view, truth is seen as being located first in nature and as existing prior to language (8). Objective rhetorics make patterns of arrangement and superficial correctness the main ends of writing instruction (9). Subjective theories, in contrast, according to Berlin, locate truth either within the individual or within a realm that is accessible only through the individual's internal apprehension (11). In this view, truth transcends the material realm, is attainable through a solitary vision, and resists expression (12). Berlin associates subjective theories with Romanticism and with Freudian psychology and sees the pedagogical approaches of keeping journals and of peer editing as arising out of a subjective orientation (14).

The transactional approach arises out of the interaction of the elements of the rhetorical situation, subject, object, audience, and language operating simultaneously (15). Berlin identifies three forms of transactional rhetoric in the twentieth century: classical, cognitive, and epistemic. If the emphasis in the transactional view sometimes appears to be on the individual, according to Berlin, the individual is conceived of as inherently transactional, arriving at truth through a transaction with the surrounding environment (16). The epistemic approach emphasizes that interlocutor, audience, and the material world are all regarded as verbal constructs (16). It emphasizes, further, that all experiences including scientific and logical ones are grounded in language (16). Berlin associates epistemic transactionalism with the work of Kenneth Burke, Richard Rorty, Hayden White, and Michel Foucault (17).

Berlin's objectivist rhetoric is related to modern approaches within the humanities that reflect the belief in the possibility of arriving at objective knowledge through the scientific method or through legal processes of adjudication of evidence. Objectivist rhetoric sometimes becomes positivistic when the observer is seen as having no effect on that which is being observed. Berlin's subjectivist rhetoric is related to antimodern approaches within the humanities that deny the possibility of objective knowledge and place emphasis on the uniqueness of the individual and on dimensions of experience that cannot be measured or quantified. His transactional rhetoric anticipates postmodernism within the humanities with its denial of the foundations that objectivity and subjectivity are based on and its affirmation of the nonfoundational and contingent nature of knowledge. The taxonomy he develops in *Rhetoric and Reality* is useful because it suggests that all three traditions have been and continue to be influential within rhetoric and composition.

Berlin develops his ideas more fully in *Rhetorics, Poetics, and Cultures,* using the term *social-epistemic rhetoric* rather than transactionalism and making clearer the relationship between social-epistemic rhetoric and postmodern thought. He observes that all language use is inherently interpretive, but he emphasizes that the language user is not a unified, coherent, and sovereign subject who can transcend language (86). He insists that language is ineluctably involved in power and politics (86). Berlin concludes his chapter on social-epistemic rhetoric by observing that students must come to see that the languages they are expected to speak, write, and embrace "are never disinterested, always bringing with them structures on the existent, the good, the possible, and the resulting regimes of power" (93).

What Berlin calls objectivism, Louise Phelps in *Composition as a Human Science* calls scientism, positivism, or strong empiricism. Positivism, according to Phelps, sees knowledge as based on two kinds of proofs: sense data and universal reason (9). The world is seen as independent of the perspective of the observer, and science is seen as value free and "objective" (10). Contextualism, in contrast, according to Phelps, is intersubjectivist, an interpretive science, and is rooted in hermeneutics (22). Science is seen as a rhetorical practice. Contextualism escapes subjectivism or imprisonment within closed, virtual language by restoring the possibility of reference through discourse (25). Phelps makes it clear that contextualism is a postmodern perspective.

Thomas Kent in *Paralogic Rhetoric* also moves interactionalism in the direct of postmodernism. He identifies paralogic rhetoric as a theory of *communicative interaction,* a term that derives from philosopher Donald Davidson's work and assumes that communication is a thoroughly hermeneutic act that cannot be converted into a logical framework or system of social conventions that determines the meaning of an utterance (x). Kent develops the approach in *Paralogic Rhetoric,* arguing that language conventions do not control the production and reception of discourse but instead are established through the give-and-take of communicative interaction (x). Kent's perspective works against the idea that disciplinary communities produce relatively stable and static conventions that can be codified and then imitated. It also works against the idea that any totalizing system can explain the language act, and Kent sees that one of the most powerful foundational elements in contemporary rhetorical study is the notion of convention (24). He emphasizes that pedagogies that emphasize teaching students rhetorical conventions are limited because learning these elements does not ensure that students can produce effective discourse (47). He explains that the hermeneutic act operates much like open-ended dialogue. Writing and reading cannot be separated from the dialogic interaction in which any specific act of writing and reading takes place (48). Kent says, "The most fundamental activity of discourse production is the hermeneutic act: the interpretive guess we must make about our hearer's or reader's code that occurs even before invention becomes possible" (38).

Theories of interaction, while emphasizing fluidity and change, also attempt to account for regularity. They therefore do not preclude discussions of genre. The work of Mikhail Bakhtin has been influential in the development of interactional accounts of genre, and Kent draws heavily on Bakhtin's essay "The Problem of Speech Genres" in developing his theory of "paralogic genres." Kent emphasizes that a genre is a public construct rather than an internal transcendental category (128). He says that a genre never stands as a synchronic category outside the concrete reality of communicative interaction and cannot be reduced to a set of conventional elements that function together as a structural or organic whole (140). He sees a genre as "an open-ended and uncodifiable strategy for hermeneutic guessing that comes into being through triangulation or what Bakhtin formulates as open-ended dialogue" (128). A genre, according to Kent, is defined by its response to other utterances and not by its conventional formal elements (143).

Interactional approaches to writing move in the direction of postmodern ones by emphasizing the necessary interconnectedness of subject and object without claiming that the two become fused or indistinct. Interactionalists see writing as taking place within a rich context that is charged politically and that is open ended and dynamic rather than closed. Writer and reader make momentary contact in a situation that involves struggle and interanimation with other readers, writers, and texts. In emphasizing the social dimensions of writing, they prepare the way for considerations of writing that take into account gender, race, class, ethnicity, sexual orientation, and other factors.

Emergent Postmodern-Feminist Rhetoric and Composition

As I make clear in chapter 1, rhetoric and composition is beginning to develop postmodern-feminist approaches to reading, writing, and teaching in the form of alternatives to modern positivism and scientism that do not necessitate rejecting scientific approaches entirely. Perusal of recent books and journal articles provides evidence of the emergence of such approaches. Two manifestations of this change are an increasing concern for ethical issues and disruption of traditional forms of academic discourse through an emphasis on autobiographical writing. These developments, which parallel developments in a number of other fields, are sometimes called the *ethical turn* and the *autobiographical turn*.

Feminist researchers in rhetoric and composition are beginning to explore the ethical dimensions of research—the rights and responsibilities of researchers and research subjects. This work recognizes that research necessarily involves intervention as well as observation and that work in rhetoric and composition frequently makes use of human subjects. Rather than conceiving of the researcher as a neutral observer, this work defines the researcher as necessarily partial, interested, biased, and engaged. The challenge, then, is to observe research subjects while treating them fairly and ethically. Some possibilities for ensuring that observations are fair and ethical are increasing the number of observers, increasing the number of observations, including descriptions of the research process in reports of research findings, qualifying conclusions, and including reflective narratives in research reports. Some possibilities for ensuring that research subjects are treated fairly and ethically include obtaining their consent if their work is quoted, obtaining their consent on the use of their material or their ideas as expressed in interviews on research reports, collaborating with them on research projects, including them in on research designs, and asking for their input on research reports.[9]

The autobiographical turn involves including personal narrative in otherwise impersonal discourse. Examples of disruptions of traditional academic discourse by postmodern feminists are abundant[10] as are the ways in which that discourse is disrupted. Dialogues, conversations, and interviews take the place of or are woven into argumentative or expository prose. First-person narratives are interspersed with third-person observation. Genres such as poetry and prose are interspersed. The visual aspects of texts take on increasing importance, and texts and graphics are juxtaposed in creative ways as are electronic media and print media.

Rhetoric and composition is beginning to find postmodern alternatives to unhealthy identification with fields more powerful than itself and is less reliant on association with other fields to confer authority on its work. Appropriations from other fields are being made carefully and critically in order to prevent asking inappropriate questions, employing inappropriate methods, and embracing perspectives that leave the field vulnerable in the face of persistent challenges by literary theorists and others. As Kirsch and Mortensen emphasize in their introduction to *Ethics and Representation in Qualitative Studies of Literacy,* "A desirable critical conversation about qualitative research and its theoretical underpinnings cannot be borrowed from other disciplines; the conversation must begin with and be sustained by scholars in composition studies themselves" (xx). Kirsch and Mortensen are by no means advocating that qualitative work in other fields be ignored. Rather, they are calling for discussions of qualitative research methods that have a critical edge, and such discussions must begin with issues directly pertinent to rhetoric and composition. Because the field of rhetoric and composition is more interdisciplinary than most, because its subject is discourse itself, because it understands feminization and marginalization all too well, and because it is finding alternatives to its modern research methods and assumptions, it has the potential to become a leader within the academy.

In chapter 7, I focus on pedagogical concerns, suggesting that postmodern-feminist pedagogical approaches are useful in developing ways of dealing with student resistance in both the literature and the composition classroom. The pedagogical strategies that have arisen out of modern-feminist and antimodern-feminist approaches, I suggest, are not sufficient to deal with the complexities of the contemporary academy. They generally do not address changing demographics that necessitate an understanding of multiple cultures, nor do they generally take into consideration students' often conservative political views that make conflict in the feminist classroom almost inevitable.

7

Employing Resistance in Postmodern-Feminist Teaching

Resistance. 1. The act, on the part of persons, of resisting, opposing, or withstanding. 2. Power or capacity of resisting. 3. Opposition of one material thing to another material thing, force, etc.

—*OED*

Resistance: a word for the fear, dislike, hesitance most people have about turning their entire lives upside down and watching everything they have ever learned disintegrate into lies. "Empowerment" may be liberating, but it is also a lot of hard work and new responsibility to sort through one's life and rebuild according to one's own values and choices.

—Kathy Kea, quoted in Patti Lather, *Getting Smart: Feminist Research and Pedagogy with/in the Postmodern*

*A*s I make clear in chapter 6, postmodern-feminist approaches to the teaching of writing are just beginning to emerge within the field of rhetoric and composition. Here I emphasize that an important dimension of a postmodern-feminist approach in both literary studies and rhetoric and composition is dealing with student resistance. Feminist antimodern expressivists, who tend to have radical- or cultural-feminist orientations, place faith in the inherent willingness on the part of students to grow and develop as writers once they are free of the constraints imposed by modern teachers and educational institutions. Modern Marxist feminists tend to place faith in the ability of the teacher to direct rebellious and frustrated students toward the development of critical perspectives and toward activism. Postmodern-feminist approaches aim to make students aware of inequalities and abuses of power but recognize that student resistance to pedagogies of resistance is a probability. In entitling this chapter as I have, therefore, I intend two meanings: (1) We have begun to develop pedagogies that resist abuses of power in various forms, but our students often resist these pedagogies; and (2) we need to develop strategies for making productive use of their resistance.

The first statement is fairly easy to support. More difficult is developing ways of redirecting the resistance of our students to our pedagogies of resistance. A good example of student resistance is the attitude of a student in a course I have taught, Literary Representations of Gender, Race, Class, and Ethnicity. This student compared the class system in India with the class system in America, concluding that the two are totally different and that America does not have an underclass. When I asked about the homeless, he explained that he has read books that make clear that most homeless people have chosen and are satisfied with their situation. Students with such attitudes, I suspect, sometimes enroll in classes that promise to deal with diversity issues because such classes provide a forum for the expression of their own prejudices. This student's attitudes are all too common at universities such as my own to which students often come from conservative backgrounds and arrive at the university with deeply entrenched prejudices against progressive movements, minorities, and homosexuals. At Michigan Tech three-fourths of the undergraduates are male, the students are conservative, the university does not have well-developed support networks in place such as the women's studies and black studies programs present at many other universities, and only a very small percentage of the students are minorities.[1]

Postmodern-feminist scholars have documented student resistance to feminist pedagogies. Dale Bauer in "The Other 'F' Word"[2] makes clear that, for feminists, teaching is largely a matter of finding ways to circumvent the damaging effects of student resistance to our pedagogies of resistance. Min-Zhan Lu in "Reading and Writing Differences: The Problematic of Experience" finds that her students, while attentive to problems of gender inequality, are indifferent to the ways in which sexism is related to other forms of oppression. Lu sees her students' inattention to issues of ethnicity as a kind of essentialism that has its parallel in forms of feminism whereby the gendered experience of the academic researcher or reader functions as a universalizing term to overwrite the experiences of others under study (242).

Because postmodern-feminist teaching is often a matter of dealing with student resistance, postmodern-feminist conceptions of resistance provide a very useful point of departure in attempting to deal with student resistance to our pedagogies of resistance.[3] The work of Judith Butler, Toni Morrison, bell hooks, and Gloria Anzaldúa is especially helpful in dealing with the difficulties students often have confronting perspectives on homosexuality, race, and gender that differ from their own. After describing the conceptions of resistance developed by these writers, I will relate their perspectives to situations I have encountered in my own classes. As I will make clear, student resistance, though often disturbing, can result in useful discussion and student learning. Indeed, a degree of resistance is no doubt necessary for student learning. The clash of values and the interanimation of perspectives can lead to the articulation of diverse opinions, to changed attitudes, and to a recognition of our own situatedness, blindnesses, and limitations. Patti Lather makes a related point in *Getting Smart:* "Rather than dismiss student resistance to our classroom practices as false consciousness, I want to explore what these resistances have to teach us about our own impositional tendencies" (76).

Postmodern-Feminist Conceptions of Resistance

Postmodern feminists often represent resistance positively, seeing it as disrupting male representations of women and as involving subversion of those representations, turning them against themselves. Such approaches focus on power but tend to see power as ubiquitous rather than centralized and to see discourse as implicated in power relations. They also tend to associate domination with Western humanism and to see the self as multiple and changing rather than unified and static. Resistance, therefore, takes more subtle and complicated forms than it does in radical feminism. The "enemy" is not always easily identifiable and not always clearly distinct from the feminist with progressive views. The structures of power that work against women are often networks of forces including social, economic, and political factors in which gender is implicated in complex ways.[4] I will discuss the works of Butler, Morrison, hooks, and Anzaldúa in turn.

Butler's work focuses largely on resistance in the context of homophobia. Some of her books, including *Gender Trouble, Bodies That Matter, The Psychic Life of Power,* and *Excitable Speech,* emphasize that gender is performative, a "doing," hence calling into question foundational conceptions of gender that see identity as prior to and determinative of action. She says in *Gender Trouble,* "Gender is always a doing. . . . There is no gender identity behind the expressions of gender; that identity is performatively constituted by the very 'expressions' that are said to be its results" (25). Invoking Foucault's genealogical inquiry, she insists that gender is not a cause but an effect (23). It is the institution of heterosexuality, according to Butler, that requires and regulates a binary conception of gender and sexuality (23). For Butler, sexuality is multiple rather than single, and lesbianism destroys the sexual categories that heterosexuality legislates (19).

> Gender is a complexity whose totality is permanently deferred, never fully what it is at any given juncture in time. An open coalition, then, will affirm identities that are alternatively instituted and relinquished according to the purposes at hand; it will be an open assemblage that permits of multiple convergences and divergencies without obedience to a normative telos of definitional closure. (16)

Butler discusses resistance in *Bodies that Matter* and *The Psychic Life of Power.* In *Bodies that Matter,* Butler argues against a Lacanian conception of resistance that sees resistance as involving the failure of compliance with the law that does not change the structure of the law (105–6). For Butler, the legitimation of homosexuality necessitates resisting the force of normalization and a resignification of the law to expand and alter its terms (111). Butler is not asking that everyone become homosexual, only that homosexuality be legitimated and accepted. Resistance for Butler involves repetitions of hegemonic forms of power that do not repeat loyally (124).

> There is no subject prior to its constructions, and neither is the sub-
> ject determined by those constructions; it is always the nexus, the
> nonspace of cultural collision, in which the demand to resignify or
> repeat the very terms which constitute the "we" cannot be summarily
> refused, but neither can they be followed in strict obedience. It is
> the space of this ambivalence which opens up the possibility of a
> reworking of the very terms by which subjectivation proceeds—and
> fails to proceed. (124)

Butler develops her conception of resistance further in *The Psychic Life of Power*. Here she attempts to identify a position that is "between" Freud and Foucault, that allows for the development of a Foucauldian perspective within psychoanalysis (88). In making her case, she distinguishes between the psyche and the subject. The psyche, which she sees as including the unconscious, is what exceeds "the imprisoning effects of the discursive demand to inhabit a coherent identity, to become a coherent subject" (88). The subject, in contrast, is the intelligible being produced, at a cost, by normative demands (88). Butler sees that resistance involves a repetition that does not consolidate the unified subject but, rather, proliferates effects that undermine the force of normalization (93).

> A subject only remains a subject through a reiteration or rearticu-
> lation of itself as a subject, and this dependency of the subject on
> repetition for coherence may constitute that subject's incoherence,
> its incomplete character. (99)

She sees that the subject's need for repetition to reinforce its coherence provides the potential for disruption of that coherence. The subject is always potentially unstable and hence resistant.

Butler also discusses resistance in the context of discussions of freedom of speech in *Excitable Speech*. Here she argues against radical feminist Catharine A. MacKinnon's work on pornography. MacKinnon tends to define speech broadly to include actions, graphics, and written texts and calls for the suppression of speech that is injurious to individuals. MacKinnon finds pornography to be damaging to women and hence calls for its elimination. Butler, however, finds MacKinnon's position to be a dangerous one. She sees that MacKinnon's collapsing of the distinction between representation and conduct and her call for enhancing the power of the state in interventions over graphic sexual representation to be serious threats to lesbian and gay politics. Such a position, according to Butler, results in unfortunate actions such as the censorship of Robert Mapplethorpe's photography. For Butler, the problem is that radicals such as MacKinnon and conservatives alike construe representation not merely as performative but as causative. They assume that gansta rap, for example, causes urban crime (22).

Butler sees that censorship produces speech and is in some sense responsible for its production (128). Speech is an effect of censorship. Speakers make their decisions only in the context of an already constrained field of possibilities (129).

The censored text takes on a new life as part of the discourse produced by the mechanism of censorship (130). The effort to constrain a term results in its proliferation (131). Butler does not think, then, that censorship is an effective means of dealing with offensive speech. Rather, she finds that dominant discourse can be expropriated so its expropriation becomes a potential site of subversive resignification (157). She thinks that appropriating cultural norms to oppose their historically sedimented effect constitutes the insurrectionary moment (159): "The effort to tighten the reins on speech undercuts those political impulses to exploit speech itself for its insurrectionary effects" (162). The name-calling associated with hate speech "may be the initiating moment of a counter-mobilization" (163). The word that wounds "becomes an instrument of resistance in the redeployment that destroys the prior territory of its operation" (163). Butler concludes that insurrectionary speech is the necessary response to injurious language (163).

If Butler focuses primarily on resistance to progressive attitudes toward sexuality, Morrison focuses on resistance to progressive attitudes toward race. In *Playing in the Dark,* she helps explain why white students might ignore racial themes as they read. Morrison emphasizes that, regardless of the race of the author, "the readers of virtually all of American fiction have been positioned as white" (xii). She finds that white authors are attentive to racial issues, seeing them as sensitive and probing (15), but readers, especially professional critics, have not been. She says, "Criticism as a form of knowledge is capable of robbing literature not only of its own implicit and explicit ideology but of its ideas as well" (9). For her, Africanism ought to be inextricable from the deliberations of literary criticism, but elaborate strategies are undertaken to "erase its presence from view" (9).

Morrison speaks of processes of exclusion among Europeans and the Europeanized (7). Within American culture, according to Morrison, European sources of cultural hegemony were dispersed, and "the process of organizing American coherence through a distancing Africanism became the operative mode of a new cultural hegemony" (8). She sees that in matters of race, "silence and evasion have historically ruled literary discourse" (9). The situation is exacerbated because the habit of ignoring race is understood to be a "graceful, even generous, liberal gesture" (10). Every well-bred instinct argues "against noticing" (10).

Morrison thinks that one reason for this "ornamental vacuum" in literary discourse is the pattern of thinking about what she calls "racialism" in terms of its consequences on the victim (11). Equally important, according to Morrison, is an investigation of "the impact of racism on those who perpetuate it" (11). In *Playing in the Dark,* she is therefore interested in what she calls "whiteness," the way in which blacks are depicted in literature written by white authors. She focuses on what "racial ideology does to the mind, imagination, and behavior of masters" (12). Morrison explores how "literary whiteness" and "literary blackness" are made as well as the consequences of these constructions (xii). She asks, "How do embedded assumptions of racial (not racist) language work in the literary enterprise that hopes and sometimes claims to be 'humanistic'?" (xii–xiii).

Her subject is Africanism, the blackness that African peoples have come to signify as well as the "views, assumptions, readings, and misreadings that accompany Eurocentric learning about these people" (7). Although Morrison is interested in the blindnesses of professional critics, her analysis also helps explain the
blindnesses of student readers. Students typically have not read much literature
by African American writers and have not been taught how to do so. They tend
to read it the way they read literature by whites, erasing black issues and black
concerns. Doing so allows them to ignore their own complicity in racism and in
domination by whites.

Like Morrison, hooks thinks that we need what she calls "the production of
a discourse on race that interrogates whiteness" (*Yearning* 54). If Morrison emphasizes the problem of ignoring racial issues, however, hooks focuses considerable attention on ways of resisting white cultural hegemony. She has been strongly
influenced by the work of Paulo Freire, speaking in *Talking Back,* for instance,
of the need for literacy programs that educate for critical consciousness (31), a
term that Freire often uses.[5] Hooks, though, moves beyond her mentor in her
explicit feminist perspective. She speaks in *Talking Back,* for instance, of "interlocking systems of domination—sex, race, and class" and of women acknowledging the "diversity and complexity of female experience" (21).

In her essay "Postmodern Blackness" included in *Yearning,* hooks makes clear
that she is aware of the limitations of postmodern perspectives, especially their lack
of concern for racial issues and their tendency to be overly academic and exclusive
(23). Hooks explains that she is alienated by postmodernism as it exists in the academy at the present. She nevertheless feels that it can become a powerful approach
in black liberation struggle if its "politics of difference" incorporates the voices
of displaced, marginalized, exploited, and oppressed black people (25). She finds
that its critique of identity politics and of the universalizing agenda of modernism can be useful in struggles to find new strategies of resistance (26). She says,
"Postmodern critiques of essentialism which challenge notions of universality and
static over-determined identity within mass culture and mass consciousness can
open up new possibilities for the construction of self and the assertion of agency"
(28). Postmodern critiques allow for the affirmation of multiple black identities
and varied black experience (28). For hooks, changing the exclusionary practices
of postmodern critical discourse is to enact a "postmodernism of resistance" (30).
The decentered subject of postmodern culture "can provide the space where ties
are severed or it can provide the occasion for new and varied forms of bonding"
(31). However, in order for postmodernism to become resistant, according to
hooks, critics, writers, and academics have to give the same critical attention to
nurturing and cultivating our ties to black community as they give to writing
articles, teaching, and lecturing (30).

For hooks, resistance need not be oppositional. She speaks in "Homeplace:
A Site of Resistance," also included in *Yearning,* of the work of black women to
create places of healing and recovery as resistance (43). She says, "Historically,

black women have resisted white supremacist domination by working to establish homeplace" (44). For hooks, then, black liberation struggle needs to recognize the role women have played in sustaining black culture. The subordination of black women has damaged black solidarity (48). At other times, however, her conception of resistance does sound oppositional. She speaks in *Outlaw Culture,* for instance, of cultural revolution necessitating doing everything differently, of decolonizing our minds and imaginations (7).

Hooks speaks in *Reel to Real* of Foucault's conception of power as a system of domination that leaves no room for freedom. She also speaks, though, of Foucault's view that there are possibilities for resistance in all power relations and of agency being located in the margins, gaps, and locations on and through the body (198). Resistance, then, according to hooks, involves "gazing" when one is not supposed to gaze, looking critically and naming that which is seen (199). Black women, according to hooks, have only been able to resist class exploitation and racist and sexist domination through struggle, reading, and looking "against the grain" (208).

Anzaldúa shifts the emphasis from race to the situation of Third World women. Her perspective is a postmodern one in that she makes clear that she is not defining Third World women as a single culture. She says, "There is no one Chicano language just as there is no one Chicano experience" (*Borderlands* 58). Chicano Spanish, she says, is as diverse linguistically as it is regionally (59). She also speaks of the need to enlist the aid of white people and to allow them to be the allies of women of color (85). She sees the self as multiple rather than single, fluid rather than static. She speaks of reality shifting and gender shifting: "One person metamorphoses into another in a world where people fly through the air, heal from mortal wounds" (70). She also speaks of playing with her Self, of being in dialogue with it (70).

Anzaldúa speaks in "Speaking in Tongues: A Letter to Third World Women Writers" of her own resistance, as a Third World woman writer, to the act of writing. She says, "To write is to confront one's demons, look them in the face, and live to write about them. Fear acts like a magnet; it draws the demons out of the closet and into the ink in our pens" (171). She speaks of writing as "dangerous" because it reveals the fears, angers, and strengths of women under a triple or quadruple oppression (171). She concludes, "Find the muse within you. The voice that lies buried under you, dig it up. Do not fake it, try to sell it for a handslap or your name in print" (173).

In *Borderlands,* Anzaldúa speaks of her resistance, her refusal to know some truth about herself bringing about paralysis and depression (48). She is resistant to knowing, to letting go, to "that deep ocean where once I dived into death" and is resistant to sex, to intimate touching, to opening herself to an alien other (48). The problem is especially acute for Third World women who are oppressed on a number of different levels. If a Third World woman doesn't change her ways, Anzaldúa says, she will remain a stone forever (49).

According to Anzaldúa, living in a state of psychic unrest, in a Borderland, is what makes writers write (73). She compares writing to a cactus needle embedded in the flesh that festers and must be plucked out (73). Writing for her is "an endless cycle of making it worse, making it better, but always making meaning out of the experience, whatever it may be" (73). For images, words, and stories to have transformative power, they must arise from the human body: "This work, these images, piercing tongue or ear lobes with cactus needle, are my offerings, are my Aztecan blood sacrifices" (75).

If women are resistant to coming to terms with themselves, men are even more so, according to Anzaldúa. She sees that men, even more than women, are fettered to gender roles. Women are more likely to break out of "bondage," according to Anzaldúa. Only gay men have had the courage to challenge current masculinity. She has encountered a few scattered and isolated gentle straight men, the beginnings of a "new breed," but they are "confused, and entangled with sexist behaviors that they have not been able to eradicate. . . . We need a new masculinity and the new man needs a movement" (84).

Some Pedagogical Contexts

The work of Butler, Morrison, hooks, and Anzaldúa is useful in explaining student resistance to pedagogies of resistance and in suggesting strategies for making productive use of their resistance. The first situation I will describe involves resistance to acceptance of homosexuality, the second resistance to discussion of racial issues, and the third resistance to discussion of gender issues. In all three examples, student resistance, though disturbing in its pervasive conservativism, was useful in that it enabled discussion and, in some cases, changed perspectives.

Context 1: Resisting Homosexuality

The first context involved an honors, first-year composition course in which I created a class e-mail list and required students to post a message at least twice during the term, either to the entire list or to me. Most students opted to post their messages to the list. After reading a cluster of essays on "Female Icons" in *Constellations*, the course reader, a student commented appreciatively on Camille Paglia's "Madonna: Venus of the Radio Waves." In the essay, Paglia speaks of Madonna's video "Justify My Love," which deals with bisexuality, and concludes that "she has introduced ravishing visual beauty and a lush Mediterranean sensuality into parched, pinched, word-drunk Anglo-Saxon feminism" (540). An e-mail message by the student who liked the essay triggered a spate of e-mail messages, most of which were opposed to the student's perspective and were hostile to bisexuality and homosexuality. Some students were clearly very bothered by Paglia's acceptance of bisexuality and her religious iconoclasm.

The messages were so highly charged and so numerous that the list began to gain a reputation, at least among first-year students, and students who were not enrolled in the class tried to subscribe. One lurker who was temporarily successful in joining our conversation introduced himself as the student who sat in the back of the class whom no one noticed. Indeed, some students did not realize he was not in the class because it was early in the term and they had not yet gotten to know each other. I unsubscribed him and one other whom a student in the class tried to add because I did not want to disrupt the pedagogical "homeplace" that we were collectively beginning to create.

Often the messages affirmed a belief in Christianity and seemed unaccepting of the perspectives of students who did not share their beliefs. One student in a very long message listed every passage in the Bible that she could find to prove definitively that homosexuality is against the Bible's teachings. Another student made it clear that he did not believe that women were equal to men, surely a risky stance to take in a class taught by a woman. There were also a number of messages by students who did not agree with the opinions being expressed. Some observed, for instance, that the Bible often contains contradictory messages and that there is frequently widespread disagreement on what certain passages mean. It was as if the relative distance of e-mail had released attitudes and opinions that would normally have been repressed.

The heated exchange may have been a result, in part, of the relatively homogeneous makeup of the class. In this particular class, seventeen of the twenty-two students were white males ages eighteen and nineteen. All five women were white. Although a few were from other midwestern states, most of the students were from Michigan. The class was diverse only in the sense that several of the students came from homes in which languages other than English were spoken, and two of the women were still in high school. Many, it became clear, were uncritical of modern mainstream culture that condemns homosexuality and takes for granted a belief in Christianity. One of the high school students, though, had a somewhat different perspective, perhaps because she was from a family that was not well-off financially. It was her acceptance of bisexuality and homosexuality that triggered the spate of messages. It is ironic, of course, that conservative Paglia was taken to have progressive ideas and that her essay was resisted by conservative students. bell hooks in her essay "Camille Paglia: 'Black' Pagan or White Colonizer," published in *Outlaw Culture,* says, "Throughout her work, Miss Camille unabashedly articulates white cultural imperialist representations of her beloved neoprimitive darkies" (85).

Instinct and experience told me that it would be counterproductive for me to intervene by taking sides with one group and alienating the other. Paulo Freire in *Pedagogy of the Oppressed* speaks of the importance for the educator to avoid alienating those being educated by becoming moralistic. The example he uses is a discussion of a scene showing a drunken man walking on the street and three young men conversing on the corner. The educator had intended to use the theme to discuss the evils of alcoholism but changed his plan when group participants came to the defense of the drunkard by calling him a decent worker and "a souse like us" (111). Freire observes that sermonizing against alcoholism and presenting an example of virtue would certainly have resulted in failure.

I responded to the e-mail exchanges by making indirect references to them in class rather than on the list. I also reminded students that their formal research assignment was to be based on topics in assigned readings and that many of the topics discussed in the e-mail messages were far afield of those topics. The research assignment asked them to choose a topic related to one of the essays we had read in *Constellations* and to construct an argumentative essay based on library research. I stipulated, further, that their audience would include me and other class members. I emphasized that their essay was not simply a summary of the sources they found but an argument that recognized the complexity of the issues involved and that was balanced in tone.

The final papers on topics such as drugs, affirmative action, education, multiculturalism, and screen violence varied in quality but in general avoided the stridency of the e-mail messages as did the presentations that were based on them. The student who was certain that the Bible unequivocally condemned homosexuals collaborated with a classmate on a paper on affirmative action. They made a case against it that was qualified and acknowledged that affirmative action does have some merits. I doubt whether this student changed her attitudes toward homosexuality as a result of the course, but she at least learned that in the eyes of some, her opinions about homosexuality are close minded and narrow and her interpretation of the Bible unconvincing. It is quite possible that her religious beliefs had never been challenged before. In grading the essays, I tried to put the e-mail messages out of my mind and to focus on the arguments in front of me. I had to resist the temptation of giving high grades to the students whom I considered to have enlightened attitudes in the e-mail exchanges and low grades to the students whom I considered to have made weak arguments in the e-mail exchanges. I hope I was successful.

Butler might say that the students in my class who repudiated homosexuality were imposing traditional norms in a situation in which those norms were being challenged. Many of the students were insisting on heterosexuality, a single gender identity, and fiercely opposing alternatives to heterosexuality such as bisexuality and homosexuality. They were resisting the resistance to a conception of gender identity as unified and stable. Butler's reflections on freedom of speech in *Excitable Speech,* however, suggest that my not censoring student discussion was an important move. From Butler's perspective, then, the openness of the e-mail list allowed for my students' outbursts against homosexuality but also provided the occasion for other students to point out the serious limitations of those outbursts. Declaring the offensive messages off limits, censoring the speech of the students repulsed by homosexuality, and taking an official stand against their speech would have resulted in a silencing of all students, including those who made good arguments in support of homosexuality or who pointed out ways in which the offensive messages were irrational or illogical.

Although Butler's work was not included in *Constellations,* the class did encounter critiques of the work of MacKinnon. A constellation of essays on pornography in *Constellations* that we discussed later in the term included an excerpt from MacKinnon's *Only Words* and two essays that defended freedom of speech, Ronald Dworkin's "Women and Pornography" and Katie Roiphe's "Catharine MacKinnon, the Antiporn Star." MacKinnon makes clear that for her pornography is sexual abuse as speech (740), and that for her, pornography is discriminatory (741). She argues that pornography should be censored because of what it takes to make it and what happens through its use (743).

Dworkin's critique of MacKinnon's position rejects the modern-liberal defense of freedom of speech as articulated by John Stuart Mill (745). Instead, Dworkin attacks MacKinnon's claim that pornography significantly increases the number of rapes and other sexual crimes (747). No reputable study has come to such a conclusion, according to Dworkin (747). Also, he sees that desire for pornography is a symptom rather than a cause of deviance (747). Dworkin also attacks MacKinnon's argument that pornography should be censored because it silences and intimidates women. His objection to this argument is that it is premised on an unacceptable proposition, that the right to free speech includes a right to circumstances that encourage one to speak and the right that others grasp and respect what one means to say (749), but Dworkin argues that these are not rights that any society can recognize or enforce. Dworkin also criticizes MacKinnon's argument that women who act in pornographic films suffer degradation. He finds that it is possible to prosecute crimes that result when women are coerced into acting in pornographic films without banning the films themselves (749).

Roiphe criticizes MacKinnon for collapsing distinctions between soft pornography and hard pornography and for seeing pornography as the root of all evil (753). She also argues, as does Butler, that there is a difference between what someone sees and what someone does (755). She finds that MacKinnon uses language that gives her description of male behavior a "patina of scientific accuracy" (755). Roiphe concludes that many feminists oppose MacKinnon's perspective, valuing freedom of speech more than they fear pornography (759).

Speech was free rather than censored in the course in the sense that the e-mail messages enabled students to express their opinions in an unguided exchange of ideas. The expression of differing opinions resulted in challenges to homophobia. I was not forced, therefore, to use my own authority as instructor to censure the offensive remarks, thus discouraging students from expressing homophobic attitudes by steering them toward other topics. In the final papers, they had to explore perspectives but in more depth and in a different genre and idiom. Their initial resistance allowed for a discussion of the issues and the subsequent exploration of topics in a more balanced way.

Context 2: Resisting Race

The second context I will describe focuses on student resistance to engaging racial issues. Although Michigan Tech's student population is predominantly male and conservative, the Literary Representations of Gender, Race, Class, and Ethnicity course has been more diverse.[6] Students sometimes took the course because they thought it would help them deal with their own struggles as minorities. I have had Asian students who were adopted and took the course because they wanted to better understand their special situation. I have also had biracial students attempting to understand why they cannot claim they are white if one of their parents is white. The resistance I have experienced to engaging racial issues often took a different form in this course than it does in other courses. One student who was part Native American expressed impatience with essays that depicted Native Americans as victims because her father, a Native American, had suffered extraordinary deprivations and hardships and had become a hard-working, responsible adult who had done an excellent job raising his family. In another section of the same course, several black students complained in a presentation that the stories we were reading included no representations of middle-class blacks. They were embarrassed, they said, by the repeated suggestion that all blacks are impoverished. I observed that we had, in fact, encountered some portrayals of middle-class blacks, though such portrayals were by no means dominant.[7] Often, though, even in this course, traditional students are in the majority, and they sometimes resist engaging racial issues by overlooking them.[8]

A response I received to a selection from Gloria Naylor's *Mama Day* included in Terry McMillan's anthology *Breaking Ice* is a good example. The response was written by a white, male student who took the course the first time I taught it in the early 1990s. The portion of the novel that we read contains two retrospective accounts of the meeting of two of the protagonists, Ophelia (nicknamed Cocoa) and George, who encounter each other for the first time at a lunch counter, though they do not actually meet until shortly thereafter when George interviews Cocoa for an office manager job. Naylor presents the event by alternating points of view in first-person narrative with Cocoa speaking first and third, George second and last. Although the portion of the novel anthologized in the McMillan anthology does not make this clear, the discussion that takes place between the two is actually between Cocoa and George's spirit, given that he died years earlier (x). Both are blacks who have had success in a predominantly white, middle-class world. Cocoa had been a successful office manager for seven years at a firm in New York but lost her job because the company went out of business. She came, however, from Willow Springs, a small island off the coasts of South Carolina and Georgia. George grew up in an orphanage on Staten Island, graduated with a degree in engineering from Columbia University, and is co-owner of his own business, Andrews and Stein Engineering Company. They are fated, later in the novel, to get married, and George is fated to die in order to save Cocoa's life. At this point, however, their relationship is strained. The passage from

Naylor's novel makes explicit references to both race and gender. In addition to making it evident that both Cocoa and George are black, Naylor has the characters reflect self-consciously on racial and gender issues. Cocoa, for instance, says, "Those were awful times for a single woman in that city of yours" (523), adding "but it took me a while to figure out that New York racism moved underground like most of the people did" (525).

The student response to the passage, although sensitive, enthusiastic, and appreciative, tended to overlook important themes, especially ones concerning race. The student was very attentive to the psychological dimensions of the story, focusing on the thought processes of the two characters. He made reference to racial issues, however, only once, when he referred to the race of the white woman Cocoa calls a "cherry vanilla" (526), but he misreads the text, thinking that the woman Cocoa is envious of for her fuller figure is white. She is actually a black woman, whom Cocoa calls a "licorice," who has a fuller figure than Cocoa.

In a first-year English course focusing on writing about literature in which I assigned *Mama Day* in its entirety, students tended to respond in a similar way. They focused on topics such as the contrast between the rural and the urban setting and Naylor's extensive discussion of herbal medicine but tended to skirt issues directly related to race. Even those students who explored the topic of voodoo, which is referred to on several occasions in the novel, tended to emphasize its religious rather than racial aspects.

Morrison's *Playing in the Dark* helps explain why students might ignore racial issues in their reading. As I have already indicated, she finds that, although writers, regardless of color, deal sensitively with racial themes in their works, ignoring racial issues is a typical reading strategy of white American readers and critics. Free-flowing discussions in class and on e-mail, therefore, are important ways of making productive use of student resistance. Other strategies for making students aware of racial themes include pointing them out explicitly in class discussions and providing contexts for reading that make them evident. I have also constructed writing assignments that make dealing with racial and class issues unavoidable.

An example of successful deployment of student resistance to engaging racial issues is the change in attitude of a white, male student enrolled in Literary Representations of Gender, Race, Class, and Ethnicity who was initially resistant to the course. The student came to my office to confess that he did not feel that the "deep meanings" we were finding in the stories were really there. He said that he reads stories for enjoyment only, not to analyze them. I'd heard the position many times before and encouraged him to raise his questions in class because it gave me an opportunity to discuss authorial intention, the situatedness of the reader, and the constraints and opportunities provided by the course topic. He did so, and the result was a lively session. I was especially pleased with this student's progress in the course. In his final collaborative paper, he joined together with the three black students mentioned earlier who had complained midway through the course that selections in the course anthology portrayed blacks as impoverished. Together this group of resistant students engaged in reflective analysis. They decided, however, to focus on gender rather than race in their paper.

I have also had some success in highlighting racial issues by juxtaposing literary texts with essays that deal explicitly with the topics the literature is exploring. In the Literary Representations of Gender, Race, Class, and Ethnicity, for instance, in addition to a collection of short stories, Ann Charters's *The Story and Its Writer,* I have used *Race, Class, and Gender: An Anthology* edited by sociologists Margaret L. Anderson and Patricia Hill Collins. Anderson and Collins have interests in women's studies; Collins also has a background in African American studies. Their text is divided into four sections: "Shifting the Center and Reconstructing Knowledge," "Conceptualizing Race, Class, and Gender," "Rethinking Institutions," and "Analyzing Social Issues," and students read essays from all four sections. Anderson and Collins explain in the introduction that they see race, class, and gender as "simultaneous and intersecting systems of relationship and meaning" (5) and "Understanding race, class, and gender means coming to see the systematic exclusion and exploitation of different groups" (4). Their goal is to allow students to see that although we are all caught in multiple systems of oppression, "we can learn to see our connection to others. . . . Resisting systems of oppression means revising the ideas about ourselves and others that have been created as a part of a system of social control" (7). They emphasize toward the end of the introduction, "The idea that objectivity is best reached only through rational thought is a specifically Western and masculine way of thinking—one that we challenge throughout the book" (8).

Anderson and Collins emphasize, then, intersections of class, race, and gender. A good example is an essay included in the anthology, "Structural Transformation and Systems of Inequality" by D. Stanley Eitzen and Maxine Baca Zinn. These authors see that "the rate of downward mobility exceeds the rate of upward mobility" for the first time in American history (203) and that the employment status of minorities is falling in all regions (204). They discuss the growing feminization of the workplace (205) and a growing underclass of low-paid, immigrant women from Mexico, Vietnam, Korea, and the Philippines in Silicon Valley (206).

I attempt to match essays in the Anderson and Collins book with stories from the literature anthology. In the unit on ethnicity, for instance, two essays on Asian American women accompanied Amy Tan's "Two Kinds." In the unit on race, an essay by Paula Gunn Allen on American Indian women accompanied stories by Louise Erdrich and Leslie Silko. In the unit on gender and sexual orientation, I paired an essay about AIDS by Evelynn Hammonds with a story about AIDS by Susan Sontag. In that unit we also read Alice Walker's *The Color Purple* and saw the film version.

White students tend to convert texts about blacks into texts about whites, to see whiteness everywhere. It is important, therefore, to make a conscious effort to make race and racial themes visible. Careful selection of the course texts is not enough. Inclusion of works by authors from diverse backgrounds and locations is not enough. Students have to be encouraged to read diverse texts in ways that do justice to the sensibilities and perspectives of their authors. They need to be encouraged to rethink, revise, reinscribe, and reiterate in order to bring about some reasonable convergence between their own worlds and those of the writer they are engaging.

Context 3: Resisting Gender

Student resistance to engaging gender issues is often similar to their resistance to engaging racial issues. Too frequently they ignore them. In a 300-level course entitled "Rhetoric and Composition," the first text I assigned was *Women Speak: The Eloquence of Women's Lives* edited by Karen A. Foss and Sonja K. Foss. *Women Speak,* which is cultural feminist in orientation, recognizes that the work women do such as homemaking and childrearing often gets ignored in male-dominated society. If rhetoric usually deals with the public realm, Foss and Foss focus on the private realm. If history records the heroic deeds of public statesmen and diplomats, they focus on work that usually goes unrecorded and unacknowledged.

Women Speak was a good place to start, because many students knew little about rhetoric and about feminism, and the book is very accessible. Foss and Foss avoid the term *rhetoric,* for instance, using *communication* and *public address* instead, lest they alienate students. They provide a very useful introduction that contains two chapters, a revisionist analysis of public address from a feminist perspective, and a discussion of what factors should be taken into consideration in analyses of communication. These chapters are followed by thirty brief and engaging narratives told by a variety of women involved in a variety of activities including architecture, dance, filmmaking, herbology, letter writing, needlework, photography, public speaking, and quilting. Foss and Foss have their own narrative on dressmaking, and the volume concludes with a discussion of shopping. The women selected to tell their stories were generally friends of Foss and Foss, women whose stories might otherwise be ignored or forgotten. One of the contributors, however, was science-fiction writer Ursula Le Guin.

The first essay I assigned asked students to do a rhetorical analysis of an activity that was important to them, using the analyses in *Women Speak* as models. I emphasized, in clarifying what was expected in the essay, that students were not obliged to focus on women's issues even though *Women Speak* did. The course, after all, was not a women's studies course, and I had selected *Women Speak* primarily because it was very accessible and because I thought it would make rhetoric palatable to students resistant to it. Most students followed the recommendations in the introduction of the text and included in their analyses a discussion of the nature of the exigence, the nature of the audience, the nature of the communicator, the nature of the text, the functions of the text, and the nature of the world created, though they didn't necessarily use this terminology. This was not surprising because the authors in *Women Speak* did not use this terminology either. I was a bit surprised, however, that the assignment produced no essays that focused specifically on gender. Paper topics such as nursing, disk jockeying, and communication in a sorority did not result in discussions of the gendered nature of these activities.

I was pleased, though, that some students developed a critical perspective on the book, which became clear when we exchanged e-mail messages with the Foss sisters. A number of male students wanted to know how the book had been received by other male students. Quite clearly, and perhaps understandably, some of the male students felt excluded by it and threatened by its woman-centeredness. Students also noticed the emphasis on white, middle-class women and thought the book, for all its inclusivity, could be even more so. Sonja Foss explained that the book was most often used in women's studies classes. She admitted, though, that the book does not include enough minority voices and said that if they were to do another edition of it, it would include more. As a way of explaining some of the limitations of the book, I attempted to describe what cultural feminism is and to discuss some of its shortcomings, especially its tendency to idealize the situation of women and to focus on white, middle-class women. I was encouraged that some students recognized some limitations of *Women Speak* and, implicitly, of cultural-feminist perspectives.

In their final papers, students had the choice of making connections among course texts, Gregory Clark's *Dialogue, Dialectic, and Conversation,* Freire's *Pedagogy of the Oppressed,* and Morrison's *Playing in the Dark,* or doing a rhetorical analysis that applied some of the concepts in these works. In the papers, students once again tended to avoid gender issues, though I was pleased that they were quite receptive to the works by Clark, Freire, and Morrison, and I was pleased that many of their papers reflected considerable sensitivity to ethnic and racial issues. Morrison's book also resulted in some productive discussions of gender issues because she critiques the work of Ernest Hemingway, and several of the women students who were taking an American literature course began to raise questions about Hemingway's portrayal of women.

Like race, gender is often invisible. Students do not always see that gender is at the root of a powerful ideological system of inequality and sociality that affects all aspects of their lives. They do not necessarily recognize their own gendered behavior or attitudes or those of their friends or individuals who hold authority over them. Making gender visible often involves initially making productive use of their resistances to it. It also involves linking gender oppression to other forms of oppression, ones that may be more obvious to them. It involves moving beyond dichotomous conceptions of gender that oversimplify and distort a complex reality.

Modern/Antimodern/Postmodern Pedagogy

Modern responses to the first situation I describe, the e-mail discussions of homosexuality, might have emphasized freedom of speech within the context of rational discourse and equality of opportunity regardless of race, gender, or sexual orientation. The situation makes clear, however, that classroom discourse is often irrational, and student attitudes and opinions are often intransigent. Had I encouraged the students who expressed deeply felt prejudices against homosexuals to explore homosexuality in their final papers, the results would no doubt have been disturbing. A ten-week term and four weeks of research, I felt, would not have been sufficient to alter perspectives that have evolved over a lifetime. I encouraged free speech, then, but not random, unreflective speech. I did not assume that the free expression of opinion would result in rational debate, nor did I assume that students would bring to class discussions carefully thought-out opinions on racial or gender issues. Rather, I recognized that discussions needed to allow students a forum for expressing resistance to the ideas being presented in course texts and in class discussions and that I needed to find ways to allow students to explore alternatives to their prejudices without alienating them.

Antimodern responses to the situations I describe would have been equally problematic. I felt that condemning my students' prejudices as might a radical feminist would be counterproductive. Mary Daly might have responded differently. News and Internet stories covering attempts by Boston College to force Daly to retire at age seventy focused on her controversial pedagogical policies, especially her barring men from her classroom on the grounds that they interfere with the learning experiences of women students. Daly's militancy has certainly contributed substantially to the development of radical-feminist thought and radical-feminist pedagogy, but as Boston College lawyers pointed out, excluding men from classes at a coeducational institution is a violation of Title IX legislation and hence discriminatory.[9] Less extreme but certainly also damaging is outright rejection of opinions of students that fall short of the progressive views we hold. If students embody opinions and prejudices that resist liberatory pedagogies, and they often do, then turning against them in self-righteous anger is not likely to work.

Postmodern-feminist conceptions of resistance are useful in explaining students' resistance to pedagogies of resistance and in developing ways of directing that resistance in productive ways. Our students typically hold opinions that conflict with the perspectives presented in the texts they are encountering in the classroom and with our own ideological positions. The classroom can become a space where individuals holding a variety of opinions meet and, sometimes, clash. Such a space can only be created, however, if teachers make use of their institutional authority not to condemn students but to redirect their conversation and their inquiry. Teachers can select texts that invite consideration of power and oppression in their complexity and that recognize that sexuality, race, and gender are interlocking systems of power. They can also attempt to facilitate careful and thoughtful discussion in contexts in which such discussion is far from guaranteed.

The strategies that Min-Zhan Lu has developed are a good example of postmodern-feminist approaches to dealing with student resistance. Lu is concerned primarily with the political uses and abuses of personal experience in feminist writing pedagogy and recommends imagining ways of using experience critically (239). For Lu, reflecting on our own experience should motivate us to care about another's differences and disrupt the material conditions that give rise to them (239). She recommends encouraging students to see the self not as an end in itself but as the opening of a perspective that allows us to conceive of transforming ourselves with the aid of others (243). Lu has students read works by what she calls feminist critics on the margin—Anzaldúa, hooks, Kobena Mercer, Audre Lorde, Adrienne Rich, Gayatri Spivak, and Trinh T. Minh-ha—and then she asks them to revise their initial papers. In the revision assignment, she has students reread the assigned story and critique their initial interpretations, asking them explicitly to approach the story from the perspective of interlocking issues of race, class, sexual identity, religion, and gender. In a second revision assignment, she asks them to take an inventory of their personal experiences of oppression along lines of race, gender, class, sex, ethnicity, age, education, physical norm, geographic region, or religion. Lu explains that the assignments can motivate students to revise their initial approach to the story and to recognize that their Protestant or nonreligious background made it initially difficult for them not to see the attitudes and actions of the characters in the story as foreign, primitive, or silly (247). She then recounts ways in which this process of taking inventory enabled students to see the story in new ways. Lu concludes that exploring the structural underpinnings of one's experience can motivate students to revise their habitual approaches to differences (249) and that, in spite of our best intentions, social isolation and amnesia can result from unreflective use of the experiential (251).[10]

If postmodern-feminist perspectives blur the distinction between student and teacher, they do so only provisionally and only temporarily. Students inevitably have diverse perspectives on issues, and the expression of those diverse perspectives needs to be encouraged and accepted as legitimate. Students need to be provided opportunities to put forth controversial, outrageous, and provocative ideas with impunity, but the teacher is also obligated, ultimately, to judge students and to coax them toward an awareness of the limitations of their perspectives and the situatedness of their ideological leanings. Employing resistance, then, involves the creation of a homeplace where it is safe to express ideas and where responses to those ideas will enable students to see them as others see them and hence to reflect on them and perhaps alter them. Such a homeplace can become a positive as much as a negative space, a place where the hidden dimensions of gender, race, class, and sexual orientation begin to become visible.

Modern principles and practices are deeply entrenched in university classrooms. Here the inheritance of positivism, scientism, and objectivism take the form of standardized tests, teacher-centered pedagogies, monological lectures, and silenced, intimidated students. The students themselves, especially at technologically oriented universities, also come to the classroom with an implicit faith in technology, in scientific progress, and, often, with a belief that their own opinions are unbiased, unprejudiced, and valid and with a reluctance to rewrite or rethink. Too frequently they come with the certainties that result from limited exposure to diverse perspectives and cultures. Their perspectives are often obdurately Western, white, and male. Unlike Woolf's common reader and Rosenblatt's aesthetic reader, many do not find pleasure in reading and do not read if they do not have to; unlike Rich, Walker, and Rosenblatt, many do not feel an urgent need to read or write. For the most part, they have been taught by teachers who have encouraged them to read and write passively, submissively, and they have not, therefore, learned how to make connections between course reading and their own lives or the world around them.

Feminist studies, feminist literary studies, and feminist rhetoric and composition are beginning to develop pedagogies that respond to these problems. I attempt to draw on all three areas, and on others as well, as I develop courses. I have made productive use, for instance, of Moira Ferguson's *Colonialism and Gender Relations from Mary Wollstonecraft to Jamaica Kincaid: East Caribbean Connections* in a British novel course that I have taught several times. Using Ferguson as a point of departure, we discuss colonialism and slavery in the context of Jane Austen's *Mansfield Park* as well as Jean Rhys's *Wide Sargasso Sea* and Jamaica Kincaid's *Annie John* and *A Small Place,* works that Ferguson analyzes. I have sometimes also included a videotape about the life of reggae singer Bob Marley. Students frequently observe at the end of the course that they had previously associated the West Indies only with vacations and resorts. They are often shocked by Ferguson's introduction of issues such as the slave trade into discussions of *Mansfield Park* and even more shocked by Kincaid's tirade against American and British tourists and corrupt Antiguan politicians in *A Small Place.* I expect these resistances, accept them, and attempt to make use of them in informal writing, formal writing, and class discussion. In this unlikely site—a somewhat random group of students many of whom are males majoring in engineering—we attempt to move beyond modern concepts and practices.

Conclusion

The student resistance I discuss above makes clear that modernism is alive and well. Another indicator is the conversation recently within feminist studies, philosophy, cultural studies, and other fields that centers around the relative merits of universalism versus particularism. Universalism is defended by liberals who argue that democratic institutions and structures depend upon a conception of universal rights of citizens and equality of opportunity. Particularists, in contrast, see appeals to universals as totalizing and totalitarian and emphasize the uniqueness of each individual and each situation.

A postmodern response to what appears to be an impasse, however, is to emphasize that discussions of universality are discursive and historical and hence particular. Universalism, therefore, is not rejected but contextualized. This is the approach Butler takes in "Competing Universalities," one of three essays in a collaboratively produced book, *Contingency, Hegemony, Universality* (2000), authored as well by Ernesto Laclau and Slavoj Žižek. Butler calls for a rethinking of history so that it is not rooted in positivism or teleology but accepts "a notion of a politically salient and shifting set of epistemes" (138). She thinks psychoanalysis should play a crucial role in this project of rethinking history, because psychoanalysis insists upon "the efficacy of unintended meaning in discourse" (158). According to Butler, psychoanalytic accounts of identification that move beyond structuralism assume that identifications are multiple rather than singular and that no identification is reducible to an identity (149). She also speaks of identification as unstable (150) and of the hope that "disidentificatory resistance" (151) is sometimes possible.

There is no need to abandon completely the modern project of fighting for universal rights and equality. It is still important and necessary to struggle for improvement of the situation of all peoples. But appeals to universal understandings of what that struggle might entail need to be particularized, because no two contexts are the same. Women in Afghanistan face challenges that are very different from those faced by women in the United States, and the contexts within which women in the United States experience brutality, discrimination, and harassment are themselves multiple. There is no single definition of freedom that will be appropriate in all contexts.

There is also no need to completely abandon other modern projects such as formalism within literary studies, empirical research within rhetoric and composition, or academic discourse. What needs to be abandoned is the idea that form exists prior to and independent of content or that evidence can be decoded free of interpretive bias. Accepting that all form has content and that all evidence must have an interpreter necessitates developing alternatives to prevailing theories, practices, and pedagogies without repudiating them entirely. It also necessitates developing alternatives to modern conceptions of genre, academic discourse, history, science, and rationality. Mind and body, reason and emotion are united, though hardly the same.

Moving beyond modern attitudes and practices can take many forms. Reading, writing, and teaching can be constructed not as activities rooted in static foundations such as the cognitive maps of readers or writers or in stable textual features but in the complex interaction of a variety of factors including social context. Language is always in play. It is not determined by either individuals or texts but is a function of the ways in which they engage each other. Texts are not objects but communicative actions authored by individuals with emotions and intentions, difficult as it may be to determine what those intentions are.

Modern thought results in classification and partition. Perspectives are seen as separate and distinct rather than as related and relational. Traditions are represented in binary ways, their blurred boundaries ignored or denied. I have tried to problematize the distinctions I make among modern-, antimodern-, and postmodern-feminist traditions. There is obviously a range of feminist traditions rather than just three, including amodern ones, that do not concern themselves directly with Western science and rationality. I make no claim to having accounted for all intellectual, social, and cultural traditions that have a bearing on feminist thought. I also attempt to make clear that the perspectives I describe manifest themselves in actual situations in complex and contradictory ways. Woolf is both modern and antimodern, and a good case can be made that her perspectives anticipate postmodern ones as well. Rich and Walker develop radical and cultural perspectives but later in their work turn toward postmodern ones. Rosenblatt's approach to language has decided modern roots though her transactional perspective on reading looks in the direction of postmodernism. The field of rhetoric and composition has strong modern and antimodern traditions that intertwine in complex ways but recently has been developing postmodern and postmodern-feminist perspectives. Postmodern feminists such as Anzaldúa, hooks, Morrison, and Butler rethink both modernism and antimodernism in productive ways.

Misrepresentations of postmodern feminism have been harmful to feminism, to the academic community, and to individuals who suffer the consequences of oppression. There are alternatives to constructions of problems in binary ways— modernism versus postmodernism, universalism versus particularism, rationality versus irrationality, objectivism versus subjectivism. Self and other, content and form, reason and emotion are not distinct entities but interacting participants in complex processes. Foundational accounts, modern as well as antimodern, reify those processes and privilege one participant or another, thus distorting relationships and establishing unnecessary hierarchies and oppositions. Equality for all and equal rights are ideals worth fighting for, but if they amount to equality and rights for some and not others, they become dangerous illusions. It is crucial at this moment in feminism's development to move beyond universals, particulars, and binaries and attempt to develop new explanations, methods, and structures that take into consideration dynamic processes, contingencies, complexities, contradictions, and power. As I have tried to demonstrate, there is evidence of the beginnings of such a transformation in the work of numerous individuals in numerous fields, but there is still considerable work to do.

NOTES
WORKS CITED AND CONSULTED
INDEX

Notes

Introduction

1. It was no doubt important in early discussions of feminism to represent feminism as a unified, coherent ideology. One of the earliest anthologies devoted to feminist approaches to literary studies, Susan Koppelman Cornillon's *Images of Women in Fiction: Feminist Perspectives,* attempts to represent feminism in this way. Although essays such as Lillian S. Robinson and Lise Vogel's "Modernism and History" are clearly Marxist in orientation, the book as a whole gives the reader the impression that the authors are contributing to the development of a single feminist perspective rather than one composed of diverse strands. Another early collection of essays on feminist approaches to literature, Josephine Donovan's *Feminist Literary Criticism* (1975) is similar. Essays in the collection do sometimes distinguish among different approaches to the study of literature from a feminist perspective, but feminism itself would seem to be monolithic. The first essay in the collection, Cheri Register's "American Feminist Literary Criticism: A Bibliographical Introduction," illustrates the point. Register identifies three feminist approaches to the study of literature: "image of women criticism," "phallic criticism," and "prescriptive criticism" (3, 8, 11). She focuses, then, on diverse critical approaches but not on diverse feminist traditions.

An exception might appear to be the 1981 volume of *Yale French Studies* entitled "Feminist Readings: French Texts/American Contexts," which marks the beginnings of the emergence of distinctions between French and Anglo-American feminist literary studies, categories that become increasingly important as feminist literary studies evolves. The guest editorial collective (Colette Gaudin, Mary Jean Green, Lynn Anthony Higgins, Marianne Hirsch, Vivian Kogan, Claudia Reeder, and Nancy Vickers) in their introductory essay, "Literary and Sexual Difference: Practical Criticism/Practical Critique" (1981) identifies some differences between Anglo-American and French feminism, the former locating patriarchal power in interpersonal relations, the latter defining how patriarchal power functions on the symbolic level (9). They also observe that the pragmatic exigencies of teaching inform the discourse of American feminist scholarship (11). For the most part, though, feminism is equated with French feminism. The issue marks the emergence of a recognition that not all feminist perspectives are the same, but it makes only passing references to differences between French feminisms and Anglo-American feminisms.

2. Feminists may also be reluctant to name feminist traditions because doing so identifies those traditions in too definitive a way. This tendency is evident in "Feminist Criticism" by Catharine Stimpson, published in 1992, a useful map of different feminist locations within literary studies. Stimpson resists identifying distinct historical stages within

feminist literary criticism, finding it more useful to discuss three activities that have "supplemented, corrected, and overlapped with each other" (259) over the past decades. She identifies three activities: the defiance of difference, the celebration of difference, and the recognition of differences.

This reluctance to chart the various feminist traditions is also evident in one of the earliest collections of essays providing feminist approaches to rhetoric and composition, *Teaching Writing: Pedagogy, Gender, and Equity* (1987) edited by Cynthia L. Caywood and Gillian R. Overing. Some of the essays in the book provide concrete discussions of pedagogical approaches to the work of Adrienne Rich and others, but there is little emphasis on feminism as a diverse and complex movement.

Louise Phelps and Janet Emig take the approach one step further in their edited collection, *Feminine Principles and Women's Experience in American Composition and Rhetoric* (1995), in that, although they use the tern "feminism" freely in the introduction, they do not do so in the title of their book, substituting the word "feminine" instead. They explain in their conclusion that the term "feminine" was their original title and that it reflects "the kinds of thinking about writing, teaching, rhetoric, and gender often discussed quietly among women but seldom published in books and journals of the field and almost never linked to feminism as a social movement or academic study" (407). They see it as "a synecdoche for the feminism still emergent in the field" (407). The final section of the book, entitled "Reconfigurations and Responses," provides useful attempts to chart the territory traversed by the portion of the book that precedes it. Janice Lauer in "Issues and Discursive Practices," for instance, identifies the many discursive practices that are employed by the book's contributors. The charts that she provides, however, are of rhetorical traditions rather than feminist traditions. Jacqueline Jones Royster praises editors Phelps and Emig for the multidimensional nature of their inquiry and for relinquishing a significant part of their authority as editors by presenting essays in alphabetical order rather than the usual system of themes, categories, or rubrics of one sort or another ("In Search" 385–86). As I have suggested, this absence of a system of themes, categories, and rubrics is characteristic of early disciplinary attempts to chart feminist approaches to an area of inquiry and can be limiting.

A more recent introduction to the emerging field of feminist rhetoric and composition, *Feminism and Composition Studies* (1998) edited by Susan Jarratt and Lynn Worsham, is a considerable advance in that it does not represent feminism as a unified ideology, though it acknowledges that its purpose is not to explore feminism's diverse traditions. Joy Ritchie and Kathleen Boardman in "Feminism in Composition: Inclusion, Metonymy, and Disruption" identify overlapping tropes—inclusion, metonymy, and disruption—rather than feminist traditions. Tropes of inclusion sought equality for women; tropes of metonymy emphasize contiguity between feminism and composition; and tropes of disruption critique hegemonic narratives through resistance, interruption, and redirection of business as usual (587).

3. Internal disputes can result in representations of opposed traditions in reductive ways. Toril Moi's *Sexual/Textual Politics* (1985), for instance, attempts an even-handed discussion of both Anglo-American and French feminism. Her preference for French feminism and her impatience with Anglo-American feminism, though, becomes quite evident as her discussion proceeds. She concludes that Anglo-American feminist literary criticism has "remained within the lineage of male-centered humanism but that it has done so without sufficient awareness of the high political costs this entails" (87). Moi treats French feminists, especially Julia Kristeva, in contrast, much more positively. But the binary opposition between Anglo-American and French feminism that underlies Moi's

discussion is too rigid. One reason why it is difficult to make a clear distinction between Anglo-American feminist critics and French ones is that so many American feminists— Jane Gallop, Barbara Johnson, Nancy K. Miller, Elaine Marks, Mary Jacobus, and Ann Roselind Jones, for instance—teach and write in the United States about French literature and theory, and their work often reflects their complex intellectual situations.

Moi's subsequent work is less reductive. Her reconsiderations of the work of Simone de Beauvoir in *Feminist Theory & Simone de Beauvoir* (1990), for instance, acknowledges that although Beauvoir appears to be a "dinosaur" to feminists inspired by French feminist theory because she seems to believe in reason, truth, and the intellect, Moi believes that Beauvoir is "the most important feminist intellectual of the twentieth century" (108). It is this connection between modernism, here exemplified by Beauvoir, and postmodernism, here exemplified by Moi, that I find to be important in understanding both movements.

4. Cheris Kramarae and Dale Spender in *The Knowledge Explosion* discuss the emergence of feminist approaches to medicine, physics, mathematics, peace studies, black studies, literary studies, religious studies, cultural studies, anthropology, philosophy, engineering, political science, history, the natural sciences, nursing, journalism, the law, education, sociology, home economics, psychology, economics, architecture, and music.

Catharine Stimpson, in her overview of feminist literary criticism published in Greenblatt and Gunn's *Redrawing the Boundaries,* observes that in the fall of 1989, the Schlesinger Library at Radcliffe College listed forty-eight journals with a feminist orientation (257).

5. Tong expands her discussion in the second edition of *Feminist Thought.*

6. See Patrocinio P. Schweickart and Elizabeth A. Flynn, Introduction, *Reading Sites.*

7. Gerald Holton in *The Advancement of Science, and Its Burdens* speaks of some unfortunate ways in which Einstein's relativity theory has influenced anthropology, ethics, religion, and literature and says that Einstein himself was disturbed by misunderstandings of his theory. According to Holton, it was Max Planck and Max Abraham who named it "theory of relativity." Einstein would have preferred the term "theory of invariance" (xliv n. 3).

8. For a useful discussion of the notorious attack by Alan Sokal on postmodern critics of science, see Jennifer Daryl Slack and M. Mehdi Semati, "Intellectual and Political Hygiene: The 'Sokal Affair.'"

9. Essays by postmodernists that Charney critiques include Paul Dombrowski's "Post-Modernism as the Resurgence of Humanism in Technical Communication Studies," Carl G. Herndl's "Teaching Discourse and Reproducing Culture: A Critique of Research and Pedagogy in Professional and Non-Academic Writing," and Nancy Roundy Blyler's "Research as Ideology in Professional Communication." Other essays in technical communication with a postmodern orientation include Ben F. Barton and Marthalee S. Barton, "Ideology and the Map: Toward a Postmodern Visual Design Practice," and Richard C. Freed, "Postmodern Practice: Perspectives and Prospects." Charney makes clearer her association of critics of empiricism with Romanticism in "From Logocentrism to Ethnocentrism: Historicizing Critiques of Writing Research."

10. The tendency to characterize modernism and postmodernism as opposites and to associate postmodernism with an opposition to science and objectivity, with obscure language, and even with anarchy is widespread beyond the academy as well. A good example of an attack on postmodernism is an article by James Drake in the *Times Literary Supplement* entitled "The Naming Disease." Drake speaks of postmodernists berating concepts of truth and objectivity thus removing any need for evidence to support doctrines. He

says, "No aspect of postmodernist scholarship is proof of anything except the decline of some university departments into a condition where . . . they wallow in diseased naming" (15). Beeb Salzer in an article in the *Chronicle of Higher Education* entitled "Postmodern Idea Inflation in the Humanities Hyperjungle" objects to the "impenetrable complexity" of postmodernist jargon that makes concepts seem more important than they actually are. He wonders whether we are becoming "posthuman creatures who don't understand one another" (B6). David Bosworth in "Echo and Narcissus: The Fearful Logic of Postmodern Thought," an essay published in the *Georgia Review,* claims that postmodernists have replaced originality with repetition, dialogue with monologue. He associates postmodernism with mechanical mimicry or obsessive self-absorption (416), with democracy of aversion not inclusion (425), and with the extinction of forms (430). Daniel Seligman in "Postmodernism, in Seventy-Five Words or Less," published in *Fortune* magazine, speaks of postmodernism as "a lot of involved nonsense" (155). He also provides a quote from the work of postmodern feminist Judith Butler suggesting that Butler's work is impenetrable by commenting "Uh-huh" (155). These references suggest that postmodernism directly threatens conventional belief systems and values.

Another example of an attack on postmodernism is Peter Sacks's *Generation X Goes to College: An Eye-Opening Account of Teaching in Postmodern America.* Although the book is about the academy within the United States, it is clearly aimed at a nonacademic audience. *Peter Sacks* is the pen name of an award-winning journalist who took a teaching position at a community college and found the experience to be so alienating and frustrating that he decided to expose the corruption he encountered. Sacks associates grade inflation and a culture of accommodation with postmodernist delegitimation of modernity (116). For Sacks, modernism is associated with trust in reason, objective reality, and the scientific method whereas postmodernism is associated with relativism and subjectivism (117). He makes connections among postmodernism, "sweeping anti-rationalism," (125) and cynicism (127), claiming that the defining characteristic of postmodernity is a return to pre-Enlightenment states of mind, "when such notions as witches, devils, satanic cults, angels, UFOs, and other unprovable explanations held so much power over people" (135). For Sacks, postmodernism legitimizes antiscientific beliefs in the fantastic (135). Sacks is clearly also disturbed by movements that disrupt modernist hierarchy and order, and feminism is surely one of them. He says, for instance,

> It is as if scientists were a cabal of middle-aged white males using their esoteric magic as a means of maintaining political power and control over the world's spiritualists and non-linearists, including women, third-world peoples, and the poor. (125)

11. The tendency to conflate modernism and Romanticism is widespread within literary studies. Marjorie Perloff in "Modernist Studies," published in Greenblatt and Gunn's *Redrawing the Boundaries,* discusses a number of literary critical works, all published in 1957 (Bayley, Kermode, Langbaum), that make the case that modernist poetry is squarely in the Romantic tradition, even though modernist writers themselves had vigorously denied such links. Later arguments, according to Perloff, make a similar case (Gelpi, Bloom, and Gilbert and Gubar). Robert Scholes's *Structuralism in Literature,* an appreciative discussion of the work of individuals who attempt to systematize and scientize literature, in effect equates Romanticism with modernism as well in that he makes connections between structuralism and Romanticism.

I am not suggesting that double-column schemas are always binary ones. Jonathan Crewe points out in "Transcoding the World: Haraway's Postmodernism," for instance, that the double-column schemas in Haraway's work are not necessarily binary because the items in one column can be seen as transcoding and historically displacing its counterpart in the other column rather than opposing it (895). Hassan's schema, though, seems clearly to be a binary one.

12. Pauline Marie Rosenau's *Post-Modernism and the Social Sciences* demonstrates that the tendency to see modernism and postmodernism as binary opposites is not limited to rhetoric and composition and literary studies. Rosenau speaks of postmodernism haunting mainstream social science and disputing its underlying assumptions (3). Rather than situating Romanticism within modernism, however, she situates it within postmodernism. She also, at times, tends to conflate intersubjectivist perspectives with postmodern ones.

13. Postmodern feminists such as Jane Flax, Donna J. Haraway, Sandra Harding, Trinh T. Minh-ha, and Gloria Anzaldúa often associate modernism with Enlightenment modernism, a project they emphasize is androcentric, sexist, racist, and colonialist. Flax in *Thinking Fragments* describes modernism as a master narrative of the Enlightenment, a narrative characterized by beliefs in:

1. A coherent, stable self
2. An objective, reliable, and universalizable foundation for knowledge
3. Unchanging truth
4. Knowledge resulting in both freedom and progress
5. Language as a transparent medium of expression
6. History as the progressive perfection of humans and the ever more complete realization of their capabilities and projects
7. An optimistic and rationalist philosophy of human nature
8. Scientific progress and the independence of the object of scientific investigation from the perceptions of the scientist. (30–31)

Donna J. Haraway in *Modest_Witness@Second_Millennium* speaks of a painting by Pablo Picasso, *Woman with Lovers,* as a sign of Western culture that, "in kinship with the Scientific Revolution, is narratively at the foundations of modernity and its sense of rationality, progress, and beauty" (155). Like Flax, Haraway is critical of the Enlightenment project, emphasizing later in the book that concepts such as freedom, justice, and knowledge are about what bell hooks calls "yearning," not about "putative Enlightenment foundations" (191). Sandra Harding in *Is Science Multicultural?* observes that modernity is usually synonymous with European modernity and with progressive social, political, economic, and institutional structures (105). She argues, however, that women's activities such as folk beliefs that occur outside mainstream science are often denigrated as "premodern." For Harding, our conception of modernity needs to be expanded so that it includes women's patterns of knowledge and ignorance as well as men's.

Trinh T. Minh-ha in *Woman, Native, Other* provides a related conception of modernism by associating the Enlightenment idea of advancement in rationality and liberty with colonialism (40). Although Gloria Anzaldúa was born and raised in the United States rather than in what Trinh calls the Third World, Anzaldúa's perspective in *Borderlands,* because she speaks as a Chicana, is somewhat similar to Trinh's. Anzaldúa associates certain twentieth-century modernist painters with an Enlightenment sensibility, speaking of "modern Western painters" who borrowed, copied, or otherwise extrapolated the art of tribal cultures and called it cubism, surrealism, or symbolism (*Borderlands* 68).

14. Like work in feminist studies, work in rhetoric and composition frequently makes direct links between late-nineteenth-century and twentieth-century modernism and the Enlightenment, often in criticisms of current-traditional rhetoric, which is seen as hav-

ing inherited scientistic and mechanistic tendencies of Enlightenment rhetoric. When rhetorical modernism is associated with the work of modernists such as I. A. Richards, Kenneth Burke, Chaim Perelman, Stephen Toulmin, and others, however, it is often seen as a period of rejuvenation.

Lester Faigley in *Fragments of Rationality* sometimes discusses modernism as it is understood within art history and architecture. He defines modernism, for instance, by referring to "The Theory and Politics of Postmodernism" by Roy Boyne and Ali Rattansi, who restrict the term to aesthetic movements that emerged in Europe in the 1880s, flourished after World War I, and became institutionalized after World War II (243, note 1). When Faigley discusses modernism within the context of the Enlightenment, however, modernism becomes a pejorative term. Louise Wetherbee Phelps's associations in *Composition as a Human Science* of modernism with Enlightenment rationality are also critical of both modernism and the Enlightenment. She sees modernism as characterized by "reason, consciousness, knowledge, meaning, communication, freedom, and other values asserted by the Enlightenment and developed in modern sciences, humanities, and public life" (5). Sharon Crowley, too, defines modernism in this way in *The Methodical Memory*, associating it with a privileging of human reason as the source and foundation of knowledge and reduction of the primary function of language to the representation of thought (4–5).

Robert J. Connors in *Composition-Rhetoric* situates modernist composition-rhetoric within the modern period as defined within literary studies and art history and criticism, identifying modern composition-rhetoric as occurring between 1910 and 1960, "a period of relative stasis that is usually associated with the pejorative uses of the term 'current-traditional rhetoric'" (13). During this period, according to Connors, pedagogical approaches emphasized formal and mechanical correctness (13). James Berlin in *Writing Instruction in Nineteenth-Century American Colleges* associates modern rhetoric with current-traditional rhetoric, which he sees as a "scientistic approach" that is linked with the faculty psychology of the eighteenth century (62). According to Berlin, current-traditional rhetoric takes only the most mechanical features of the work of eighteenth-century rhetoricians George Campbell, Hugh Blair, and Richard Whately (62).

Although Susan Miller is primarily concerned, in *Rescuing the Subject,* with the history of rhetoric, her conception of modernism, like Louise Phelps's, derives largely from philosophical perspectives, and like Phelps, she is critical of the modernist project. She sees modernist approaches to writing as emphasizing the stability of meaning (16) as well as a "unified, consistent, controlling author" (16). In her most recent book, *Assuming the Positions,* Miller speaks of modern views of cultural reproduction (145) and modernist views of authorship (146).

15. While modernism within feminist studies and rhetoric and composition is often associated with Enlightenment modernism, it has quite a different meaning within literary studies. Although literary scholars have defined it in numerous ways, there seems to be a consensus, as David Brooks's entry in the *Encyclopedia of Literature and Criticism* makes clear, that it is a late-nineteenth-century and early-twentieth-century phenomenon characterized by radical ruptures from past ideas and practices. The entry on "Modernist Theory and Criticism" written by Vicky Mahaffey for the *Johns Hopkins Guide to Literary Theory and Criticism* is similar:

> *Modernist* is a term most often used in literary studies to refer to an experimental, avant-garde style of writing prevalent between World War I and World War II, although it is sometimes applied more generally to the en-

tire range of divergent tendencies within a longer period, from the 1890s to the present. (512)

If there is disagreement about exactly when the movement began, exactly when it ended, who the major modernist writers were, what the movement is, or where it occurred, there is usually agreement that a relevant historical benchmark is World War I and the intellectual, social, and aesthetic changes that took place in its wake. There is also likely to be agreement that some important modernist writers are T. S. Eliot, James Joyce, Virginia Woolf, D. H. Lawrence, Gertrude Stein, and Ezra Pound.

Marjorie Perloff's overview of modernist literary studies in "Modernist Studies" in *Redrawing the Boundaries* defines modernism in the way that is traditional within literary studies, although she is especially concerned with detailing the different ways in which the movement had been evaluated as the twentieth century had progressed. Perloff does mention that a number of studies of modernism see it as an extension of early-nineteenth-century Romanticism (159). She does not mention connections, though, between aesthetic modernism and modernism as it has been conceptualized in other fields. Malcolm Bradbury and James McFarlane's *Modernism: A Guide to European Literature: 1890–1930* also defines modernism as a late-nineteenth-century and early-twentieth-century phenomenon apparently unrelated to earlier philosophical traditions.

Andreas Huyssen in *After the Great Divide* emphasizes the differences between Enlightenment modernity and twentieth-century modernity. He observes, for instance, that Jurgen Habermas's project of a critical social theory "revolves around a defense of enlightened modernity, which is *not* identical with the aesthetic modernism of literary critics and art historians" (201).

16. The term *antimodern* has been used occasionally within literary studies quite differently from the way I am using the term. It is sometimes used to describe a realist tradition that reacted against literary modernism. Literary critic David Lodge, for instance, entitles a chapter of *Working with Structuralism* "Modernism, Antimodernism, and Postmodernism" and uses antimodernism in this way. Marianne DeKoven in "The Politics of Modernist Form" also uses the term in this way as does Fredric Jameson in *Postmodernism*. DeKoven sees Georg Lukács as the "most influential Marxist antimodernist" (675). Jameson finds Hassan's position as well as Lukács's antimodern (56). I am suggesting, though, that realism and Marxism are modern rather than antimodern traditions.

Brian May in *The Modernist as Pragmatist* uses the term *antimodernism* in yet another way, speaking of critics such as Hugh Kenner and A. Walton Litz as celebrators of modernism whereas revisionist critics such as Vincent Pecora, Astradur Eysteinsson, and, to some extent, Jameson, as being antimodern in that they abjure modernism (6). May sees himself as anti-antimodern in that he takes issue with the perspectives of the revisionists. Theodore Ziolkowski in *The View from the Tower: Origins of an Antimodernist Image* uses the term to describe the situation of four writers, Yeats, Jeffers, Rilke, and Jung, who saw themselves outside of and opposed to the twentieth-century modernist writers such as poets Pound, Eliot, and Stevens or novelists Joyce, Woolf, and Lewis (xii).

Although Saree Makdisi in *Romantic Imperialism* sees Romanticism as the historical designation of a number of enormously varied engagements with the multitudinous discourses of modernization (7), she also sees Romantic poetry as "a privileged site for the exploration of alternatives to modernization, or the celebration of anti-modern exoticism" (8).

Bruno Latour in *We Have Never Been Modern* uses the term antimodern, as I do, to refer to a tradition that opposes modernism. Latour sees antimoderns as individuals who firmly believe that the West has rationalized and disenchanted the world, that it has truly peopled the social with cold and rational monsters which saturate all of space, that it has definitively transformed the premodern cosmos into a mechanical interaction of pure matters. (123)

Latour is critical of antimoderns and moderns alike, finding that "except for the plus or minus sign, moderns and antimoderns share all the same convictions" (123). For Latour, antimoderns are always on the defensive, are antirevolutionary. They "never managed to innovate" and were unsuccessful in putting "the brakes on the moderns' frenzy" (135).

17. *Poststructuralism* is often used synonymously with *postmodernism* to describe intellectual and aesthetic traditions occurring toward the later part of the twentieth century. Postmodernism, though, is sometimes seen as the broader term, encompassing art and architecture as well as literature. Seyla Benhabib in "Sexual Difference and Collective Identities: The New Global Constellation" distinguishes between postmodernism and poststructuralism as follows:

> While the former designates a movement with wide currency in many different fields, the latter refers to a specific moment in the evolution of high theory, in the European—but particularly French—context, when Marxist and psychoanalytic paradigms, as well as the models of Claude Levi-Strauss and Ferdinand de Saussure, which had dominated French theory construction from the early 1960s onward, came to an end. (335)

I suggest, however, that the modernist structuralism Benhabib sees as coming to an end was dramatically altered as it evolved into new forms of modernism put forth by individuals such as Benhabib herself and into poststructuralism and postmodernism.

18. The term *postfeminism* is controversial because it tends to suggest that the struggle for women's equality is over. I am using it positively, as does Ann Brooks in *Postfeminisms: Feminism, Cultural Theory, and Cultural Forms*. For Brooks, *post* suggests a process of ongoing transformation and change rather than an overcoming and replacement of a perspective (1). Jane Kalbfleisch, in "When Feminism Met Postfeminism: The Rhetoric of a Relationship," discusses the dissatisfaction many feminists have had with the term *postfeminism* but attempts to work out a nonbinary relationship between feminism and postfeminism.

19. For an overview of postmodernist literary studies, see John Carlos Rowe, "Postmodernist Studies." Rhetoricians and compositionists who have provided a postmodern perspective on the field include Susan Miller, Jasper Neel, John Schilb, Patricia Harkin, James Berlin, Louise Phelps, and Lester Faigley. Feminist compositionists such as Gesa E. Kirsch, Joy Ritchie, Patricia A. Sullivan, and Mary Lay critique research methods that valorize the researcher's objectivity and call for methods that establish more interactive, collaborative, and reciprocal relations between researchers and participants.

20. Marxist feminists also sometimes criticize postmodern feminists for not being sufficiently attentive to material reality. Teresa Ebert in *Ludic Feminism and After* is critical of what she calls ludic postmodern feminism, which she sees as deriving from continental philosophical traditions that emphasize play, desire, and discursivity (153). For Ebert, ludic postmodern feminism denies the reality of social totality and thus denies the possibility of knowing anything other than metanarratives (7). Ebert argues in favor of what she calls resistance postmodernism, which she sees as critiquing the reified, naturalized identities and inadequately materialized theories of modern feminisms (155–56). In reducing continental feminist perspectives to a single metaphor, however, and in using this characterization as the basis for dismissal, Ebert misrepresents a feminist tradition that

has complex origins and tendencies. Also, it is not always clear how Ebert's resistance postmodernism is postmodern considering that it is so heavily indebted to modernist Marxism. Like Ebert, Carol A. Stabile in "Feminism and the Ends of Postmodernism" is critical of the work of postmodern feminists, providing a materialist critique of the work of Judith Butler and Ernesto Laclau and Chantel Mouffe.

The exchange between postmodern feminist Susan J. Hekman and standpoint theorists Nancy Harstock, Patricia Hill Collins, Sandra Harding, and Dorothy Smith occasioned by Hekman's essay "Truth and Method: Feminist Standpoint Theory Revisited" is another example of an attack on postmodern feminism by feminists with Marxist tendencies. For the most part, Hekman writes appreciatively of standpoint theory, seeing it as the beginning of a paradigm shift in the concept of knowledge (342). She finds that although feminist standpoint theory arose out of the Enlightenment tradition, it deconstructed that tradition and in the process created a new paradigm (401). She feels that it often falls short of its promise, however, because it emphasizes the materiality of women's standpoint but tends to ignore its discursivity, seeing instead a dichotomy between concepts and reality (348). For Hekman, feminist standpoint theory needs to reject the definition of knowledge and truth as either universal or relative. In other words, it needs to embrace a postmodern perspective. Harstock, Collins, Harding, and Smith reply to Hekman, sometimes appreciatively, but often aggressively, frequently defending their own approaches, which are often modernist Marxist in orientation, and dismissing Hekman's call for a postmodern approach to standpoint theory. Hekman explores her postmodern perspective more fully in *Gender and Knowledge: Elements of a Postmodern Feminism.* Rosemary Hennessy in *Materialist Feminism and the Politics of Discourse* provides a very thorough and useful discussion of ways in which standpoint theory can be rethought from a postmodern, materialist perspective.

21. Haraway in *Modest_Witness@Second_Millennium* says, "I remain a child of the Scientific Revolution, the Enlightenment, and technoscience. My modest witness cannot ever be simply oppositional. Rather s/he is suspicious, implicated, knowing, ignorant, worried, and hopeful" (3).

22. Jameson in *Postmodernism* sees Lyotard's "vital commitment to the new and the emergent" as being "part and parcel of a reaffirmation of the authentic older high modernisms very much in Adorno's spirit" (60).

23. Linda Hutcheon in *A Poetics of Postmodernism* constructs postmodernism as a critique of modernism rather than a repudiation of it. She describes postmodernism as questioning "centralized, totalized, hierarchized, closed systems" (41). Robert B. Ray in "Postmodernism" suggests that postmodernism's beginnings could be traced to 1984 after the Supreme Court ruling that copyright laws did not prohibit home off-the-air videotaping, to 1954 when most American homes had television, or as far back as 1852 when the Bon Marché, the first department store, opened in Paris, one year after the Crystal Palace and three years before the Louvre (132).

Although Huyssen's representation of postmodernism in *After the Great Divide* differs in many ways from the account I provide here, our discussions converge in his main point about contemporary postmodernism.

> It operates in a field of tension between tradition and innovation, conservatism and renewal, mass culture and high art, in which the second terms are no longer automatically privileged over the first; a field of tension which can no longer be grasped in categories such as progress vs. reaction, left vs. right, present vs. past, modernism vs. realism, abstraction vs. representation, avantgarde vs. Kitsch. (217)

Henry A. Giroux in "Rethinking the Boundaries of Educational Discourse" concludes his essay by reminding the reader that his main purpose is not to pit modernism, postmodernism, and postmodern feminism against each other but to "see how they converge as part of a broader political project linked to the reconstruction of democratic public life" (44).

24. For a very useful discussion of Kristeva's complicated relationship to feminism see Kelly Oliver, *Reading Kristeva: Unraveling the Double-bind.* As Oliver explains, Kristeva has been quite critical of the feminist movement, mainly because she became disillusioned with politics as a result of her trip to China in 1974 (153). According to Oliver, Kristeva rejects feminist movements that maintain a fixed notion of a feminine essence because they ignore differences among individual women (153). Oliver finds, however, that there are similarities between Kristeva's perspective and that of Judith Butler. For both, sexed bodies are multiple, and both see that feminism needs to operate without fixed identities of woman, feminine, or even female (157). The claim, which I endorse, is interesting given Butler's accusation, in *Gender Trouble,* that Kristeva is homophobic (86–88).

25. Marilyn Edelstein in "Toward a Feminist Postmodern *Poléthique*: Kristeva on Ethics and Politics" argues, as well, that Kristeva's work is postmodern feminist. She sees "Women's Time" as helping feminism avoid becoming a master narrative about woman (199). She also provides a useful summary of criticisms of Kristeva's work by numerous feminists including Gayatri Chakravorty Spivak, Eleanor Kuykendall, Rita Felski, and Ann Roselind Jones for focusing on the individual rather than the social or political dimensions of experience or for denying individual agency. Edelstein takes the position, though, that Kristeva's work does deal with broader, sociosymbolic, political spheres and that her subject is capable of agency (202–3).

1. Modern/Antimodern/Postmodern: Rewritings

1. I am emphasizing here Kant's indebtedness to Descartes and his Enlightenment roots. He is sometimes associated with pre-Romanticism, however. See, for instance, Julia Kristeva's *Strangers to Ourselves* (170–73) and Norman Hampson, *The Enlightenment* (196–98).

2. Mill speaks appreciatively of positivism and of Auguste Comte in his essay, "Auguste Comte and Positivism." Leslie Stephen in *The English Utilitarians,* though, speaks of Mill's troubled epistolary relationship with Comte, which ultimately came to an end. According to Stephen, Mill came to recognize their "hopeless differences" and came to think that Comte's doctrine of the spiritual power implied "a despotism of the worst kind" (51).

3. According to Alice Rossi, although Mill wrote "The Subjection of Women" in 1861, three years after the death of his wife, Harriet Taylor, the essay was a joint endeavor in that the ideas formulated in the essay were the result of more than twenty years of intimacy and intellectual collaboration between the two (184).

4. Marshall Berman in *All That is Solid Melts into Air* attempts to define a space in which Marx's thought and the modernist converge.

> Both are attempts to evoke and to grasp a distinctively modern experience. Both confront this realm with mixed emotions, awe and elation fused with a sense of horror. Both see modern life as shot through with contradictory impulses and potentialities, and both embrace a vision of ultimate or ultramodernity. (120–21)

5. Nancy F. Cott in *The Grounding of Modern Feminism,* a history of the feminist

movement in the United States, says, "The tradition that most obviously nourished women's rights advocates was Enlightenment rationalism, its nineteenth-century political legacy liberalism, and its social representation bourgeois individualism" (16).

6. This brief analysis does not adequately address the many contradictions in *The Second Sex*. As Penelope Deutscher in her essay on Simone de Beauvoir in *Yielding Gender* points out, Beauvoir's arguments in *The Second Sex* are characterized by instability, ambivalence, and conflicting elements (193).

7. Jane Gallop in *Around 1981* points out that American feminist literary criticism is highly eclectic, drawing on diverse traditions and producing surprisingly sophisticated theoretical positions. Toril Moi in *Sexual/Textual Politics,* in contrast, sees the Cornillon book as based on the assumption that "art can and should reflect life accurately and inclusively in every detail" (45).

8. Essays published elsewhere such as Sue Ellen Holbrook's "Women's Work: The Feminizing of Composition" explore a similar theme.

9. Feminist literary scholars and Marxist critics, among others, have emphasized the conservatism of the perspectives of male modernist writers and artists. See, for instance, Bridget Elliott and Jo-Ann Wallace's chapter "Whose Modernism?" in *Women Artists and Writers.*

10. For discussions of the racial dimensions of modernism see Houston A. Baker, Jr., *Modernism and the Harlem Renaissance* and Paul Gilroy, *The Black Atlantic.* See also Sandra Harding, ed., *The "Racial" Economy of Science* and Harding, *Is Science Multicultural?* In *Is Science Multicultural?* Harding makes a connection between modernity and colonialism: "Crucial to the advance of both European expansion and of modern science was the European appropriation in some respects and destruction in others of the scientific and technological traditions of non-European cultures" (111).

11. For a good example of a radical feminist critique of Freud, Wilhelm Reich, and R. D. Laing, see Juliet Mitchell's *Psychoanalysis and Feminism.* Mitchell sees Freud as examining the "eternal" structures of patriarchy (380). She calls for a struggle, a cultural revolution against patriarchy (414).

12. Shulamith Firestone's *The Dialectic of Sex* is often seen as radical feminist, but I see it as a form of socialist feminism in that she embraces both technology and socialism or what she calls cybernetic socialism (238).

13. Although Gilbert and Gubar move toward a postmodern conception of gender identity in *Sexchanges,* volume 2 of *No Man's Land,* their "Sexual Linguistics," originally published in *New Literary History* in 1985 and included in revised form in volume 1 of *No Man's Land,* is cultural feminist in impulse.

14. Wlad Godzich in his foreword to Bakhtin and Medvedev's *The Formal Method in Literary Scholarship* associates the work with poststructuralism: "This book can be seen as an attempt to abort the structuralist stage in order to achieve a stand that we would readily associate with our own poststructuralism" (x).

15. Cherríe Moraga and Gloria Anzaldúa use the term *women of color* in their title. They also use the term *Third World Woman* in their introduction (xxiv), though, and the term is used to describe one of the subsections of the book.

16. M. Jacqui Alexander and Chandra Talpade Mohanty in *Feminist Genealogies, Colonial Legacies, Democratic Futures,* however, make clear their dissatisfaction with some forms of postmodern discourse in which the stability and analytic utility of the categories of race, class, gender, and sexuality are dissolved completely (xvii).

17. Linda Singer in "Feminism and Postmodernism" emphasizes that attempting to isolate specific sites of conjunction, consensus, or agreement is difficult because the two terms actually represent a diversity of viewpoints, voices, and textual strategies (465).

18. Patricia Waugh in *Practicing Postmodernism/Reading Modernism* comments on continuities between modernity and postmodernity: "I want to suggest, somewhat tentatively, that despite differences in the theoretical construction of modernity and postmodernity, common to them both is the inheritance of a particular ideal of subjectivity defined in terms of transcendence and pure rationality" (130).

19. Paula M. L. Moya in "Postmodernism, 'Realism,' and the Politics of Identity: Cherrie Moraga and Chicana Feminism" in Chandra Talpade Mohanty and M. Jacqui Alexander's *Feminist Genealogies, Colonial Legacies, Democratic Futures* is wary of postmodern approaches to identity that reject essentialized conceptions of identity so completely that they replace unstable and fragmented identities with fixed and unitary ones (136).

2. Reading Global Feminisms

1. As Susan Stanford Friedman points out in *Mappings*, continental and Anglo-American feminisms are interwoven in feminist discourse (189). Neither Anglo-American nor continental feminism is monolithic, and both have been influenced by the work of Simone de Beauvoir and others. In its continental and Anglo-American varieties, modern feminisms influenced by the work of Marx, Freud, and other male writers coexist with antimodern feminisms that repudiate culture as it has been passed down in patriarchal societies and with postmodern feminisms that critique androcentric culture without rejecting it entirely.

2. Michael M. J. Fischer in "Is Islam the Odd-Civilization Out?" demonstrates that binary conceptions of relationships between West and non-West are too simple. Fischer objects to constructions of the Middle East as some land of absolutes and the polar opposite of the postmodern West. For one thing, according to Fischer, the Muslim world is a demographic presence in Europe and America. For another, the ethical and political objectives of postmodern theorizing originated in the Muslim world of North Africa and were rapidly recognized and carried out into the world by Indian writers such as Homi Bhabha, Salman Rushdie, and Gayatri Spivak (59). Fischer sees that postmodernity emerged in the aftermath of the Algerian revolution in the 1960s and that some theorists of postmodernity in France, Hélène Cixous, Jacques Derrida, Jean-François Lyotard, and Pierre Bourdieu, for instance, were influenced by the Algerian struggle for independence (54). Cixous and Derrida were born in Algeria.

3. Leila Ahmed in *Women and Gender in Islam* contends that family law is the cornerstone of the system of male privilege set up by establishment Islam (242). As'ad AbuKhalil in "Toward the Study of Women and Politics in the Arab World: The Debate and the Reality" emphasizes ways in which conceptions of female inferiority are inscribed in Arab culture: "Notwithstanding the claims of Muslim apologists and the attempts of some feminists to reinterpret Islam in ways favorable to women, the ideas of female inferiority are clearly present in the Qur'anic text where the beating of women by their husbands is sanctioned" (7). Raga' El-Nimr in "Women in Islamic Law," however, claims that any fair investigation of the teaching of Islam shows clear evidence of woman's equality with man in terms of political rights (101). Elizabeth Warnock Fernea states in the conclusion of *In Search of Islamic Feminism*, "Islamic belief is also the stated basis of most of the behavior I felt to be 'feminist'" (416).

4. Shahnaz Khan in "Muslim Women: Negotiations in the Third Space" argues that seeing religion as the overriding influence in Islamic societies feeds Orientalist assumptions about the role of religion in the lives of individual women (467).

5. As'ad AbuKhalil in "Toward the Study of Women and Politics in the Arab World"

emphasizes that Islam has played a legitimating role in various contexts in Islamic countries but that it has not been the sole, dominant, hegemonic ideology (8).

3. Woolf's (Anti)Modern Reading

1. Woolf's work has been discussed within many different critical and intellectual traditions and is, in many ways, a complex combination of them all. Situating Virginia Woolf's work within the contexts of modernism, antimodernism, and postmodernism feminisms, therefore, is especially difficult. Some of the contexts in which Woolf's work has been discussed include lesbianism (Eileen Barrett), childhood sexual abuse (DeSalvo), geopolitical literacy (Friedman), fascism (Carlston), World War I (Levenback), manic-depressive illness (Caramagno), empire (Phillips), and colonialism (McNees). Her work has also been compared with that of numerous authors including Samuel Johnson (Rosenberg), Doris Lessing (Saxton and Tobin), Vita Sackville-West (Raitt), and Eudora Welty (Harrison). It has also been situated within numerous literary traditions including realist or formalist versions of modernism, Wordsworthian Romanticism, postmodernism, a version of modernism that is gendered female, radical, cultural, postmodern feminisms, and numerous other literary and nonliterary traditions.

Eileen Barrett in her introduction to *Virginia Woolf: Lesbian Readings* speaks of Virginia Woolf as one of the twentieth-century's best-known lesbians (3). Louise DeSalvo discusses Woolf's work in the context of her childhood sexual abuse. Susan Stanford Friedman discusses Woolf's globalism in *Mappings,* a work I discuss in chapter 2. Erin G. Carlston in *Thinking Fascism* argues that fascist discourses share a vernacular with non- and antifascist discourses and that fascism itself could supply the vocabulary and the methodology of even the most rigorously antifascist critiques such as Woolf's *Three Guineas* (5). Karen L. Levenback in *Virginia Woolf and the Great War* suggests that the Great War remained a constant presence in Woolf's writing as well as in her life (8). Thomas C. Caramagno in *The Flight of the Mind* argues that the manic-depressive illness that Woolf suffered from is periodic but that her novels were produced by "a sane, responsive, insightful woman" (2). Kathy J. Phillips in *Virginia Woolf Against Empire* discusses Woolf's work in relation to the context of empire broadly defined to include economics, gender relations, and war as these forces operate both at home and abroad (xi). In her introduction, Phillips observes that although empire is a central topic in Woolf's books, she never directly portrays any of the colonized people as characters (xxxiv). Eleanor McNees in "Colonizing Virginia Woolf: *Scrutiny* and Contemporary Cultural Views" observes that the mature novels of Woolf's middle period, *Mrs. Dalloway, To the Lighthouse,* and *The Waves,* have received considerable attention by postcolonial critics (46). She finds that contemporary cultural critics have chosen to interpret Woolf's novels "as subversive postcolonial texts in which patriarchy and imperialism are synonymous" (46).

Beth Carole Rosenberg in *Virginia Woolf and Samuel Johnson: Common Readers* finds that Woolf directly alludes to Johnson in at least twenty-six essays (49). Ruth Saxton and Jean Tobin's edited collection, *Woolf and Lessing,* is the first to examine the relationship between the two writers. Suzanne Raitt in *Vita and Virginia* argues that Woolf and Sackville-West "lived their sex as a coincidence and sometimes as a conflict of various and varying roles: wife, lesbian, writer" (16). Suzan Harrison is interested in Woolf's influence on Welty's development as a writer (5).

Tony E. Jackson in *The Subject of Modernism* makes a connection between modernism and realism arguing that "it is *as* modernism that realism can be said to become itself for the first time" (14). Michael Tratner in *Modernism and Mass Politics* finds that both modernism and realism were concerned with mass politics but differed in their approaches to it. Christopher Reed in "Through Formalism: Feminism and Virginia Woolf's Relation to Bloomsbury Aesthetics" sees that Woolf's commitment to formalism was strongest in the mid-1920s when she was interested in taking a stand against naive mimetic perspectives (27), but that in general she was ambivalent about both aesthetic and literary formalism (21). C. J. Mares in "Reading Proust: Woolf and the Painter's Perspective" identifies what he calls Woolf's "formalist aesthetics" (339) and makes connections between her formalism and the aesthetic theories of her Bloomsbury contemporaries, Roger Fry and Clive Bell (334). Like Reed, though, Mares sees that she made a distinction between artistic form and literary form and was ambivalent about formalist approaches to the novel (342).

Ellen Tremper in *"Who Lived at Alfoxton?" Virginia Woolf and English Romanticism* makes connections between the writing of Wordsworth and Woolf's work, seeing her short stories as biographical proof of her relation to Romanticism and "the literary laboratories in which she made her self-enlightening comments and experiments on interiority or self-consciousness perfected in her longer fictions" (32). Edward A. Hungerford in "'deeply and consciously affected.': Virginia Woolf's Reviews of the Romantic Poets" documents Woolf's interest in Wordsworth, Coleridge, Shelley, and Keats (97).

Pamela L. Caughie in *Virginia Woolf and Postmodernism* is careful not to claim that Woolf *is* a postmodernist but nevertheless argues that postmodernism is a useful frame of reference for her work. Leila Brosnan in *Reading Virginia Woolf's Essays and Journalism* makes a convincing case that Woolf's approach to the essay and to the reader of the essay is postmodern. Brosnan makes evident the usefulness of a Bakhtinian approach to Woolf's essays, emphasizing that many of them are conversational and create a space for an active reader.

Sandra M. Gilbert and Susan Gubar in *No Man's Land* see Woolf and T. S. Eliot as modernist rivals (1: 149). Bonnie Kime Scott in *Refiguring Modernism* shows how attention to the work of Woolf, Rebecca West, and Djuna Barnes changes our conception of when modernism occurred and what events were important to it. Bridget Elliott and Jo-Ann Wallace in *Women Artists and Writers* argue that women developed diverse strategies for negotiating unequal and uneasy relationships with their male modernist counterparts (17), though they see that Woolf's association with Bloomsbury isolated her from the larger context of women's modernism (58). Genevieve Sanchis Morgan in "The Hostess and the Seamstress" sees that Woolf's works argue for a "poetics of domesticity" (91). Marianne DeKoven in *Rich and Strange* focuses on modernist writers' irresolvable ambivalence toward the possibility of radical social change and sees this ambivalence as differently inflected for male and female modernists (4), contrasting Joseph Conrad's *Heart of Darkness* with Woolf's *The Voyage Out*. DeKoven speaks of "women modernists" in her essay "The Politics of Modernist Form" (676).

Krista Ratcliffe makes connections between Woolf's work and that of radical feminists Adrienne Rich and Mary Daly in *Anglo-American Feminist Challenges to the Rhetorical Traditions*. Jane Marcus frequently focuses on radical feminist themes such as Woolf's resistance to patriarchal culture, but she also discusses Woolf's interest in female culture (see, for instance, *Art and Anger*).

Toril Moi in *Sexual/Textual Politics* sees Woolf's writing as deconstructive in form, engaging with and thereby exposing the duplicitous nature of discourse (9). Moi also sees Woolf as having a skeptical attitude toward the male-humanist concept of an essential human identity and argues that for Woolf all meaning is a ceaseless play of difference (9). Makiko Minow-Pinkney in *Virginia Woolf and the Problem of the Subject* uses the work of Julia Kristeva to illuminate Woolf's novels, arguing that Kristeva offers Woolf a new concept of subjectivity, a concept of the subject in process (17).

Judy Little, in *The Experimental Self: Dialogic Subjectivity in Woolf, Pym, and Brooke-Rose*, argues that Woolf relationalizes the symbolic, juggling "an amazing heteroglossia of discourses" and focusing on their interaction (27). Rebecca Saunders in "Language, Subject, Self: Reading the Style of *To the Lighthouse*," drawing on the work of Julia Kristeva, Jacques Lacan, and others, argues that the unresolved arguments about the self in Woolf's style is "an impressively rigorous uncertainty" (211).

2. For a useful overview of the complex relationships between modernism and feminism see Rita Felski's *The Gender of Modernity.*

3. See, for instance, James L. Machor, *Readers in History,* Cathy N. Davidson's *Reading in America,* Nancy Glazener's *Reading for Realism,* and Alberto Manguel's *A History of Reading.*

4. Modernism is often seen as a departure from realism rather than realism's antithesis. Malcolm Bradbury and James McFarlane, in *Modernism: A Guide to European Literature 1890–1930,* for instance, see modernism as a "various sequence running through different subversions of the realist impulse: Impressionism, Post-Impressionism, Cubism, Vorticism, Futurism, Expressivism, Dada, and Surrealism" (50). René Wellek in *A History of Modern Criticism* makes a connection between Woolf's philosophical propensities and that of G. E. Moore. He sees Moore as advocating a modern realism, and whereas Wellek is hesitant to label Woolf's philosophical disposition, he does see that in her criticism she aims "at grasping an object" (66). Wellek also finds that Woolf concludes "Phases of Fiction," which I discuss in this chapter, with an admission of the inevitability of mimesis (78).

5. I do not mean to suggest that *male* modernist reading can be defined simply or easily. Kathryne V. Lindberg in *Reading Pound Reading,* for instance, speaking of Ezra Pound's concept of reading, says, "Indeed, the very possibility of hermeneutical mastery propounded by systematic aesthetics is everywhere put into question by his notion of reading, which is decidedly against 'ideas' and markedly resistant to generalizations identified as 'modernism'" (4).

6. Individuals commonly associated with Bloomsbury include Roger Fry, Maynard Keynes, Lytton Strachey, Leonard Woolf, Duncan Grant, Desmond MacCarthy, Vanessa Bell, Virginia Woolf, and Dora Carrington.

7. Tuzyline Jita Allan in "A Voice of One's Own" makes a connection between the "disinterested voice" Woolf speaks of in "The Modern Essay" and T. S. Eliot's dissociated sensibility and sees this as the theoretical ideal that informs the *Common Reader* essays.

8. David Lodge in *Twentieth-Century Literary Criticism* speaks of "Tradition and the Individual Talent" as anti-intentionalist.

9. Michael Kaufmann in "A Modernism of One's Own" argues that Woolf's critical views and formulations continue to be seen through the lens of Eliot's criticism despite the fact that Eliot wrote for small, specialized audiences, whereas Woolf had a considerably wider readership (137). Rosenberg and Dubino in their introduction mention numerous critical works, including recent ones, in which Eliot's critical essays are taken seriously but Woolf's are not (7).

10. Karen Schiff in "Moments of Reading and Woolf's Literary Criticism" uses this passage to describe a "moment of reading," (185) a point in the reading process when "something interrupts the flow (either of the narrative or of the experience of reading) to expose an enriching new complex of realizations or sensations" (178). Schiff compares Woolf's moments with Wordsworth's, finding that Wordsworth's "emotion recollected in tranquility" is deliberate whereas Woolf's moments are not (191).

11. Steve Ferebee in "Bridging the Gulf: The Reader In and Out of Virginia Woolf's Literary Essays" argues that Woolf's approach to reading is subjectivist. Tremper devotes considerable attention to Woolf's interest in reading, making connections between Woolf's attention to individual consciousness, which Tremper sees as a Romantic concern, and reading.

12. Feminist literary scholar Jane Marcus emphasizes Woolf's radical feminism when she discusses Woolf's identification of the literary canon as patriarchal. She sees Woolf's jokes, slips, and asides as signals to the woman reader that woman reader and woman writer together conspire against the power of patriarchal language (*Art and Anger* 148). Marcus's emphasis, however, is often cultural feminist. In "Other People's I's (Eyes): The Reader, Gender, and Recursive Reading in *To the Lighthouse* and *The Waves*," for instance, Marcus finds that Woolf explicates a practice of gender-different experiences in descriptions of Mr. and Mrs. Ramsey in *To the Lighthouse.*

Sandra M. Gilbert and Susan Gubar allude to the radical-feminist Woolf in their title "Milton's Bogey: Patriarchal Poetry and Women Readers," an essay in *The Madwoman in the Attic,* and the cultural feminist Woolf in their title *Shakespeare's Sisters* but argue in *No Man's Land* that her relationships with her literary foremothers is ambivalent, sometimes revealing what Harold Bloom calls the anxiety of influence and what they call the female "affiliation complex" (*No Man's Land* 224).

13. Susan Sanford Friedman in "Virginia Woolf's Pedagogical Scenes of Reading: *The Voyage Out, The Common Reader,* and Her 'Common Readers'" provides a cultural-feminist analysis of reading, focusing on differences between male and female readers and arguing that in *The Voyage Out,* women, on the whole, excel in reading the book of life whereas men control the production and interpretation of the printed word (6). Mark Hussey in "Reading and Ritual in Virginia Woolf's *Between the Acts*" also provides a cultural feminist perspective, arguing that the novel is the capstone of Woolf's works, "embodying in its largest context her perennial themes of male destructiveness and female creativity" (98).

14. Beth Rigel Daugherty in "Readin', Writin', and Revisin': Virginia Woolf's 'How Should One Read a Book'" compares earlier versions of the essay with this version, concluding, "What Woolf says about the relationship between the writer and reader in this essay and what she does as she moves from draft to final version also demonstrate the crucial role the common reader plays in her revising process" (159).

15. Juliet Dusinberre in *Virginia Woolf's Renaissance* says that for Woolf "one of the most difficult and ongoing struggles had always laid in the uneasy territory she herself occupied somewhere between amateurism and professionalism" (6).

16. Anne E. Fernald in "Pleasure and Belief in 'Phases of Fiction'" compares "Phases of Fiction" with a twenty-three-page, typescript draft entitled "Notes of a Day's Walk," which is embedded in a single, extended narrative that opens in a city church. Fernald finds that "the church setting flouts the difference between Woolf and thinkers of her father's generation, it announces her modernity. Even the discussion of belief as an instinct, with its vague musings about a kind of racial memory, suggests an interest more generally scientific (be it biological, psychological, or anthropological) than personal" (199).

4. Rich and Walker on Writing and Mothering: Radical/Cultural Feminist and Womanist Perspectives

1. I discuss Simone de Beauvoir as a structuralist feminist in "Emergent Feminist Technical Communication." There seems to be little critical agreement on how to situate Beauvoir's work in relation to feminism. For an overview that emphasizes the nega-

tive reception of Beauvoir's work, see Toril Moi, "Politics and the Intellectual Woman: Clichés in the Reception of Simone de Beauvoir's Work" in *Feminist Theory and Simone de Beauvoir*.

2. The considerable feminist literature on the relationship between writing and mothering should have prepared me for the challenges I faced when I, too, attempted to balance a full-time job, writing, and mothering, but I had clearly not sufficiently attended to that literature, no doubt because at the time it did not concern me directly. Kate was born on Labor Day weekend, 1988, when I was 43 and interim head of my department. It was a short pregnancy given that I did not have medical confirmation until month four when I could no longer ignore my tight-fitting clothes and Kate's kicking. I naively agreed to remain as head the following academic year even though I was lame duck (a new head had been hired as a result of an external search but delayed his arrival for a year). The emergency C-section as a result of high blood pressure should have been sufficient warning that, for me at least, a full-time administrative position, writing, and mothering would not work.

I minimized my writing commitments that year but had agreed to give a paper at the Conference on College Composition and Communication seven months hence. I started working on the paper after Kate was about a month old. I could find only four hours a week at the computer, though, so I began composing in my head while Kate was nursing. After more than a month of this, I eagerly presented the results of my efforts to two colleagues for comments. They both were encouraging but agreed that my ideas needed more development—I had written three pages.

Things have gotten somewhat easier, but writing is still a challenge. Before Kate started school, she was mostly cared for in our home and sometimes in a day-care home or a day-care center. From kindergarten through fourth grade she went to an after-school program when she didn't have other activities during the week. She has also had full-time activities several weeks during the summer. I can usually work quite productively in my study during the week. Weekends and summers present more of a challenge, however. Recently, I attempted to find more time to write by teaching overloads fall and spring terms so that I did not have to teach during the winter term. The approach definitely resulted in increased productivity, but the overloads were exhausting.

3. Alice Templeton in *The Dream and the Dialogue: Adrienne Rich's Feminist Poetics* does not focus on Rich's radical feminism, and she is dealing with Rich's poetry rather than her prose, but her discussion of the development of Rich's feminist poetics complements mine in that she sees that Rich moves from a Romantic aesthetic to a dialogic one. We differ, however, in our conception of the relationship between Romanticism and modernism. As I argue in the introduction and in chapter 1, I see the two as distinct traditions whereas Templeton sees modernism as an extension of Romanticism (17). Jane Hedley in "Surviving to Speak New Language: Mary Daly and Adrienne Rich" also suggests that Rich's perspective shifts from a form of radical feminism similar to Mary Daly's to a conception of language as open ended and context oriented (99).

4. In a very useful essay, Paula Bennett distinguishes among four traditions of lesbian poetry: the early modernist Romantic lyric; modernist poetry; the poetry of identity politics; and poststructuralist, post–lesbian-feminist poetry. Bennett makes only brief reference to Rich, associating her with identity politics (105). She sees Rich as a precursor of but distinct from post–lesbian-feminists.

5. Kathy Rugoff in "Sappho on Mount Sinai: Adrienne Rich's Dialogue with Her Father" speculates that Rich's disillusionment with her father and with patriarchy may have been a result of Rich's father's "failure to deal with the Holocaust or to recognize

the need for its discussion" (11). She also observes, though, that Rich's reductive and bipolar view of men changes in her collection of poetry, *Your Native Land, Your Life,* published in 1986, as she begins to view men "within a larger context, not simply as oppressor" (16).

6. Jean Perreault in *Writing Selves* emphasizes that Rich's prose "inscribes a textual self that is unstable, provisional, urgently self-disclosing, attentive to its own processes, and explicit in displaying them" (46–47). Perreault might argue, then, that Rich's sensibility throughout her essays is a postmodern one, a position I do not hold. Krista Ratcliffe in *Anglo-American Feminist Challenges to the Rhetorical Tradition* also suggests that Rich's metaphors of a dream of a common language and a politics of location can be found throughout her work. I suggest, however, that Rich did not embrace the postmodern perspective implied by the metaphor of a politics of location until fairly late in her career.

7. The question of Walker's adhering to essentialized representations of gender and race in her conception of womanism is taken up by Tuzyline Jita Allan in *Womanist and Feminist Aesthetics.* Allan does think the concept is limited in this way but finally affirms the concept of womanism (121).

8. Barbara Christian says of Walker in *Black Feminist Criticism,*

> In refusing to elevate sex above race, by insisting on the black woman's responsibility to herself and to other women of color, Walker aligns herself neither with prevailing white feminist groups nor with blacks who refuse to acknowledge male dominance in the world. Because her analysis does not yield to easy generalizations and nicely packaged clichés, she continues to resist the trends of the times without discarding the truths upon which they are based. (92)

9. Alice Walker's daughter, Rebecca, describes the parenting arrangements her mother and her white, Jewish father worked out in her autobiography *Black, White, and Jewish.* Her parents divorced when she was eight, and she stayed with each of them two years at a time—with her mother in New York City and San Francisco and with her father and stepmother in Washington, D.C., the Bronx, New York, and Larchmont, New York. She speaks of visiting her parents' extended families, in rural Georgia in the case of her mother and in Brooklyn, New York in the case of her father, and of spending summers at camp. These arrangements were clearly difficult for her, and she had abundant unsupervised time that resulted in experimentation with sex and drugs. Her life takes a turn for the better, however, when she attends a private high school where she has supportive teachers, attends Yale University, and begins to travel extensively with her mother. As a young adult, she decided to change her name from Rebecca Leventhal to Rebecca Walker. Her autobiography suggests that her mother's writing took its toll on her as she was growing up but that Alice Walker's success as a writer had much to do with Rebecca's becoming a successful adult. Alice Walker provides additional perspectives on her marriage, her divorce, and her daughter in somewhat fictionalized stories in *The Way Forward Is with a Broken Heart.*

10. Susan Willis in *Specifying* sees literacy and education as crucial to the way Walker depicts the process of liberation (126). Jacqueline Jones Royster in *Traces of a Stream* focuses on Walker's essays as literacy practices, emphasizing the ways in which Walker's essays merge oral and literate practices (31).

11. For a discussion of Alice Walker's rediscovery of Zora Neale Hurston, see Rachel Stein's chapter "Returning to the Sacred Tree: Black Women, Nature, and Political Re-

sistance in Alice Walker's *Meridian*" in *Shifting the Ground*. Dianne F. Sadoff in "Black Matrilineage: The Case of Alice Walker and Zora Neale Hurston" finds that "Walker designates her precursor an author of black legend and black female liberation, a woman who facilitates what Adrienne Rich calls 're-vision' and who enables female possibility; her dedication—that is, her inscription and devotion—to Hurston acknowledges that, without predecessors, a writer cannot write, since texts enable other texts." (7)

Numerous other writers have dealt with the relationship between the two. See, for instance, Lillie P. Howard, ed. *Alice Walker and Zora Neale Hurston*. Howard mentions a number of other writers who discuss the Hurston-Walker connection (xii–xiii).

12. Tuzyline Jita Allan in "A Voice of One's Own" compares the essays of Virginia Woolf with those of Alice Walker finding both sameness and difference. Allan sees Walker as rewriting and re-visioning Woolf in an "attempt to foreground the significant fact of difference among women, in spite of the rallying force of their gender sameness" (137).

5. Pragmatic Reading and Beyond: Rosenblatt and Feminism

1. Ann E. Berthoff in "Democratic Practice, Pragmatic Vistas: Louise Rosenblatt and the Reader's Response" argues that Rosenblatt exemplifies pragmatism at its best (78).

2. For a useful introduction to the work of Peirce, see Nathan Houser's introduction to *The Essential Peirce: Selected Philosophical Writings*, volume 1. Houser discusses Peirce's theory of signs and his conception of the sign as fundamentally triadic in that it involves both an object and an interpretant (xxxvi). He also discusses Peirce's pragmatism or theory of meaning or inquiry (xxxix). He concludes that Peirce is a semiotic realist in that he sees that the mind represents the world and in that he provides a semiotic account of pragmatism (xli).

3. Richard Beach in *A Teacher's Introduction to Reader-Response Theories* associates Rosenblatt's work with experiential theories of response, theories that are primarily interested in describing specific processes of a reader's experience (49).

4. Hurston's commitment to literature takes the form, primarily, of her writing numerous literary works. She was also a teacher of literature, if only briefly. In *Dust Tracks on the Road*, Hurston speaks of her being so impressed by her English teacher, Dr. Lorenzo Dow Turner, that she wanted to become one as well (166). Robert Hemenway in *Zora Neale Hurston* speaks of the difficulties Hurston actually had when she briefly held academic positions at North Carolina College for Negroes and Florida Normal (254–56, 295).

5. Rosenblatt said in a 22 April 1998 phone conversation with the author that she did not know Hurston at Barnard because their times there did not overlap but that she did once meet her at a party at the home of Leo Huberman in the 1930s when both Rosenblatt and Huberman were on the Commission on Human Relations. She remembers Hurston as a dynamic personality, and she said she has read everything Hurston has written.

6. Elizabeth Jane Harrison in "Zora Neale Hurston and Mary Hunter Austin's Ethnographic Fiction: New Modernist Narratives" finds that Hurston employed postmodern ethnographic techniques after discarding Boasian models by including dialogues and scenes in *Tell My Horse* that "reveal her interference in the cultures she observes" (50). Alice Gambrell in *Women Intellectuals, Modernism, and Difference*, however, argues for a more complex relationship between the Columbia-based anthropologists influenced by Boas and the literary innovations emerging from the Harlem Renaissance.

7. Paul Gilroy in *The Black Atlantic* discusses Hurston's modernism, contrasting it to that of Richard Wright: "Her folksy and assertively feminine perspective is thought to indicate the direction of a more positive counterpart to the overpoliticized and rugged masculinity of Wright's more pessimistic and more self-consciously modernist work" (176).

8. Rosenblatt spoke of her parents' objections to her going into anthropology in the 22 April 1998 phone conversation with the author. In an interview with Nicholas J. Karolides published in *Language Arts* in 1999, she speaks of being torn between doing graduate work in literature or anthropology. She says she chose literature but decided to go abroad to a country with a different language. She also says that after she had her doctorate, she did two years of graduate work in anthropology (161).

9. In the 22 April 1998 phone conversation with the author, Rosenblatt explained her connection with John Dewey. She never took a course with Dewey because Dewey never taught courses at Barnard. She was associated with him, however, through the Conference on Methods in Philosophy and the Sciences that Dewey founded in the 1930s. The group of several hundred people met two times a year at the New School for Social Research to discuss matters related to philosophy and the sciences. The group originated as a way of opposing European totalitarianism and is still in existence today. Rosenblatt was one of the few women in the group and served at one time as secretary. Rosenblatt discusses her association with the Conference in her preface to the 1994 edition of *The Reader, the Text, the Poem* (xiv).

10. Dewey has an excellent record when it comes to attempting to improve gender and race relations. As Larry Hickman points out in *John Dewey's Pragmatic Technology*, he was a founding member of the National Association for the Advancement of Colored People, a member of the Men's League for Women's Suffrage, and a leading member of the American Civil Liberties Union (200). Some of the language he uses in *Democracy and Education*, though, is disturbing, for instance: "Why does a savage group perpetuate savagery, and a civilized group civilization?" By 1934, however, when he wrote *Art as Experience*, he seems to have become critical of nationalism, imperialism, and colonialism in his criticism of museums for segregating art and separating it from common life and in his identification of the institution of the museum as a "distinctively modern institution" (8).

11. Clarence J. Karier, Paul Violas, and Joel Spring in *Roots of Crisis* see Dewey as uncritically embracing science and technology: "The new theology, for Dewey, had become science and technology, which in a way, had become a creator of new values and ends" (101). Jean Quandt in *From the Small Town to the Great Community* also emphasizes Dewey's uncritical acceptance of science. She sees Dewey as affirming that "with the rise of science and the conquest of nature, the meaning of man's freedom was finally becoming clear" (114). A more-recent assessment of Dewey's attitude toward science and technology, however, Larry Hickman's *John Dewey's Pragmatic Technology*, finds Dewey calling for responsible technology, which involves "the choice, the implementation, and the testing of goals" (202).

12. Dewey speaks of Mill's absolutistic tendencies in *The Public and Its Problems*. He observes that when Mill was writing, certain normative and regulative social laws were assumed to exist (195–96).

13. For an appreciative discussion of the application of Dewey's teaching philosophy in the college classroom, see Stephen M. Fishman and Lucille McCarthy, *John Dewey and the Challenge of Classroom Practice*. Fishman and McCarthy contrast Dewey's approach to education with those of both right-wing and left-wing theorists, finding that, for Dewey, we have a natural tendency to connect with others. Fishman and McCarthy see that right-wing and left-wing theorists, in contrast, see individuals as primarily self-interested, rational agents (221).

14. Rosenblatt indicates in "Looking Back and Looking Forward" that she did two years of graduate work in anthropology with Franz Boas and Ruth Benedict (156). In

her preface to the 1994 edition of *The Reader, the Text, the Poem,* Rosenblatt speaks of being influenced by Whitehead, Russell, Wittgenstein, and by the ordinary language philosophers, especially Gilbert Ryle, John Austin, and John Searle (xiv).

15. In the 22 April 1998 phone conversation, Rosenblatt said that "contemporary" was the term used to describe recent developments in literature when she was in college and graduate school and felt that "modernism" is a more-recent term. She saw her dissertation, *L'Idee de l'art pour l'art dans la litterature anglaise pendant la periode victorienne,* as discussing many of the individuals who would now be considered modern. She has always been interested, she said, in the work of Joyce, Yeats, and others.

16. Rosenblatt affirms her commitment to pragmatism in "Epilogue: Against Dualisms": "Truly pragmatist, my theory seeks to answer problems encountered in actual practice and evaluates the solutions according to their implications or consequences for actual life." She refers to her position as a "pragmatist antifoundational epistemology" (180).

17. Annika Hallin in "A Rhetoric for Audiences" argues that Rosenblatt had already found the efferent stance to be the unfortunate rule in literary education in 1938 and continued to see it as a persistent problem in subsequent years (291).

18. Mailloux makes a distinction between Rosenblatt's transactional approach to reading and Iser's interactional approach ("The Turns of Reader-Response Criticism" 47).

19. In Iser's later works, he discusses what he calls "literary anthropology." His conception of anthropology, however, is curiously devoid of discussions of the context within which reading takes place. In both *Prospecting* and *The Fictive and the Imaginary,* he is primarily concerned with the nature of representation. In *The Fictive and the Imaginary,* for instance, he says, "There can be no representation without performance, and the source of performance is always different from what is to be represented" (281). Representation, then, can result in "staging," giving appearance to something that by nature is intangible (296).

20. In a postscript to a letter to me, Rosenblatt explained her use of the generic *he* in both books.

> You might be amused at my troubles with the generic "he." When I wrote the first edition of *Lit. as Ex* (that goes back at least to 1936), I was reacting against the fact that whenever the subject was "teacher," the literature used "she." My use of the generic "he" was a feminist gesture, to counteract the notion that teaching was a feminine, and hence rightfully lower-paid occupation! And as I wrote much of *The Reader, the Text, the Poem* in the fifties (the second chapter was published in 1964, but I sent it out to a journal and it was refused in 1956, as I recall) [*sic*]. Fighting the New Critics, I couldn't carry on that particular linguistic battle at the time, and couldn't start to rewrite the whole manuscript when it finally was published in 1978. And as I don't like any of the simple substitutions for "he," it would mean a complete rewriting. My more recent articles meet the problem by eliminating it, but it does require a different approach, a difficulty since I stress the individual reader as belonging to various groups (and certainly sex-stereotyping is something I was pointing out from *Lit as Ex* on) but still as being unique.

21. Rosenblatt's husband of many years, Sidney Ratner, died in 1996. Ratner was clearly a valuable professional colleague as well. Her son, whom she had when she was 43, has a teenage daughter.

22. Nicholas Karolides, in his introduction to his interview with Louise Rosenblatt, lists the many awards she has received during her career. In 1999 she was named Outstanding Educator in the Language Arts by members of the Elementary Section of the National Council of Teachers of English.

6. Toward Postmodern-Feminist Rhetoric and Composition

1. There is ample evidence that rhetoric and composition has been marginalized within English studies. The Modern Language Association of America (MLA) has for years been dominated by literary specialists. There have been a number of attempts to include rhetoricians and compositionists in the conversation of MLA including the creation of the Division on the History and Theory of Rhetoric and Composition and the creation of a book series that includes works on composition such as Patricia Harkin and John Schilb's *Contending with Words* and John Clifford and Schilb's *Writing Theory and Critical Theory*. Given, though, that the *1998 PMLA Directory* lists sixty-nine divisions devoted to literary topics and only two devoted to rhetoric and composition (the Division on the History and Theory of Rhetoric and Composition and the Division on the Teaching of Writing), there hardly seems to have been a major shift in emphasis within the organization.

2. An article by Allison Schneider in the 28 May 1999 issue of the *Chronicle of Higher Education* speaks of composition professors at public colleges being at the bottom of the salary spectrum in 1998–99, earning an average of $41,164 (A14). Law and finance professors were at the top of the scale whereas faculty in language and literature averaged $49,478.

3. For an early investigation of the relationship between literary studies and composition studies, see Winifred Bryan Horner, ed. *Composition and Literature: Bridging the Gap*. As the title suggests, the essays attempt to bridge the gap between composition studies and literary studies, and so conflict between the two fields is not a central focus. James Slevin in "Depoliticizing and Politicizing Composition Studies," an essay in *The Politics of Writing Instruction*, speaks of the "despicable inequality" that characterizes the profession of rhetoric and composition (2) and of the continuing "misuse of graduate students and part-time faculty" (15). Robert J. Connors in "Rhetoric in the Modern University: The Creation of an Underclass," an essay in the same volume, documents the marginalization of rhetoric within the modern university and of the creation of a "cadre of graduate assistants, low-level instructors, part-timers, and departmental fringe people who became the permanent composition underclass" (65). For an analysis of the "contingent labor" in composition, see Eileen Schell, *Gypsy Academics and Mother-Teachers*. See also Schell, "Conference on the Growing Use of Part-time/Adjunct Faculty: Reflections from NCTE Participants." James A. Berlin speaks in *Rhetorics, Poetics, and Cultures* of the absence of the story of rhetoric in historical accounts of the history of English studies such as Arthur N. Applebee's *Tradition and Reform in the Teaching of English* and Gerald Graff's *Professing Literature* (xiii) and speaks of its history of marginalization (xiv).

John Clifford and John Schilb's edited volume, *Writing Theory and Critical Theory*, emphasizes connections between theories that inform both composition studies and literary studies, though there is evidence of conflicts between the two fields in essays in the collection such as David R. Shumway's "Science, Theory, and the Politics of Empirical Studies." Peter Elbow in *What is English?* addresses the problem of the conflict between the two fields, especially in his chapter, "The Question of Literature." Elbow is clearly an advocate for composition studies and argues that "literature is not some different special entity but just one among many forms of discourse or language" (99). Theresa Enos in

Gender Roles and Faculty Lives in Rhetoric and Composition speaks of respondents to her survey observing that literature specialists are the biggest danger to writing faculty (39).

4. For a perspective on the situation, see Linda Brodkey's "Making a Federal Case out of difference: The Politics of Pedagogy, Publicity, and Postponement" in Clifford and Schilb's *Writing Theory and Critical Theory*, Ben W. McClelland's "A Writing Program Administrator's Response," Mark Andrew Clark's "Topic or Pedagogy?", and Patricia Harkin's "Narrating Conflict" in the same volume.

5. Ellen L. Barton points out in "Empirical Studies in Composition," however, that Hairston in her 1985 essay, "Breaking Our Bonds and Reaffirming Our Connections," makes clear her commitment to humanistic research when she says, "It's important, however, for us to realize that ours is a humanistic discipline, and that we cannot yield to what Lewis Thomas calls 'physics envy,' the temptation to seek status by doing only empirical experiments that can be objectively normed and statistically validated" (279).

6. The language Linda Flower uses in her introduction to *Reading-to-Write: Exploring a Cognitive and Social Process* places considerably greater emphasis on the interpretive process of the writer/researcher: "The individual writer/researcher must define the heart of the question as he or she sees it, must draw the inferences that create a pattern of meaning, and must test that meaning against other possible ones. Research and writing of this sort are what an individual mind makes of its context" (11).

7. Feminist analyses of science have arisen recently out of a number of fields. See, for instance, Nancy Tuana, ed. *Feminism and Science* and Tuana, *The Less Noble Sex.*

8. I am assuming a close correspondence between transactionalism and interactionalism. Berlin in *Rhetoric and Reality* shows how "transactional" is different from objectivist and subjectivist approaches to rhetoric. Keith Gilyard in *Voices of the Self* uses the term transactional to describe a tradition "in which humans are viewed as continually negotiating with an evolving environment" (13). As I indicated in chapter 5, Louise M. Rosenblatt in *The Reader, the Text, the Poem* uses the term *transactional* within the context of the reading of literature. Rosenblatt borrows the term from Dewey and in so doing maintains, to an extent, Dewey's modernist conception of the merging of subject and object. Rosenblatt in "Viewpoints: Transaction Versus Interaction" explains that the term *transactional* suggests that the observer, the observing, and the observed are part of a total situation whereas the term interaction suggests separable elements or entities acting on one another, a mechanistic rather than a fluid process (98). Within an interactional perspective, however, subject and object do not merge but, rather, maintain their separate identities. The term *transaction* can be problematic because it can be confused with the category used to describe writing to communicate with others in James Britton's taxonomy, a category that Britton and his colleagues see as opposed to expressive writing.

9. For a useful, feminist perspective on ethics, see Gesa E. Kirsch, *Ethical Dilemmas.*

10. I discuss the autobiographical turn in rhetoric and composition in "Elbow's Radical and Postmodern Politics."

7. Employing Resistance in Postmodern-Feminist Teaching

1. Although minorities are increasing in substantial numbers at universities across the country, Michigan Tech's demographics parallel that of a number of other universities. Doreen Starke-Meyerring in "'Lost and Melted in the Pot': Multicultural Literacy in Predominantly White Classrooms" cites a U. S. Department of Education statistic of 1991 that indicates that only ten percent or less of the students in almost half of the states of the United States were minorities (139). William A. Kennedy in a summary comparison of 2000–01 first-year students at Michigan Tech with students nationwide says that

less than half of the Michigan Tech students said they had socialized with someone from a different ethnic group whereas more than two-thirds of the national sample reported such an experience.

2. In a subsequent essay, Dale Bauer and Katherine Rhoades explore the theme of student resistance and focus, once again, on student evaluations of feminist teachers.

3. I also discuss classroom resistance in "Strategic, Counter-Strategic, and Reactive Resistance in the Feminist Classroom."

4. For a poststructuralist approach to multicultural pedagogy, see Kathy Dixon, editor of *Outbursts in Academe.* For a Feminist/Poststructuralist approach, see Barbara Frey Waxman, *Multicultural Literatures through Feminist/Poststructuralist Lenses.* For a critique of postmodern feminist misappropriations of the work of women of color, however, see Paula M. L. Moya. "Postmodernism, 'Realism,' and the Politics of Identity."

5. Freire's emphasis on dialogue is in some ways Bakhtinian hence postmodern. Freire's Marxist perspective seems, at times, however, to be hierarchical rather than dialogic. He uses the generic "he" throughout the first edition of *Pedagogy of the Oppressed,* for instance, though he eliminates the problem in subsequent editions. When Freire speaks of dialogue, then, he is speaking, as often as not, of the challenges faced by educated teachers who are attempting to bring literacy to people who have been deprived of it. He is addressing middle-class radicals, privileged individuals committed to entering the world of the oppressed, the Brazilian underclass suffering from poverty and illiteracy, in order to transform it.

6. John R. Maitino and David R. Peck in *Teaching American Ethnic Literatures* provide a historical context for the emergence of multi-ethnic literature, for its scholarly treatment, and for its inclusion in literature courses. J. Paul Hunter in "Facing Others, Facing Ourselves" observes that teaching multicultural texts makes different demands on us than does teaching more traditional texts (24).

7. Michael M. J. Fischer in "Ethnicity and the Post-Modern Arts of Memory" speaks of class-linked differential reactions among ethnic groups. In speaking of responses to the work of Chinese American Maxine Hong Kingston, he observes that some Chinese Americans whose families did not experience "the railroads, sweatshops, and Chinatowns" resent the work of some Chinese Americans such as Kingston for "giving further credence to stereotypes."

8. The strongest student I ever had in the course was gay and had read widely in the areas of gay literature, women's literature, and minority literature. In a discussion of Willa Cather's "Paul's Case," he provided background on Cather's lesbianism and demonstrated that the story is a coded one that attempts to explore homosexuality without doing so overtly.

9. Mary Daly's "untenuring" at Boston College prompted considerable news coverage. For a sympathetic discussion of the situation, see Trish Wilson's "Mary Daly."

10. Other works that explore ways of incorporating liberatory pedagogies in classroom contexts are C. Mark Hurlburt and Michael Blitz, *Composition and Resistance,* David Downing's edited book *Changing Classroom Practices,* Patricia A. Sullivan and Donna J. Qualley's edited book *Pedagogy in the Age of Politics,* James A. Berlin and Michael J. Vivion's collection *Cultural Studies in the English Classroom,* Victor Villanueva's *Bootstraps,* Keith Gilyard's *Voices of the Self,* and David Bleich's *Know and Tell.* Textbooks used in writing classes also often reflect attention to political and social concerns and include works in substantial numbers by women and minorities.

Works Cited and Consulted

Abrams, M. H. *The Mirror and the Lamp: Romantic Theory and the Critical Tradition.* New York: Norton, 1953.

AbuKhalil, As'ad. "Toward the Study of Women and Politics in the Arab World: The Debate and the Reality." *Feminist Issues* 13 (1993): 3–22.

Abu-Lughod, Lila, ed. *Remaking Women: Feminism and Modernity in the Middle East.* Princeton: Princeton UP, 1998.

Adams, Alice. "Maternal Bonds: Recent Literature on Mothering." *Signs* 20 (1995): 414–27.

Ahmed, Leila. *Women and Gender in Islam: Historical Roots of a Modern Debate.* New Haven: Yale UP, 1992.

Alcoff, Linda. "Cultural Feminism Versus Post-Structuralism: The Identity Crisis in Feminist Theory." *Signs* 13 (1988): 405–36.

Alexander, M. Jacqui, and Chandra Talpade Mohanty, eds. *Feminist Genealogies, Colonial Legacies, Democratic Futures.* New York: Routledge, 1997.

Allan, Tuzyline Jita. "A Voice of One's Own: Implications of Impersonality in the Essays of Virginia Woolf and Alice Walker." *The Politics of the Essay: Feminist Perspectives.* Ed. Ruth-Ellen Boetcher Joeres and Elizabeth Mittman. Bloomington: Indiana UP, 1993. 131–47.

———. *Womanist and Feminist Aesthetics: A Comparative Review.* Athens: Ohio UP, 1995.

Allen, Paula Gunn. "Angry Women Are Building: Issues and Struggles Facing American Indian Women Today." Anderson and Collins, *Race, Class, and Gender* 32–36.

Althusser, Louis. *For Marx.* New York: Verso, 1985.

Anderson, Margaret L., and Patricia Hill Collins, eds. *Race, Class, and Gender: An Anthology.* New York: Wadsworth, 1995.

———. "Shifting the Center and Reconstructing Knowledge." Anderson and Collins, *Race, Class, and Gender* 1–9.

Anzaldúa, Gloria. *Borderlands/La Frontera: The New Mestiza.* San Francisco: Aunt Lute, 1987.

———. "Speaking in Tongues: A Letter to Third World Women Writers." *This Bridge Called My Back: Writings of Radical Women of Color.* Ed. Cherríe Moraga and Anzaldúa. Watertown: Persephone, 1981. 165–74.

Applebee, Arthur N. *Tradition and Reform in the Teaching of English: A History.* Urbana: NCTE, 1974.

Austen, Jane. *Mansfield Park.* 1814. Ed. Tony Tanner. New York: Penguin, 1966.

Baker, Houston A., Jr. *Modernism and the Harlem Renaissance*. Chicago: U of Chicago P, 1987.

Bakhtin, M. M. "Content, Material, and Form in Verbal Art." *Art and Answerability: Early Philosophical Essays*. By Bakhtin. Trans. Vadim Liapunov. Ed. Michael Holquist and Vadim Liapunov. Austin: U of Texas P, 1990. 257–325.

———. *The Dialogic Imagination: Four Essays*. Trans. Caryl Emerson and Michael Holquist. Ed. Holquist. Austin: U of Texas P, 1981.

———. "The Problem of Speech Genres." *Speech Genres and Other Late Essays*. Trans. Vern W. McGee. Ed. Caryl Emerson and Michael Holquist. Austin: U of Texas P, 1986. 60–102.

———. *Problems of Dostoevsky's Poetics*. Ed. and trans. Caryl Emerson. Minneapolis: U of Minnesota P, 1984.

———. *Rabelais and His World*. Trans. Hélenè Iswolsky. Bloomington: Indiana UP, 1984.

Barker, E. Ellen. "Creating Generations: The Relationship Between Celie and Shug in Alice Walker's *The Color Purple*." *Critical Essays on Alice Walker*. Ed. Ikenna Dieke. Westport: Greenwood, 1999. 55–65.

Barnes, Linda Laube. "Gender Bias in Teachers' Written Comments." *Gender in the Classroom: Power and Pedagogy*. Ed. Susan L. Gabriel and Isaiah Smithson. Urbana: U of Illinois P, 1990. 140–59.

Barrett, Eileen. *Virginia Woolf: Lesbian Readings*. New York: New York UP, 1997.

Barrett, Michele. "Virginia Woolf Meets Michel Foucault." *Virginia Woolf Miscellany* 52 (1998): 4–5.

Bartholomae, David, and Anthony Petrosky. *Facts, Artifacts, and Counterfacts: Theory and Method for a Reading and Writing Course*. Upper Montclair: Boynton, 1986.

Barton, Ben F., and Marthalee S. Barton. "Ideology and the Map: Toward a Postmodern Visual Design Practice." *Professional Communication: The Social Perspective*. Ed. Nancy Roundy Blyler and Charlotte Thralls. Newbury Park: Sage, 1993. 49–78.

Barton, Ellen. "Empirical Studies in Composition." *Coll. English* 59 (1997): 815–27.

Bateson, Mary Catherine. *Composing a Life*. New York: Penguin, 1989.

Bauer, Dale M. *Feminist Dialogics: A Theory of Failed Community*. Albany: State U of New York P, 1988.

———. "The Other 'F' Word: The Feminist in the Classroom." *Coll. English* 52 (1990): 385–96.

Bauer, Dale M., and Katherine Rhoades. "The Meanings and Metaphors of Student Resistance." *Antifeminism in the Academy*. Ed. VèVè Clark, Shirley Nelson Garner, Margaret Higonnet, and Ketu H. Katrak. New York: Routledge, 1996. 95–113.

Bayley, John. *The Romantic Survival: A Study in Poetic Evolution*. London: Constable, 1957.

Beach, Richard. *A Teacher's Introduction to Reader-Response Theories*. Urbana: NCTE, 1993.

Beauvoir, Simone de. *The Second Sex*. New York: Knopf, 1952.

Bechtel, Judith. "Why Teaching Writing Always Brings Up Questions of Equity." Caywood and Overing 179–83.

Belenky, Mary Field, Blythe McVicker Clinchy, Nancy Rule Goldberger, and Jill Mattuck Tarule. *Women's Ways of Knowing: The Development of Self, Voice, and Mind*. New York: Basic, 1986.

Benhabib, Seyla. "Sexual Difference and Collective Identities: The New Global Constellation." *Signs* 24 (1999): 335–61.

Bennett, Paula. "Lesbian Poetry in the United States, 1890–1990: A Brief Overview." *Professions of Desire: Lesbian and Gay Studies in Literature.* Ed. George E. Haggerty and Bonnie Zimmerman. New York: MLA, 1995. 98–110.

Bentley, Arthur F. *Inquiry into Inquiries.* Boston: Beacon, 1954.

Berlin, James A. "Rhetoric and Ideology in the Writing Class." *Coll. English* 50 (1988): 477–94.

———. *Rhetoric and Reality: Writing Instruction in American Colleges, 1900–1985.* Carbondale: Southern Illinois UP, 1987.

———. *Rhetorics, Poetics, and Cultures: Refiguring English Studies.* Urbana: NCTE, 1996.

———. *Writing Instruction in Nineteenth-Century American Colleges.* Carbondale: Southern Illinois UP, 1984.

Berlin, James A., and Michael J. Vivion, eds. *Cultural Studies in the English Classroom.* Portsmouth: Boynton, 1992.

Berman, Marshall. *All That Is Solid Melts into Air: The Experience of Modernity.* New York: Simon, 1982.

Berman, Ruth. "From Aristotle's Dualism to Materialist Dialectics: Feminist Transformation of Science and Society." *Gender/Body/Knowledge: Feminist Reconstructions of Being and Knowing.* Ed. Alison M. Jagger and Susan R. Bordo. New Brunswick: Rutgers UP, 1989. 224–55.

Berthoff, Ann E. "Democratic Practice, Pragmatic Vistas: Louise Rosenblatt and the Reader's Response." *The Experience of Reading: Louise Rosenblatt and Reader-Response Theory.* Ed. John Clifford. Portsmouth: Boynton, 1991. 77–84.

Bhabha, Homi. "The Third Space." *Identity: Community, Culture, Difference.* Ed. Jonathan Rutherford, 207–21. London: Lawrence, 1990. 207–21.

Bizzell, Patricia. "Beyond Anti-Foundationalism to Rhetorical Authority: Problems Defining 'Cultural Literacy.'" *Coll. English* 52 (1990): 661–75.

Bizzell, Patricia, and Bruce Herzberg. Introduction: Enlightenment Rhetoric. *The Rhetorical Tradition: Readings from Classical Times to the Present.* Ed. Bizzell and Herzberg. Boston: Bedford, 1990. 637–69.

Bleich, David. "Genders of Writing." *JAC* 9.1–2 (1989): 10–25.

———. *Know and Tell: A Writing Pedagogy of Disclosure, Genre, and Membership.* Portsmouth: Boynton, 1998.

———. *Readings and Feelings: An Introduction to Subjective Criticism.* Urbana: NCTE, 1975.

———. *Subjective Criticism.* Baltimore: Johns Hopkins UP, 1978.

Bloom, Harold. *The Visionary Company.* Ithaca: Cornell UP, 1961.

Bloom, Lynn Z. *Composition Studies as a Creative Art: Teaching, Writing, Scholarship, Administration.* Logan: Utah State UP, 1998.

Blyler, Nancy Roundy. "Research as Ideology in Professional Communication." *Technical Communication Quarterly* 4 (1995): 285–313.

Bordo, Susan. "Feminism, Postmodernism, and Gender-Skepticism." Nicholson 133–56.

Bosworth, David. "Echo and Narcissus: The Fearful Logic of Postmodern Thought." *Georgia Review* 51 (1997): 409–37.

Boyne, Roy, and Ali Rattansi. "The Theory and Politics of Postmodernism: By Way of an Introduction." *Postmodernism and Society.* Ed. Boyne and Rattansi. New York: St. Martin's, 1990. 1–45.

Bradbury, Malcolm, and James McFarlane. *Modernism: A Guide to European Literature 1890–1930.* 1976. New York: Penguin, 1991.

Braddock, Richard, Richard Lloyd-Jones, and Lowell Schoer. *Research in Written Composition.* Urbana: NCTE, 1963.

Bridwell, Lillian, and Richard Beach, eds. *New Directions in Composition Research.* New York: Guilford, 1984.

Britton, James, Tony Burgess, Nancy Martin, Alex McLeod, and Harold Rosen. *The Development of Writing Abilities 11–18.* London: Macmillan, 1975.

Brodkey, Linda. "Making a Federal Case out of Difference: The Politics of Pedagogy, Publicity, and Postponement." Clifford and Schilb 236–61.

Brody, Miriam. *Manly Writing: Gender, Rhetoric, and the Rise of Composition.* Carbondale: Southern Illinois UP, 1993.

Brooks, Ann. *Postfeminisms: Feminism, Cultural Theory, and Cultural Forms.* New York: Routledge, 1997.

Brooks, David. "Modernism." *Encyclopedia of Literature and Criticism.* Ed. Martin Coyle, Peter Garside, Malcolm Kelsall, and John Peck. London: Routledge, 1991. 119–29.

Brosnan, Leila. *Reading Virginia Woolf's Essays and Journalism: Breaking the Surface of Silence.* Edinburgh: Edinburgh UP, 1997.

Bruffee, Kenneth A. *Collaborative Learning: Higher Education, Interdependence, and the Authority of Knowledge.* Baltimore: Johns Hopkins UP, 1993.

Bullock, Richard, and John Trimbur, eds. *The Politics of Writing Instruction: Postsecondary.* Portsmouth: Boynton, 1991.

Butler, Judith. *Bodies That Matter: On the Discursive Limits of "Sex."* New York: Routledge, 1993.

———. *Excitable Speech: A Politics of the Performative.* New York: Routledge, 1997.

———. *Gender Trouble: Feminism and the Subversion of Identity.* New York: Routledge, 1990.

———. "Gender Trouble, Feminist Theory, and Psychoanalytic Discourse." Nicholson 324–40.

———. *The Psychic Life of Power: Theories in Subjection.* Stanford: Stanford UP, 1997.

Butler, Judith, Ernesto Laclau, and Slavoj Žižek. *Contingency, Hegemony, Universality: Contemporary Dialogues on the Left.* London: Verso, 2000.

Caramagno, Thomas C. *The Flight of the Mind: Virginia Woolf's Art and Manic-Depressive Illness.* Berkeley: U of California P, 1996.

Carlston, Erin G. *Thinking Fascism: Sapphic Modernism and Fascist Modernity.* Stanford: Stanford UP, 1998.

Cather, Willa. "Paul's Case." Charters 254–68.

Caughie, Pamela L. "Let It Pass: Changing the Subject, Once Again." Jarratt and Worsham 111–31.

———. *Virginia Woolf and Postmodernism: Literature in Quest and Question of Itself.* Urbana: U of Illinois P, 1991.

Caywood, Cynthia L., and Gillian R. Overing, eds. *Teaching Writing: Pedagogy, Gender, and Equity.* Albany: State U of New York P, 1987.

Charney, Davida. "Empiricism Is Not a Four-Letter Word." *CCC* 47.4 (1996): 567–93.

———. "From Logocentrism to Ethnocentrism: Historicizing Critiques of Writing Research." *Technical Communication Quarterly* 7 (1998): 9–32.

Charters, Ann, ed. *The Story and Its Writer: An Introduction to Short Fiction.* 4th ed. Boston: Bedford, 1995.

Chodorow, Nancy. *The Reproduction of Mothering: Psychoanalysis and the Sociology of Gender.* Berkeley: U of California P, 1978.

Christian, Barbara. *Black Feminist Criticism: Perspectives on Black Women Writers.* New York: Pergamon, 1985.

Cisneros, Sandra. "Little Miracles, Kept Promises." *Rereading America: Cultural Contexts for Critical Thinking and Writing.* Ed. Gary Colombo, Robert Cullen, and Bonnie Lisle. 2nd ed. Boston: Bedford, 1992. 221–32.

Clark, Gregory. *Dialogue, Dialectic, and Conversation: A Social Perspective on the Function of Writing.* Carbondale: Southern Illinois UP, 1990.

Clark, Mark Andrew. "Topic or Pedagogy?" Clifford and Schilb 271–77.

Clark, Suzanne. *Sentimental Modernism: Women Writers and the Revolution of the Word.* Bloomington: Indiana UP, 1991.

Clifford, John, and John Schilb, eds. *Writing Theory and Critical Theory: Research and Scholarship in Composition.* New York: MLA, 1994.

Coleridge, S. T. *Biographia Literaria.* Vol. 1. 1817. Ed. J. Shawcross. New York: Oxford UP, 1907.

Collins, Patricia Hill. *Black Feminist Thought: Knowledge, Consciousness, and the Politics of Empowerment.* New York: Routledge, 1990.

———. "Comment on Hekman's 'Truth and Method: Feminist Standpoint Theory Revisited': Where's the Power?" *Signs* 22 (1997): 375–81.

Connors, Robert J. *Composition-Rhetoric: Backgrounds, Theory, and Pedagogy.* Pittsburgh: U of Pittsburgh P, 1997.

———. "Composition Studies and Science." *Coll. English* 45 (1983): 1–20.

———. "Rhetoric in the Modern University: The Creation of an Underclass." Bullock and Trimbur 55–84.

Cooper, Charles R., and Lee Odell, eds. *Research on Composing: Points of Departure.* Urbana: NCTE, 1978.

Cornell, Drucilla. *At the Heart of Freedom: Feminism, Sex, and Equality.* Princeton: Princeton UP, 1998.

Cornillon, Susan Koppelman, ed. *Images of Women in Fiction: Feminist Perspectives.* Bowling Green, Ohio: Bowling Green UP, 1972.

Cott, Nancy F. *The Grounding of Modern Feminism.* New Haven: Yale UP, 1987.

Crewe, Jonathan. "Transcoding the World: Haraway's Postmodernism." *Signs* 22 (1997): 891–905.

Crowley, Sharon. *The Methodical Memory: Invention in Current-Traditional Rhetoric.* Carbondale: Southern Illinois UP, 1990.

Daeumer, Elisabeth, and Sandra Runzo. "Transforming the Composition Classroom." Caywood and Overing 45–62.

Daly, Mary. *Gyn/Ecology: The Metaethics of Radical Feminism.* Boston: Beacon, 1978.

Daugherty, Beth Rigel. "Readin', Writin', and Revisin': Virginia Woolf's 'How Should One Read a Book?'" Rosenberg and Dubino 159–75.

Davidson, Cathy N., ed. *Reading in America: Literature and Social History.* Baltimore: Johns Hopkins UP, 1989.

DeKoven, Marianne. "The Politics of Modernist Form." *New Literary History* 23 (1992): 675–90.

———. *Rich and Strange: Gender, History, Modernism.* Princeton: Princeton UP, 1991.

Derrida, Jacques. *Of Grammatology.* Trans. Gayatri Chakravorty Spivak. Baltimore: Johns Hopkins UP, 1976.

DeSalvo, Louise. *Virginia Woolf: The Impact of Childhood Sexual Abuse on Her Life and Work.* New York: Ballantine, 1990.

Descartes, René. *Discourse on Method*. 1637. *Discourse on Method and Other Writings*. New York: Penguin, 1960. 36–97.

———. *Meditations*. 1641. *Discourse on Method and Other Writings*. New York: Penguin, 1960. 101–69.

Deutscher, Penelope. *Yielding Gender: Feminism, Deconstruction, and the History of Philosophy*. New York: Routledge, 1997.

Dewey, John. *Art as Experience*. New York: Capricorn, 1934.

———. *Democracy and Education*. New York: Macmillan, 1961.

———. *Liberalism and Social Action*. New York: Capricorn, 1935.

———. *The Public and Its Problems*. 1927. Chicago: Swallow, 1954.

Diamond, Irene, and Lee Quinby, eds. *Feminism and Foucault: Reflections on Resistance*. Boston: Northeastern UP, 1988.

Di Stefano, Christine. "Dilemmas of Difference: Feminism, Modernity, and Postmodernism." Nicholson 63–82.

Dixon, Kathy, ed. *Outbursts in Academe: Multiculturalism and Other Sources of Conflict*. Portsmouth: Heinemann, 1998.

Dombrowski, Paul. "Post-Modernism as the Resurgence of Humanism in Technical Communication Studies." *Technical Communication Quarterly* 4 (1995): 165–85.

Donovan, Josephine, ed. *Feminist Literary Criticism: Explorations in Theory*. Lexington: U of Kentucky P, 1975.

Downing, David, ed. *Changing Classroom Practices: Resources for Literary and Cultural Studies*. Urbana: NCTE, 1994.

Drake, James. "The Naming Disease." *Times Literary Supplement* (4 Sept. 1998): 14–15.

Dusinberre, Juliet. *Virginia Woolf's Renaissance: Woman Reader or Common Reader?* Iowa City: U of Iowa P, 1997.

Dworkin, Ronald. "My Reply to Stanley Fish (and Walter Benn Michaels): Please Don't Talk about Objectivity Any More." *The Politics of Interpretation*. Ed. W. J. T. Mitchell. Chicago: U of Chicago P, 1983. 287–313.

———. "Women and Pornography." Schilb, Flynn, and Clifford 744–52. Rpt. of *New York Review of Books*. 21 Oct. 1993, 36+.

Eagleton, Terry. *Literary Theory: An Introduction*. Minneapolis: U of Minnesota P, 1983.

Ebert, Teresa. *Ludic Feminism and after: Postmodernism, Desire, and Labor in Late Capitalism*. Ann Arbor: U of Michigan P, 1996.

Echols, Alice. *Daring to Be Bad: Radical Feminism in America 1967–1975*. Minneapolis: U of Minneapolis P, 1989.

Edelstein, Marilyn. "Toward a Feminist Postmodern *Poléthique*: Kristeva on Ethics and Politics." *Ethics, Politics, and Difference in Julia Kristeva's Writing*. Ed. Kelly Oliver. New York: Routledge, 1993. 196–214.

Eitzen, D. Stanley, and Maxine Baca Zinn. "Structural Transformation and Systems of Inequality." Anderson and Collins, *Race, Class, and Gender* 202–06. Rpt. of *The Reshaping of America: Social Consequences of the Changing Economy*. Englewood Cliffs: Prentice, 1989. 131–43.

Elbow, Peter. *What is English?* New York: MLA, 1990.

Eliot, T. S. "Tradition and the Individual Talent." 1919. *Twentieth-Century Literature*. Ed. David Lodge. London: Longman, 1972. 71–77.

———. "What Is a Classic?" *On Poetry and Poets*. New York: Farrar, 1957. 52–74.

Elliott, Bridget, and Jo-Ann Wallace. *Women Artists and Writers: Modernist (Im)Positionings*. London: Routledge, 1994.

Emig, Janet. *The Composing Processes of Twelfth Graders.* Urbana: NCTE, 1971.
———. "Inquiry Paradigms and Writing." *CCC* 33 (1982): 64–75.
Enos, Theresa. *Gender Roles and Faculty Lives in Rhetoric and Composition.* Carbondale: Southern Illinois UP, 1996.
Epstein, Cynthia Fuchs. *Deceptive Distinctions: Sex, Gender, and the Social Order.* New Haven: Yale UP, 1988.
Erdrich, Louise. "The Red Convertible." Charters 448–55.
Faigley, Lester. "Competing Theories of Process: A Critique and a Proposal." *Coll. English* 48 (1986): 527–42.
———. *Fragments of Rationality: Postmodernity and the Subject of Composition.* Pittsburgh: U of Pittsburgh P, 1992.
Felski, Rita. "The Doxa of Difference." *Signs* 23 (1997): 1–21.
———. *The Gender of Modernity.* Cambridge: Harvard UP, 1995.
Ferebee, Steve. "Bridging the Gulf: The Reader In and Out of Virginia Woolf's Literary Essays." *Coll. Lang. Assn. Jour.* 30 (1987): 343–61.
Ferguson, Margaret, and Jennifer Wicke, eds. *Feminism and Postmodernism.* Durham: Duke UP, 1994.
Ferguson, Moira. *Colonialism and Gender Relations from Mary Wollstonecraft to Jamaica Kincaid: East Caribbean Connections.* New York: Columbia UP, 1993.
Fernald, Anne E. "Pleasure and Belief in 'Phases of Fiction'." Rosenberg and Dubino 193–211.
Fernea, Elizabeth Warnock. *In Search of Islamic Feminism: One Woman's Global Journey.* New York: Doubleday, 1998.
Fetterley, Judith. *The Resisting Reader: A Feminist Approach to American Fiction.* Bloomington: Indiana UP, 1978.
Firestone, Shulamith. *The Dialectic of Sex: The Case for Feminist Revolution.* New York: Bantam, 1970.
Fischer, Michael M. J. "Ethnicity and the Post-Modern Arts of Memory." *Writing Culture: The Poetics and Politics of Ethnography.* Ed. James Clifford and George E. Marcus. Berkeley: U of California P, 1986. 194–233.
———. "Is Islam the Odd-Civilization Out?" *New Perspectives Quarterly* 9 (Spring 1992): 54–59.
Fish, Stanley. *Doing What Comes Naturally: Change, Rhetoric, and the Practice of Theory in Literary and Legal Studies.* Durham: Duke UP, 1989.
———. *Is There a Text in This Class?: The Authority of Interpretive Communities.* Cambridge: Harvard UP, 1980.
———. *Self-Consuming Artifacts: The Experience of Seventeenth-Century Literature.* Berkeley: U of California P, 1972.
Fishman, Stephen M., and Lucille McCarthy. *John Dewey and the Challenge of Classroom Practice.* Urbana: NCTE, 1998.
Flax, Jane. *Disputed Subjects: Essays on Psychoanalysis, Politics, and Philosophy.* New York: Routledge, 1993.
———. "The End of Innocence." *Feminists Theorize the Political.* Ed. Judith Butler and Joan W. Scott. New York: Routledge, 1992. 445–63.
———. "Postmodernism and Gender Relations in Feminist Theory." Nicholson 39–62.
———. *Thinking Fragments: Psychoanalysis, Feminism, and Postmodernism in the Contemporary West.* Berkeley: U of California P, 1990.
Flint, Kate. "Reading Uncommonly: Virginia Woolf and the Practice of Reading." *Yearbook of English Studies* 26 (1996): 187–98.

Flower, Linda. "Cognition, Context, and Theory Building." *CCC* 40 (1989): 282–311.

Flower, Linda, Victoria Stein, John Ackerman, Margaret J. Kantz, Kathleen McCormick, and Wayne C. Peck. *Reading-to-Write: Exploring a Cognitive and Social Process.* New York: Oxford UP, 1990.

Flynn, Elizabeth A. "Composing as a Woman." *CCC* 39 (1988): 423–35.

———. "Composition Studies from a Feminist Perspective." Bullock and Trimbur 137–54.

———. "Elbow's Radical and Postmodern Politics." *Writing with Peter: A Collection of Essays in Honor of Peter Elbow.* Ed. Pat Belanoff, Marcia Dickson, Sheryl Fontaine, and Charles Moran. Logan: Utah State UP, 2002. 34–47.

———. "Emergent Feminist Technical Communication." *Technical Communication Quarterly* 6 (Summer 1997): 313–20.

———. "Feminist Theories/Feminist Composition." *Coll. English* 57 (1995): 201–12.

———. "Strategic, Counter-Strategic, and Reactive Resistance in the Feminist Classroom." *Insurrections: Approaches to Resistance in Composition Studies.* Ed. Andrea Greenbaum. Albany: SUNY P, 2001. 17–34.

Foss, Karen A., and Sonja K. Foss, eds. *Women Speak: The Eloquence of Women's Lives.* Prospect Heights: Waveland, 1991.

Foucault, Michel. *The Archaeology of Knowledge.* New York: Harper, 1972.

———. *Discipline and Punish: The Birth of the Prison.* New York: Vintage, 1977.

———. *The Order of Things: An Archaeology of the Human Sciences.* New York: Vintage, 1970.

Freed, Richard C. "Postmodern Practice: Perspectives and Prospects." *Professional Communication: The Social Perspective.* Ed. Nancy Roundy Blyler and Charlotte Thralls. Newbury: Sage, 1993. 196–214.

Freire, Paulo. *Pedagogy of the Oppressed.* New York: Seabury, 1970.

Freud, Sigmund. "A Metapsychological Supplement to the Theory of Dreams." *The Standard Edition of the Complete Psychological Works of Sigmund Freud.* Trans. James Strachey. Vol. 14. London: Hogarth, 1957. 222–35.

———. "On Narcissism: An Introduction." *The Standard Edition of the Complete Psychological Works of Sigmund Freud.* Trans. James Strachey. Vol. 14. London: Hogarth, 1957. 73–102.

———. "On the History of the Psycho-Analytic Movement." *The Standard Edition of the Complete Psychological Works of Sigmund Freud.* Trans. James Strachey. Vol. 14. London: Hogarth, 1957. 7–66.

Friedan, Betty. *The Feminine Mystique.* New York: Dell, 1963.

Friedman, Susan Stanford. "Beyond White and Other: Relationality and Narratives of Race in Feminist Discourse." *Signs* 21 (Autumn 1995): 1–49.

———. *Mappings: Feminism and the Cultural Geographies of Encounter.* Princeton: Princeton UP, 1998.

———. "Virginia Woolf's Pedagogical Scenes of Reading: *The Voyage Out, The Common Reader,* and Her 'Common Readers.'" *Modern Fiction Studies* 38 (1992): 101–25.

Gadamer, Hans-Georg. *Truth and Method.* New York: Continuum, 1975.

Gallop, Jane. *Around 1981: Academic Feminist Literary Theory.* New York: Routledge, 1992.

Gambrell, Alice. *Women Intellectuals, Modernism, and Difference: Transatlantic Culture 1919–1945.* Cambridge: Cambridge UP, 1997.

Gaudin, Colette, Mary Jean Green, Lynn Anthony Higgins, Marianne Hirsch, Vivian Kogan, Claudia Reeder, and Nancy Vickers. Introduction. "Literary and Sexual Difference: Practical Criticism/Practical Critique." In "Feminist Readings: French Texts/American Contexts." *Yale French Studies* 62 (1981): 2–18.

Gelpi, Albert. *A Coherent Splendor: The American Poetic Renaissance, 1910–1950.* Cambridge: Cambridge UP, 1987.

Gere, Anne R. *Intimate Practices: Literacy and Cultural Work in U.S. Women's Clubs, 1880–1920.* Champaign: U of Illinois P, 1997.

Gilbert, Sandra M., and Susan Gubar. *The Madwoman in the Attic: The Woman Writer and the Nineteenth-Century Literary Imagination.* New Haven: Yale UP, 1979.

———. *No Man's Land: The Place of the Woman Writer in the Twentieth Century.* 3 vols. New Haven: Yale UP, 1988–94.

———. *Sexchanges.* New Haven: Yale UP, 1989. Vol. 2. of *No Man's Land: The Place of the Woman Writer in the Twentieth Century.* 3 vols. 1988–94.

———. "Sexual Linguistics." *New Lit. Hist.* 16 (1985): 515–43.

———, eds. *Shakespeare's Sisters: Feminist Essays on Women Poets.* Bloomington: Indiana UP, 1979.

———. *The War of the Words.* New Haven: Yale UP, 1988. Vol. 1 of *No Man's Land: The Place of the Woman Writer in the Twentieth Century.* 3 vols. 1988–94.

Gilligan, Carol. *In a Different Voice: Psychological Theory and Women's Development.* Cambridge: Harvard UP, 1982.

Gilman, Charlotte Perkins. *Women and Economics: The Economic Factor Between Men and Women as a Factor in Social Evolution.* 1898. New York: Harper, 1966.

Gilroy, Paul. *The Black Atlantic: Modernity and Double Consciousness.* Cambridge: Harvard UP, 1993.

Gilyard, Keith. *Voices of the Self: A Study of Language Competence.* Detroit: Wayne State UP, 1991.

Giroux, Henry A. "Rethinking the Boundaries of Educational Discourse: Modernism, Postmodernism, and Feminism." *Coll. Lit.* 17.2–3 (1990): 1–50.

Glazener, Nancy. *Reading for Realism: The History of a U.S. Literary Institution.* Durham: Duke UP, 1997.

Glenn, Cheryl. *Rhetoric Retold: Regendering the Tradition from Antiquity through the Renaissance.* Carbondale: Southern Illinois UP, 1997.

Godzich, Wlad. Foreword. *The Formal Method in Literary Scholarship: A Critical Introduction to Sociological Poetics.* By M. M. Bakhtin and P. N. Medvedev. Trans. Albert J. Wehrle. Cambridge: Harvard UP, 1985.

Graff, Gerald. *Professing Literature: An Institutional History.* Chicago: U of Chicago P, 1987.

Graham, Margaret Baker, and Patricia Goubil-Gambrell. "Hearing Voices in English Studies." *JAC* 15 (1995): 103–19.

Grimm, Nancy Maloney. *Good Intentions: Writing Center Work for Postmodern Times.* Portsmouth: Boynton, 1999.

Gross, Paul R., and Norman Levitt. *Higher Superstition: The Academic Left and Its Quarrels with Science.* Baltimore: Johns Hopkins UP, 1994.

Hairston, Maxine. "Breaking Our Bonds and Reaffirming Our Connections." *CCC* 36 (1985): 272–82.

———. "Diversity, Ideology, and Teaching Writing." *CCC* 43 (1992): 179–93.

———. "The Winds of Change: Thomas Kuhn and the Revolution in the Teaching of Writing." *CCC* 33 (1982): 76–88.

Hallin, Annika. "A Rhetoric for Audiences: Louise Rosenblatt on Reading and Action." *Reclaiming Rhetorica: Women in the Rhetorical Tradition.* Ed. Andrea Lunsford. Pittsburgh: U of Pittsburgh P, 1995. 285–303.

Hammonds, Evelynn. "Race, Sex, AIDS: The Construction of 'Other.'" Anderson and Collins, *Race, Class, and Gender* 402–13.

Hampson, Norman. *The Enlightenment: An Evaluation of its Assumptions, Attitudes, and Values.* Middlesex, England: Penguin, 1968.

Haraway, Donna J. *Modest_Witness@Second_Millennium.FemaleMan_Meets_OncoMouse: Feminism and Technoscience.* New York: Routledge, 1997.

———. "Situated Knowledges: The Science Question in Feminism and the Privilege of Partial Perspective." *Technology and the Politics of Knowledge.* Ed. Andrew Feenberg and Alastair Hannay. Bloomington: Indiana UP, 1995. 175–94.

Harding, Sandra. "Comment on Hekman's 'Truth and Method: Feminist Standpoint Theory Revisited': Whose Standpoint Needs the Regimes of Truth and Reality?" *Signs* 22 (1997): 382–91.

———. *Is Science Multicultural?: Postcolonialism, Feminism, and Epistemologies.* Bloomington: Indiana UP, 1998.

———. *The "Racial" Economy of Science: Toward a Democratic Future.* Bloomington: Indiana UP, 1993.

———. *Whose Science? Whose Knowledge?: Thinking from Women's Lives.* Ithaca: Cornell UP, 1991.

Harkin, Patricia. "Narrating Conflict." Clifford and Schilb 278–85.

Harkin, Patricia, and John Schilb, eds. *Contending with Words: Composition and Rhetoric in a Postmodern Age.* New York: MLA, 1991.

Harrison, Elizabeth Jane. "Zora Neale Hurston and Mary Hunter Austin's Ethnographic Fiction: New Modernist Narratives." *Unmanning Modernism: Gendered Re-Readings.* Ed. Harrison and Shirley Peterson. Knoxville: U of Tennessee P, 1997. 44–58.

Harrison, Suzan. *Eudora Welty and Virginia Woolf: Gender, Genre, and Influence.* Baton Rouge: Louisiana State UP, 1997.

Harstock, Nancy. "Comment on Hekman's 'Truth and Method: Feminist Standpoint Theory Revisited': Truth or Justice?" *Signs* 22 (1997): 367–74.

———. "Foucault on Power: A Theory for Women?" Nicholson 157–75.

Hartmann, Susan M. *The Other Feminists: Activists in the Liberal Establishment.* New Haven: Yale UP, 1998.

Hassan, Ihab. *The Dismemberment of Orpheus: Toward a Postmodern Literature.* 2nd ed. Madison: U of Wisconsin P, 1982.

Hawkesworth, Mary. "Confounding Gender." *Signs* 22 (1997): 649–85.

Hays, Janice. "Intellectual Parenting and a Developmental Feminist Pedagogy of Writing." Phelps and Emig 153–90.

Hedley, Jane. "Surviving to Speak New Language: Mary Daly and Adrienne Rich." *Language and Liberation: Feminism, Philosophy, and Language.* Ed. Christina Hendricks and Kelly Oliver. Albany: State U of New York P, 1999. 99–127.

Heilbrun, Carolyn, and Catharine Stimpson. "Theories of Feminist Criticism: A Dialogue." *Feminist Literary Criticism: Explorations in Theory.* Ed. Josephine Donovan. Lexington: U of Kentucky P, 1975. 61–73.

Hekman, Susan J. *Gender and Knowledge: Elements of a Postmodern Feminism.* Boston: Northeastern UP, 1990.

———. "Reply to Harstock, Collins, Harding, and Smith." *Signs* 22 (1997): 399–402.

————. "Truth and Method: Feminist Standpoint Theory Revisited." *Signs* 22 (1997): 341–65.

Hemenway, Robert E. *Zora Neale Hurston: A Literary Biography.* Urbana: U of Illinois P, 1977.

Hennessy, Rosemary. *Materialist Feminism and the Politics of Discourse.* New York: Routledge, 1994.

Herndl, Carl G. "Teaching Discourse and Reproducing Culture: A Critique of Research and Pedagogy in Professional and Non-Academic Writing." *CCC* 44 (1993): 349–63.

Al-Hibri, Azizah. "Reproduction, Mothering, and the Origins of Patriarchy." *Mothering: Essays in Feminist Theory.* Ed. Joyce Trebilcot. Totawa: Rowman, 1983. 81–93.

Hickman, Larry A. *John Dewey's Pragmatic Technology.* Bloomington: Indiana UP, 1990.

Hillocks, George, Jr. *Research on Written Composition: New Directions for Teaching.* Urbana: ERIC, 1986.

Holbrook, Sue Ellen. "Women's Work: The Feminizing of Composition." *Rhetoric Rev.* 9 (1991): 201–29.

Holton, Gerald. *The Advancement of Science, and Its Burdens.* 1986. With a New Introduction. Cambridge: Harvard UP, 1998.

————. *Science and Anti-Science.* Cambridge: Harvard UP, 1993.

hooks, bell. *Outlaw Culture: Resisting Representations.* New York: Routledge, 1994.

————. *Reel to Real: Race, Sex, and Class at the Movies.* New York: Routledge, 1996.

————. *Talking Back: thinking feminist, thinking black.* Boston: South End, 1989.

————. *Teaching to Transgress: Education as the Practice of Freedom.* New York: Routledge, 1994.

————. *Yearning: race, gender, and cultural politics.* Boston: South End, 1990.

Horner, Winifred Bryan, ed. *Composition and Literature: Bridging the Gap.* Chicago: U of Chicago P, 1983.

Houser, Nathan, and Christian Kloesel, eds. *The Essential Peirce: Selected Philosophical Writings (1867–1893).* Bloomington: Indiana UP, 1992.

Howard, Lillie P., ed. *Alice Walker and Zora Neale Hurston: The Common Bond.* Westport: Greenwood, 1993.

Humm, Maggie. *Modern Feminisms: Political, Literary, Cultural.* New York: Columbia UP, 1992.

Hungerford, Edward A. "'deeply and consciously affected . . . ': Virginia Woolf's Reviews of the Romantic Poets." Rosenberg and Dubino 97–115.

Hunter, J. Paul. "Facing Others, Facing Ourselves." *Global Perspectives on Teaching Literature: Shared Visions and Distinctive Visions.* Ed. Sandra Ward Lott, Maureen S. G. Hawkins, and Norman McMillan. Urbana: NCTE, 1993. 19–29.

Hurlburt, C. Mark, and Michael Blitz, eds. *Composition and Resistance.* Portsmouth: Boynton, 1991.

Hurston, Zora Neale. *Dust Tracks on the Road: An Autobiography.* Ed. Robert Hemenway. 2nd ed. Urbana: U of Illinois P, 1942.

————. *Mules and Men.* 1935. New York: Negro UP, 1969.

————. *Tell My Horse.* 1938. New York: Harper, 1990.

Hussey, Mark. "Reading and Ritual in Virginia Woolf's *Between the Acts.*" *Anima* 15 (1989): 89–99.

Hutcheon, Linda. *A Poetics of Postmodernism: History, Theory, Fiction.* New York: Routledge, 1988.

————. *The Politics of Postmodernism.* New York: Routledge, 1989.

Huyssen, Andreas. *After the Great Divide: Modernism, Mass Culture, Postmodernism.* Bloomington: Indiana UP, 1986.

Irigaray, Luce. *je,tu,nous: Toward a Culture of Difference.* New York: Routledge, 1993.

Iser, Wolfgang. *The Act of Reading: A Theory of Aesthetic Response.* Baltimore: Johns Hopkins UP, 1978.

————. *The Fictive and the Imaginary: Charting Literary Anthropology.* Baltimore: Johns Hopkins UP, 1993.

————. *Prospecting: From Reader Response to Literary Anthropology.* Baltimore: Johns Hopkins UP, 1989.

Jackson, Tony E. *The Subject of Modernism: Narrative Alteration in the Fiction of Eliot, Conrad, Woolf, and Joyce.* Ann Arbor: U of Michigan P, 1994.

James, William. *Pragmatism and Four Essays from The Meaning of Truth.* 1907. New York: World, 1955.

Jameson, Fredric. *Postmodernism, or, the Cultural Logic of Late Capitalism.* Durham: Duke UP, 1991.

Jardine, Alice, and Paul Smith, eds. *Men in Feminism.* New York: Routledge, 1987.

Jarratt, Susan C. Introduction: As We Were Saying . . . Jarratt and Worsham 1–18.

————. *Rereading the Sophists: Classical Rhetoric Refigured.* Carbondale: Southern Illinois UP, 1991.

Jarratt, Susan C., and Lynn Worsham, eds. *Feminism and Composition Studies: In Other Words.* New York: MLA, 1998.

Jarvis, Darryl S. L. "Postmodernism: A Critical Typology." *Politics and Society* 26 (1998): 95–142.

Jay, Martin. "Habermas and Modernism." *Habermas and Modernity.* Ed. Richard J. Bernstein. Cambridge: MIT P, 1985. 125–39.

Jayaratne, Toby, and Abigail J. Stewart. "Quantitative and Qualitative Methods in the Social Sciences: Current Feminist Issues and Practical Strategies." *Beyond Methodology: Feminist Scholarship as Lived Research.* Ed. Mary Margaret Fonow and Judith A. Cook. Bloomington: Indiana UP, 1991. 85–106.

Joseph, Suad. "Comment on Majid's 'The Politics of Feminism in Islam': Critique of Politics and the Politics of Critique." *Signs* 23 (1998): 363–69.

Kalbfleisch, Jane. "When Feminism Met Postfeminism: The Rhetoric of a Relationship." *Generations: Academic Feminists in Dialogue.* Ed. Devoney Looser and E. Ann Kaplan. Minneapolis: U of Minnesota P, 1997. 250–66.

Kanneh, Kadiatu. "Black Feminisms." *Contemporary Feminist Theories.* Ed. Stevi Jackson and Jackie Jones. New York: New York UP, 1998. 86–97.

Kant, Immanuel. *Critique of Pure Reason.* 1787. New York: St. Martin's, 1965.

Karier, Clarence J., Paul Violas, and Joel Spring. *Roots of Crisis: American Education in the Twentieth Century.* Chicago: Rand, 1973.

Kaufmann, Michael. "A Modernism of One's Own: Virginia Woolf's *TLS* Reviews and Eliotic Modernism." Rosenberg and Dubino 137–55.

Keller, Evelyn Fox. *A Feeling for the Organism: The Life and Times of Barbara McClintock.* San Francisco: Freeman, 1983.

————. *Reflections on Gender and Science.* New Haven: Yale UP, 1985.

Kennedy, William A. "Teaching at Tech: A Snapshot of the Freshman Class." *Tech Topics* 16 (Feb. 2001): 2.

Kent, Thomas. *Paralogic Rhetoric: A Theory of Communicative Interaction.* Lewisburg: Bucknell UP, 1993.

Kermode, Frank. *Romantic Image*. London: Routledge, 1957.

Khan, Shahnaz. "Muslin Women: Negotiations in the Third Space." *Signs* 23 (1998): 463–94.

Kincaid, Jamaica. *Annie John*. 1983. New York: Plume, 1985.

———. *A Small Place*. New York: Plume, 1988.

Kirsch, Gesa E. *Ethical Dilemmas in Feminist Research: The Politics of Location, Interpretation, and Publication*. Albany: State U of New York P, 1999.

Kirsch, Gesa E., and Peter Mortensen. Introduction: Reflections on Methodology in Literacy Studies. *Ethics and Representation in Qualitative Studies of Literacy*. Ed. Mortensen and Kirsch. Urbana: NCTE, 1996. xix–xxxiv.

Kirsch, Gesa E., and Joy S. Ritchie. "Beyond the Personal: Theorizing a Politics of Location in Composition Research." *CCC* 46 (1995): 7–29.

Kirsch, Gesa E., and Patricia A. Sullivan, eds. *Methods and Methodology in Composition Research*. Carbondale: Southern Illinois UP, 1992.

Kramarae, Cheris, and Dale Spender. *The Knowledge Explosion: Generations of Feminist Scholarship*. New York: Teachers, 1992.

Kristeva, Julia. "About Chinese Women." Moi, *Kristeva Reader* 138–59.

———. *Desire in Language: A Semiotic Approach to Literature and Art*. Ed. Leon S. Roudiez. New York: Columbia UP, 1980.

———. Interview with Suzanne Clark and Kathleen Hulley. "Cultural Strangeness and the Subject in Crisis." *Julia Kristeva Interviews*. Ed. Ross Mitchell Guberman. New York: Columbia UP, 1996. 35–58.

———. *Language, the Unknown: An Initiation into Linguistics*. New York: Columbia UP, 1989.

———. "The New Type of Intellectual: The Dissident." Moi, *Kristeva Reader* 292–300.

———. "Revolution in Poetic Language." Moi, *Kristeva Reader* 89–136.

———. "Semiotics: A Critical Science and/or a Critique of Science." Moi, *Kristeva Reader* 74–88.

———. "Stabat Mater." Moi, *Kristeva Reader* 160–86.

———. *Strangers to Ourselves*. Trans. Leon S. Roudiez. New York: Columbia UP, 1991.

———. "The System and the Speaking Subject." Moi, *Kristeva Reader* 24–33.

———. "Women's Time." Moi, *Kristeva Reader* 187–213.

———. "Word, Dialogue, and Novel." *Desire in Language: A Semiotic Approach to Literature and Art*. Ed. Leon S. Roudiez. New York: Columbia UP, 1980. 64–91.

Kuhn, Thomas. *The Structure of Scientific Revolutions*. 2nd ed. Chicago: U of Chicago P, 1970.

Lamb, Catherine E. "Beyond Argument in Feminist Composition." *CCC* 42 (1991): 11–24.

Langbaum, Robert. *The Poetry of Experience: The Dramatic Monologue in Modern Literary Tradition*. New York: Norton, 1957.

Lather, Patti. *Getting Smart: Feminist Research and Pedagogy with/in the Postmodern*. New York: Routledge, 1991.

Latour, Bruno. *We Have Never Been Modern*. Trans. Catherine Porter. Cambridge: Harvard UP, 1993.

Lauer, Janice M. "Issues and Discursive Practices." Phelps and Emig 353–60.

Lauer, Janice M., and J. William Asher. *Composition Research: Empirical Designs*. New York: Oxford UP, 1988.

Lay, Mary. "Feminist Theory and the Redefinition of Technical Communication." *Jour. of Business and Technical Communication* 5 (1991): 348–70.

Lazarre, Jane. *The Mother Knot.* Boston: Beacon, 1985.

Lears, Jackson T. *No Place of Grace: Antimodernism and the Transformation of American Culture, 1888–1920.* Chicago: U of Chicago P, 1994.

Lethen, Helmut. "Modernism Cut in Half: The Exclusion of the Avant-Garde and the Debate on Postmodernism." *Approaching Postmodernism: Papers Presented at a Workshop on Postmodernism 21–23 Sept. 1984, U of Utrecht.* Ed. Douwe Fokkema and Hans Bertens. Philadelphia: Benjamins, 1986. 233–38.

Levenback, Karen L. *Virginia Woolf and the Great War.* Syracuse: Syracuse UP, 1998.

Lindberg, Kathryne V. *Reading Pound Reading: Modernism After Nietzsche.* New York: Oxford UP, 1987.

Little, Judy. *The Experimental Self: Dialogic Subjectivity in Woolf, Pym, and Brooke-Rose.* Carbondale: Southern Illinois UP, 1996.

Lloyd-Jones, Richard. Introduction. *Research on Written Composition: New Directions for Teaching.* By George Hillocks, Jr. Urbana: ERIC, 1986. xiii–xiv.

Locke, John. *An Essay Concerning Human Understanding.* 1690. Chicago: Encyclopedia Britannica, 1952.

———. *Of Civil Government, Second Treatise.* 1689. Chicago: Regnery, 1955.

Lodge, David. *Twentieth-Century Literary Criticism: A Reader.* London: Longman, 1972.

———. *Working with Structuralism: Essays and Reviews on Nineteenth- and Twentieth-Century Literature.* Boston: Routledge, 1981.

Logan, Shirley W. *With Pen and Voice: The Rhetoric of Nineteenth-Century African American Women.* Carbondale: Southern Illinois UP, 1995.

Lu, Min-Zhan. "Reading and Writing Differences: The Problematic of Experience." Jarratt and Worsham 239–51.

Lubbock, Percy. *The Craft of Fiction.* 1921. New York: Viking, 1957.

Lunsford, Andrea, and Lisa Ede. "Rhetoric in a New Key: Women and Collaboration." *Rhetoric Review* 8 (1990): 234–41.

Lyotard, Jean-François. *The Postmodern Condition: A Report on Knowledge.* Minneapolis: U of Minnesota P, 1984.

Maccoby, Eleanor Emmons, and Carol Nagy Jacklin. *The Psychology of Sex Differences.* Stanford: Stanford UP, 1974.

Machor, James L. *Readers in History: Nineteenth-Century American Literature and the Contexts of Response.* Baltimore: Johns Hopkins UP, 1993.

MacKinnon, Catharine A. *Feminism Unmodified: Discourses on Life and Law.* Cambridge: Harvard UP, 1987.

———. "Only Words." Schilb, Flynn, and Clifford 737–44. Excerpted from Catharine A. MacKinnon, *Only Words.* Cambridge: Harvard UP, 1993.

Mahaffey, Vicki. "Modernist Theory and Criticism." *The Johns Hopkins Guide to Literary Theory and Criticism.* Ed. Michael Groden and Martin Kreiswirth. Baltimore: Johns Hopkins UP, 1994. 512–14.

Mailloux, Steven. "The Turns of Reader-Response Criticism." *Conversations: Contemporary Critical Theory and the Teaching of Literature.* Ed. Charles Moran and Elizabeth F. Penfield. Urbana: NCTE, 1990. 38–54.

Maitino, John R., and David R. Peck, eds. *Teaching American Ethnic Literatures: Nineteen Essays.* Albuquerque: U of New Mexico P, 1996.

Majid, Anouar. "The Politics of Feminism in Islam." *Signs* 23 (1998): 321–61.

Makdisi, Saree. *Romantic Imperialism: Universal Empire and the Culture of Modernity.* New York: Cambridge UP, 1998.

Manguel, Alberto. *A History of Reading.* New York: Penguin, 1996.

Marcus, Jane. *Art and Anger: Reading like a Woman.* Columbus: Ohio State UP, 1988.

———. "Other People's I's (Eyes): The Reader, Gender, and Recursive Reading in *To the Lighthouse* and *The Waves.*" *Reader* 22 (1989): 53–67.

Mares, C. J. "Reading Proust: Woolf and the Painter's Perspective." *Compar. Lit.* 41 (1989): 327–59.

Marx, Karl. *Capital.* 1867. *The Marx and Engels Reader.* Ed. Robert C. Tucker. New York: Norton, 1972. 191–318.

———. *Manifesto of the Communist Party.* 1848. *The Marx and Engels Reader.* Ed. Robert C. Tucker. New York: Norton, 1972. 335–62.

Marx, Karl, and Friedrich Engels. *The German Ideology.* 1845–46. *The Marx and Engels Reader.* Ed. Robert C. Tucker. New York: Norton, 1972. 110–64.

May, Brian. *The Modernist as Pragmatist: E. M. Forster and the Fate of Liberalism.* Columbia: U of Missouri P, 1997.

Mayer, Ann Elizabeth. "Comment on Majid's 'The Politics of Feminism in Islam.'" *Signs* 23 (1998): 369–77.

McClelland, Ben W. "A Writing Program Administrator's Response." Clifford and Schilb 262–70.

McHale, Brian. *Constructing Postmodernism.* New York: Routledge, 1993.

McMillan, Terry, ed. *Breaking Ice: An Anthology of Contemporary African-American Fiction.* New York: Penguin, 1990.

McNees, Eleanor. "Colonizing Virginia Woolf: *Scrutiny* and Contemporary Cultural Views." Rosenberg and Dubino 41–58.

Mill, John Stuart. "Auguste Comte and Positivism." 1865. *Essays on Ethics, Religion, and Society.* Ed. J. M. Robson, F. E. L. Priestley, and D. P. Dryer. Toronto: U of Toronto P, 1969. 261–368.

———. *Autobiography.* 1873. New York: Holt, 1890.

———. "An Economic and Social Forecast." *Principles of Political Economy.* 1848. Excerpted in *John Stuart Mill: A Selection of His Works.* Ed. John M. Robson. New York: St. Martin's, 1966. 322–42.

———. *On Liberty.* 1859. *John Stuart Mill: A Selection of His Works.* Ed. John M. Robson. New York: St. Martin's, 1966. 1–147.

———. "The Subjection of Women." 1873. Excerpted in *The Feminist Papers: From Adams to de Beauvoir.* Ed. Alice S. Rossi. New York: Columbia UP, 1973. 196–238.

———. *Utilitarianism.* 1861. *John Stuart Mill: A Selection of His Works.* Ed. John M. Robson. New York: St. Martin's, 1966. 149–228.

Miller, Susan. *Assuming the Positions: Cultural Pedagogy and the Politics of Commonplace Writing.* Pittsburgh: U of Pittsburgh P, 1998.

———. *Rescuing the Subject: A Critical Introduction to Rhetoric and the Writer.* Carbondale: Southern Illinois UP, 1989.

———. *Textual Carnivals: The Politics of Composition.* Carbondale: Southern Illinois UP, 1991.

Millett, Kate. *Sexual Politics.* New York: Doubleday, 1970.

Minow-Pinkney, Makiko. *Virginia Woolf and the Problem of the Subject: Feminine Writing in the Major Novels.* New Brunswick: Rutgers UP, 1987.

Mitchell, Juliet. *Psychoanalysis and Feminism.* New York: Vintage, 1974.

Modelski, Tania. *Feminism Without Women: Culture and Criticism in a "Postfeminist" Age.* New York: Routledge, 1991.

Modern Language Association of America. *Directory.* Vol. 113. New York: MLA, 1998.

Mohanty, Chandra Talpade, Ann Russo, and Lourdes Torres. *Third World Women and the Politics of Feminism.* Bloomington: Indiana UP, 1991.

Moi, Toril. *Feminist Theory and Simone de Beauvoir.* Oxford: Blackwell, 1990.

——, ed. *The Kristeva Reader.* New York: Columbia UP, 1986.

——. "Politics and the Intellectual Woman: Clichés in the Reception of Simone de Beauvoir's Work." Moi *Feminist Theory* 21–61.

——. *Sexual/Textual Politics: Feminist Literary Theory.* New York: Routledge, 1985.

Mojab, Shahrzad. "'Muslim' Women and 'Western' Feminists: The Debate on Particulars and Universals." *Monthly Rev.* 7 (1998) 19–30.

Molony, Barbara. "Japan's 1986 Equal Employment Opportunity Law and the Changing Discourse on Gender." *Signs* 20 (1995): 268–302.

Moraga, Cherrie, and Gloria Anzaldúa, eds. *This Bridge Called My Back: Writings by Radical Women of Color.* Watertown: Persephone, 1981.

Morgan, Genevieve Sanchis. "The Hostess and the Seamstress: Virginia Woolf's Creation of a Domestic Modernism." *Unmanning Modernism: Gendered Re-Readings.* Ed. Elizabeth Jane Harrison and Shirley Peterson. Knoxville: U of Tennessee P, 1997. 90–104.

Morrison, Toni. *Playing in the Dark: Whiteness and the Literary Imagination.* New York: Vintage, 1992.

Mortensen, Peter, and Gesa E. Kirsch, eds. *Ethics and Representation in Qualitative Studies of Literacy.* Urbana: NCTE, 1996.

Moya, Paula M. L. "Postmodernism, 'Realism,' and the Politics of Identity: Cherrie Moraga and Chicana Feminism." *Feminist Genealogies, Colonial Legacies, Democratic Futures.* Ed. Chandra Talpade Mohanty and M. Jacqui Alexander. New York: Routledge, 1995. 125–50.

Naylor, Gloria. *Mama Day.* New York: Vintage, 1988.

Neel, Jasper. *Aristotle's Voice: Rhetoric, Theory, and Writing in America.* Carbondale: Southern Illinois UP, 1994.

——. *Plato, Derrida, and Writing.* Carbondale: Southern Illinois UP, 1988.

Nicholson, Linda J., ed. *Feminism/Postmodernism.* New York: Routledge, 1990.

——. Introduction. Nicholson 1–16.

El-Nimr, Raga'. "Women in Islamic Law." *Feminism and Islam: Legal and Literary Perspectives.* Ed. Mai Yamani. New York: New York UP, 1996. 87–102.

Noddings, Nel. *Caring: A Feminine Approach to Ethics and Moral Education.* Berkeley: U of California P, 1984.

Noordhof, Paul. "Scientism." *The Oxford Companion to Philosophy.* Ed. Ted Honderich. New York: Oxford UP, 1995. 814.

Norris, Christopher. "Modernism." *The Oxford Companion to Philosophy.* Ed. Ted Honderich. New York: Oxford UP, 1995. 583.

North, Stephen M. *The Making of Knowledge in Composition: Portrait of an Emerging Field.* Upper Montclair: Boynton, 1987.

Nussbaum, Martha C. *Sex and Social Justice.* New York: Oxford UP, 1999.

Oliver, Kelly. *Reading Kristeva: Unraveling the Double-bind.* Bloomington: Indiana UP, 1993.

Olsen, Tillie. *Silences.* New York: Dell, 1965.

Olson, Gary A. "Jacques Derrida on Rhetoric and Composition: A Conversation." *JAC* 10.1 (1990): 1–21.

———. "Resisting a Discourse of Mastery: A Conversation with Jean-François Lyotard." *JAC* 15.3 (1995): 391–410.

Ostriker, Alicia. *Writing Like a Woman.* Ann Arbor: U of Michigan P, 1983.

Oyewumi, Oyeronke. "De-confounding Gender: Feminist Theorizing and Western Culture, a Comment on Hawkesworth's 'Confounding Gender.'" *Signs* 23 (1998): 1049–62.

Paglia, Camille. "Madonna: Venus of the Radio Waves." Schilb, Flynn, and Clifford 534–40. Rpt. of *Sex, Art, and American Culture.* New York: Vintage, 1992.

Pathak, Zakia, and Saswati Sengupta. "Between Academy and Street: A Story of Resisting Women." *Signs* 22 (1997): 545–77.

Pearce, Lynne. *Feminism and the Politics of Reading.* London: Arnold, 1997.

Perloff, Marjorie. "Modernist Studies." *Redrawing the Boundaries: The Transformation of English and American Literary Studies.* Ed. Stephen Greenblatt and Giles Gunn. New York: MLA, 1992. 154–78.

Perreault, Jeanne. *Writing Selves: Contemporary Feminist Autography.* Minneapolis: U of Minnesota P, 1995.

Peterson, Linda H. "Gender and the Autobiographical Essay: Research Perspectives, Pedagogical Practices." *CCC* 42 (1991): 170–83.

Phelps, Louise Wetherbee. *Composition as a Human Science: Contributions to the Self-Understanding of a Discipline.* New York: Oxford UP, 1988.

Phelps, Louise Wetherbee, and Janet Emig, eds. *Feminine Principles and Women's Experience in American Composition and Rhetoric.* Pittsburgh: U of Pittsburgh P, 1995.

Phillips, Kathy J. *Virginia Woolf Against Empire.* Knoxville: U of Tennessee P, 1994.

"Positivism." *The Compact Edition of the Oxford English Dictionary.* New York: Oxford UP, 1971. 1153–54.

Purves, Alan C. Foreword. *Composition Research: Empirical Designs.* By Janice M. Lauer and J. William Asher. New York: Oxford UP, 1988. v–viii.

Quandahl, Ellen. "The Anthropological Sleep of Composition." *JAC* 14 (1994): 413–29.

Quandt, Jean B. *From the Small Town to the Great Community: The Social Thought of Progressive Intellectuals.* New Brunswick: Rutgers UP, 1970.

Raitt, Suzanne. *Vita and Virginia: The Work and Friendship of V. Sackville-West and Virginia Woolf.* Oxford: Clarendon, 1993.

Ratcliffe, Krista. *Anglo-American Feminist Challenges to the Rhetorical Traditions: Virginia Woolf, Mary Daly, Adrienne Rich.* Carbondale: Southern Illinois UP, 1996.

Ray, Robert B. "Postmodernism." *Encyclopedia of Literature and Criticism.* Ed. Martin Coyle, et al. Detroit: Gale, 1991. 131–47.

Reddy, Maureen. "Maternal Reading: Lazarre and Walker." *Narrating Mothers: Theorizing Maternal Subjectivities.* Knoxville: U of Tennessee P, 1991. 222–38.

Reed, Christopher. "Through Formalism: Feminism and Virginia Woolf's Relation to Bloomsbury Aesthetics." *Twentieth-Century Literature* 38 (1992): 20–43.

Register, Cheri. "American Feminist Literary Criticism: A Bibliographical Introduction." *Feminist Literary Criticism: Explorations in Theory.* Ed. Josephine Donovan. Lexington: U of Kentucky P, 1975. 1–28.

"Resistance." *The Compact Edition of the Oxford English Dictionary.* New York: Oxford UP, 1971. 2509.

Reynolds, Nedra. "Interrupting Our Way to Agency: Feminist Cultural Studies and Composition." Jarratt and Worsham 58–73.

Rhys, Jean. *Wide Sargasso Sea.* New York: Norton, 1966.

Rich, Adrienne. "The Antifeminist Woman." Rich, *On Lies, Secrets, and Silence* 69–84.

———. *Blood, Bread, and Poetry: Selected Prose 1979–1985.* New York: Norton, 1986.

———. "Blood, Bread, and Poetry: The Location of the Poet." Rich, *Blood, Bread, and Poetry* 167–87.

———."Compulsory Heterosexuality and Lesbian Existence." Rich, *Blood, Bread, and Poetry* 23–75.

———. Foreword. Rich, *Blood, Bread, and Poetry* vii–xiv.

———. "Notes Toward a Politics of Location." Rich, *Blood, Bread, and Poetry* 210–31.

———. *Of Woman Born: Motherhood as Experience and Institution.* New York: Norton, 1976.

———. *On Lies, Secrets, and Silence: Selected Prose 1966–1978.* New York: Norton, 1979.

———. "Split at the Root: An Essay on Jewish Identity." Rich, *Blood, Bread, and Poetry* 100–23.

———. "Teaching Language in Open Admissions." Rich, *On Lies, Secrets, and Silence* 51–68.

———. "Toward a More Feminist Criticism." Rich, *Blood, Bread, and Poetry* 85–99.

———. "Toward a Woman-Centered University." Rich, *On Lies, Secrets, and Silence* 125–55.

———. "What Does a Woman Need to Know?" Rich, *Blood, Bread, and Poetry* 1–10.

———. "When We Dead Awaken: Writing as Re-Vision." Rich, *On Lies, Secrets, and Silence* 33–49.

———. *Your Native Land, Your Life: Poems.* New York: Norton, 1986.

Richards, I. A. *Practical Criticism: A Study of Literary Judgment.* New York: Harcourt, 1929.

Ritchie, Joy, and Kathleen Boardman. "Feminism in Composition: Inclusion, Metonymy, and Disruption." *CCC* 50 (1999): 585–606.

Robinson, Lillian S., and Lise Vogel. "Modernism and History." *Images of Women in Fiction: Feminist Perspectives.* Ed. Susan Koppelman Cornillon. Bowling Green: Bowling Green U Popular P, 1972. 278–307.

Roiphe, Katie. "Catharine MacKinnon, the Antiporn Star." Schilb, Flynn, and Clifford 752–59. Rpt. of *The Morning After.* New York: Little, 1993.

Rorty, Richard. *Consequences of Pragmatism (Essays: 1972–1980).* Minneapolis: U of Minnesota P, 1982.

Rosenau, Pauline Marie. *Post-Modernism and the Social Sciences: Insights, Inroads, and Intrusions.* Princeton: Princeton UP, 1992.

Rosenberg, Beth Carole. *Virginia Woolf and Samuel Johnson: Common Readers.* New York: St. Martin's, 1995.

Rosenberg, Beth Carole, and Jeanne Dubino, eds. *Virginia Woolf and the Essay.* New York: St. Martin's, 1997.

Rosenblatt, Louise M. "Epilogue: Against Dualisms." Rosenblatt, *The Reader, the Text, the Poem* 176–89.

———. *L'Idee de l'art pour l'art dans la litterature anglaise pendant la periode victorienne.* 1931. New York: AMS, 1976.

———. Interview with Nicholas J. Karolides. "Theory and Practice: An Interview with Louise M. Rosenblatt." *Lang. Arts* 77 (1999): 158–70.

———. Letter to the author. 5 May 1987.

———. *Literature as Exploration.* 1938. New York: Noble, 1976.

———. *Literature as Exploration.* 1938. 5th ed. New York: MLA, 1995.

———. "Looking Back and Looking Forward." *Dialogue in a Major Key: Women Scholars Speak.* Ed. Mary H. Maguire. Urbana: NCTE, 1995.

———. "On the Aesthetic as the Basic Model of the Reading Process." *Theories of Reading, Looking, and Listening.* Ed. Harry R. Garvin. Lewisburg: Bucknell UP, 1981. 17–32.

———. Preface. Rosenblatt, *The Reader, the Text, the Poem* ix–xv.

———. *The Reader, the Text, the Poem: The Transactional Theory of the Literary Work.* Carbondale: Southern Illinois UP, 1978.

———. "Retrospect." *Transactions with Literature: A Fifty-Year Perspective.* Ed. Edmund J. Farrell and James R. Squire. Urbana: NCTE, 1990. 97–107.

———. Telephone interview with Elizabeth A. Flynn. 22 Apr. 1998.

———. "The Transactional Theory of Reading and Writing." *Theoretical Models and Processes of Reading.* 4th ed. Ed. R. R. Ruddell, M. R. Ruddell, and Harry Singer. Newark: Internl. Reading Assn., 1994. 1057–92.

———. "Viewpoints: Transaction Versus Interaction—A Terminological Rescue Operation." *Research in the Teaching of English* 19 (1985): 96–107.

———. "Whitman's *Democratic Vistas* and the New 'Ethnicity.'" *Yale Review: A National Quarterly* 67 (1978): 187–204.

Ross, Ellen. "New Thoughts on 'the Oldest Vocation': Mothers and Motherhood in Recent Feminist Scholarship. *Signs* 20 (1955): 397–413.

Rossi, Alice S. *The Feminist Papers: From Adams to de Beauvoir.* New York: Columbia UP, 1973.

Rossiter, Margaret W. *Women Scientists in America: Before Affirmative Action 1940–1972.* Baltimore: Johns Hopkins UP, 1995.

———. *Women Scientists in America: Struggles and Strategies to 1940.* Baltimore: Johns Hopkins UP, 1982.

Rowe, John Carlos. "Postmodernist Studies." *Redrawing the Boundaries: The Transformation of English and American Literary Studies.* Ed. Stephen Greenblatt and Giles Gunn. New York: MLA, 1992.

Royster, Jacqueline Jones. "In Search of Ways In." Phelps and Emig 385–91.

———. *Traces of a Stream: Literacy and Social Change among African American Women.* Pittsburgh: U of Pittsburgh P, 2000.

Rubin, Donnalee. *Gender Influences: Reading Student Texts.* Carbondale: Southern Illinois UP, 1993.

Ruddick, Sara. *Maternal Thinking: Toward a Politics of Peace.* Boston: Beacon, 1989.

Rugoff, Kathy. "Sappho on Mount Sinai: Adrienne Rich's Dialogue with Her Father." *Multicultural Literatures Through Feminist/Poststructuralist Lenses.* Ed. Barbara Frey Waxman. Knoxville: U of Tennessee P, 1993. 1–21.

Russ, Joanna. "What Can a Heroine Do? Or Why Women Can't Write." *Images of Women in Fiction: Feminist Perspectives.* Ed. Susan Koppelman Cornillon. Bowling Green: Bowling Green U Popular P, 1972. 3–20.

Saadawi, Nawal, and Mary E. Willmurth. "A Feminist in the Arab World." *Women and Therapy* 17 (1995): 435–42.

Sacks, Peter. *Generation X Goes to College: An Eye-Opening Account of Teaching in Postmodern America.* Chicago: Open Court, 1996.

Sadker, Myra, and David Sadker. "Confronting Sexism in the College Classroom."

Gender in the Classroom: Power and Pedagogy. Ed. Susan L. Gabriel and Isaiah Smithson. Urbana: U of Illinois P, 1990. 176–87.

Sadoff, Dianne F. "Black Matrilineage: The Case of Alice Walker and Zora Neale Hurston." *Signs* 11 (1985): 4–26.

Salzer, Beeb. "Postmodern Idea Inflation in the Humanities Hyperjungle." *Chronicle of Higher Education* 21 Nov. 1997: B6.

Saunders, Rebecca. "Language, Subject, Self: Reading the Style of *To the Lighthouse.*" *Novel* (1993): 192–213.

Saussure, Ferdinand de. *Course in General Linguistics.* 1915. New York: McGraw, 1959.

Saxton, Ruth, and Jean Tobin, eds. *Woolf and Lessing: Breaking the Mold.* New York: St. Martin's, 1994.

Schell, Eileen E. "Conference on the Growing Use of Part-time/Adjunct Faculty: Reflections from NCTE Participants." *Forum: Newsletter of the Non–Tenure-Track Faculty Special Interest Group, Conference on College Composition and Communication,* 1998. Ed. Roberta Kirby-Werner. *CCC* 49 (1998) A1-A24.

———. *Gypsy Academics and Mother-Teachers: Gender, Contingent Labor, and Writing Instruction.* Portsmouth: Boynton, 1997.

Schiff, Karen. "Moments of Reading and Woolf's Literary Criticism." Rosenberg and Dubino 176–92.

Schilb, John. *Between the Lines: Relating Composition Theory and Literary Theory.* Portsmouth: Boynton. 1996.

Schilb, John, Elizabeth A. Flynn, and John Clifford, eds. *Constellations: A Contextual Reader for Writers.* 2nd ed. New York: Harper, 1995.

Schiller, F. C. S. "Pragmatism." *The Compact Edition of the Oxford English Dictionary.* New York: Oxford UP, 1971. 2266.

Schneider, Alison. "Law and Finance Professors Are Top Earners in Academe, Survey Finds." *Chronicle of Higher Educ.* 28 May 1999: A14.

Scholes, Robert. *Structuralism in Literature: An Introduction.* New Haven: Yale UP, 1974.

Schweickart, Patrocinio P. "Reading Ourselves: Toward a Feminist Theory of Reading." *Gender and Reading: Essays On Readers, Texts, and Contexts.* Ed. Elizabeth A. Flynn and Schweickart. Baltimore: Johns Hopkins UP, 1986. 31–62.

Schweickart, Patrocinio P., and Elizabeth A. Flynn, eds. *Reading Sites: Social Difference and Reader Response.* New York: MLA (forthcoming).

Scott, Bonnie Kime. *Refiguring Modernism: The Women of 1928.* Vol. 1. Bloomington: Indiana UP, 1995.

Seligman, Daniel. "Postmodernism, in Seventy-five Words or Less." *Fortune* 155 (22 July 1996). 19 Oct. 1998 <http://web7.searchbank.com/infotrac/session/864/556/26182316 w3/71!xm_180>.

Showalter, Elaine. *A Literature of Their Own: British Women Novelists from Brontë to Lessing.* Princeton: Princeton UP, 1977.

Shumway, David R. "Science, Theory, and the Politics of Empirical Studies in the English Department." Clifford and Schilb 148–58.

Silko, Leslie. "Storyteller." Charters 1145–56.

Silver, Brenda R. Introduction: The Uncommon Reader. *Virginia Woolf's Reading Notebooks.* Princeton: Princeton UP, 1983.

Simons, Marlise. "After the Rape, a Lifetime of Shame. It's Morocco." *New York Times on the Web* 1 Feb. 1999. 1–3. New York Times. 1 Feb. 1999 <http://www.nytimes.com/yr/mo/day/news/worl00d/morocco-singlemoms.html>.

Singer, Linda. "Feminism and Postmodernism." *Feminists Theorize the Political.* Ed. Judith Butler and Joan W. Scott. New York: Routledge, 1992. 464–75.

Slack, Jennifer Daryl, and M. Mehdi Semati. "Intellectual and Political Hygiene: The 'Sokal Affair.'" *Critical Studies in Mass Communication* 14 (1997): 201–27.

Slevin, James. "Depoliticizing and Politicizing Composition Studies." Bullock and Trimbur 1–21.

Smith, Dorothy E. "Comment on Hekman's 'Truth and Method: Feminist Standpoint Theory Revisited.'" *Signs* 22 (1997): 392–98.

Sommers, Nancy. "Between the Drafts." *CCC* 43 (1992): 23–31.

Sontag, Susan. "The Way We Live Now." Charters 1191–204.

Spacks, Patricia Meyer. *The Female Imagination.* New York: Avon, 1992.

Spellmeyer, Kurt. *Common Ground: Dialogue, Understanding, and the Teaching of Composition.* Englewood Cliffs: Prentice, 1993.

Spender, Dale. *Man Made Language.* London: Routledge, 1980.

Spivak, Gayatri Chakravorty. *Outside in the Teaching Machine.* New York: Routledge, 1993.

Stabile, Carol A. "Feminism and the Ends of Postmodernism." *Materialist Feminism: A Reader in Class, Difference, and Women's Lives.* Ed. Rosemary Hennessy and Chrys Ingraham. New York: Routledge, 1997. 395–408.

Starke-Meyerring, Doreen. "'Lost and Melted in the Pot': Multicultural Literacy in Predominantly White Classrooms." *Outbursts in Academe: Multiculturalism and Other Sources of Conflict.* Ed. Kathleen Dixon. Portsmouth: Boynton, 1998. 135–57.

Stein, Rachel. "Returning to Sacred Tree: Black Women, Nature, and Political Resistance in Alice Walker's *Meridian.*" *Shifting the Ground: American Women Writers' Revisions of Nature, Gender, and Race.* Charlottesville: UP of Virginia, 1997.

Stephen, Leslie. *The English Utilitarians.* 1900. Vol. 3. New York: Kelley, 1968.

Stimpson, Catharine R. "Feminist Criticism." *Redrawing the Boundaries: The Transformation of English and American Literary Studies.* Ed. Stephen Greenblatt and Giles Gunn. New York: MLA, 1992. 251–70.

Sullivan, Patricia A. "Feminism and Methodology in Composition Studies." *Methods and Methodology in Composition Research.* Ed. Gesa E. Kirsch and Sullivan. Carbondale: Southern Illinois UP, 1992.

Sullivan, Patricia A., and Donna J. Qualley, eds. *Pedagogy in the Age of Politics: Writing and Reading (in) the Academy.* Urbana: NCTE, 1994.

Taha, Mahmoud Mohammed. *The Second Message of Islam.* Trans. Abdullahi Ahmed an-Na'im. Syracuse: Syracuse UP, 1987.

Tan, Amy. "Two Kinds." Charters 1215–23.

Tannen, Deborah. *You Just Don't Understand: Women and Men in Conversation.* New York: Morrow, 1990.

Templeton, Alice. *The Dream and the Dialogue: Adrienne Rich's Feminist Poetics.* Knoxville: U of Tennessee P, 1994.

Tong, Rosemarie. *Feminist Thought: A Comprehensive Introduction.* Boulder: Westview, 1989.

———. *Feminist Thought: A More Comprehensive Introduction.* 2nd ed. Boulder: Westview, 1998.

Toulmin, Stephen. *Cosmopolis: The Hidden Agenda of Modernity.* New York: Free, 1990.

Tratner, Michael. *Modernism and Mass Politics: Joyce, Woolf, Eliot, Yeats.* Stanford: Stanford UP, 1995.

Tremper, Ellen. *"Who Lived at Alfoxton?" Virginia Woolf and English Romanticism.* Lewisburg: Bucknell UP, 1998.

Trimbur, John. "Agency and the Death of the Author: A Partial Defense of Modernism." *JAC* 20 (2000): 283–98.

Trinh T. Minh-ha. *Woman, Native, Other: Writing Postcoloniality and Feminism.* Bloomington: Indiana UP, 1989.

Tuana, Nancy, ed. *Feminism and Science.* Bloomington: Indiana UP, 1989.

———. *The Less Noble Sex: Scientific, Religious, and Philosophical Conceptions of Woman's Nature.* Bloomington: Indiana UP, 1993.

Villanueva, Victor. *Bootstraps: From an American Academic of Color.* Urbana: NCTE, 1993.

Walker, Alice. "Beauty: When the Other Dancer Is the Self." Walker, *In Search of Our Mothers' Gardens* 384–93.

———. "Beyond the Peacock: The Reconstruction of Flannery O'Connor." Walker, *In Search of Our Mothers' Gardens* 42–59.

———. "The Black Writer and the Southern Experience." Walker, *In Search of Our Mothers' Gardens* 15–21.

———. "Choice: A Tribute to Dr. Martin Luther King, Jr." Walker, *In Search of Our Mothers' Gardens* 142–45.

———. *The Color Purple.* New York: Washington, 1982.

———. "Coretta King: Revisited." Walker, *In Search of Our Mothers' Gardens* 146–57.

———. "Father." Walker, *Living by the Word: Essays* 9–17.

———. "From an Interview." Walker, *In Search of Our Mothers' Gardens* 231–43.

———. "Gifts of Power: The Writings of Rebecca Jackson." Walker, *In Search of Our Mothers' Gardens* 71–82.

———. "If the Present Looks like the Past, What Does the Future Look Like?" Walker, *In Search of Our Mothers' Gardens* 290–312.

———. "In Search of Our Mothers' Gardens." Walker, *In Search of Our Mothers' Gardens* 231–43.

———. *In Search of Our Mothers' Gardens: Womanist Prose.* 1967. New York: Harcourt, 1983.

———. "In the Closet of the Soul." Walker, *Living by the Word: Essays* 78–92.

———. "A Letter to the Editor of *Ms.*" Walker, *In Search of Our Mothers' Gardens* 273–77.

———. *Living by the Word: Selected Writings 1973–1987 by Alice Walker.* New York: Harcourt, 1988.

———. "Looking for Zora." Walker, *In Search of Our Mothers' Gardens* 93–116.

———. "My Big Brother Bill." Walker, *Living by the Word* 41–50.

———. "One Child of One's Own: A Meaningful Digression within the Work(s)." Walker, *In Search of Our Mothers' Gardens* 361–83.

———. "Recording the Seasons." Walker, *In Search of Our Mothers' Gardens* 223–28.

———. "Saving the Life That Is Your Own: The Importance of Models in the Artist's Life." Walker, *In Search of Our Mothers' Gardens* 3–14.

———. "A Talk: Convocation 1972." Walker, *In Search of Our Mothers' Gardens* 33–41.

———. "A Thousand Words." Walker, *Living by the Word* 99–113.

———. "The Unglamorous but Worthwhile Duties of the Black Revolutionary Artist, or of the Black Writer Who Simply Works and Writes." Walker, *In Search of Our Mothers' Gardens* 130–38.

———. "A Writer Because of, Not in Spite of, Her Children." Walker, *In Search of Our Mothers' Gardens* 66–70.

———. "Zora Neale Hurston: A Cautionary Tale and a Partisan View." Walker, *In Search of Our Mothers' Gardens* 83–92.

Walker, Rebecca. *Black, White, and Jewish: Autobiography of a Shifting Self.* New York: Riverhead, 2001.

Wall, Cheryl A., ed. *Zora Neale Hurston: Novels and Stories.* New York: Lib. of Amer., 1995.

Waugh, Patricia. "Postmodernism and Feminism." *Contemporary Feminist Theories.* Ed. Stevi Jackson and Jackie Jones. New York: New York UP, 1998.

———. *Practicing Postmodernism/Reading Modernism.* London: Arnold, 1992.

Waxman, Barbara Frey. *Multicultural Literatures through Feminist/Poststructuralist Lenses.* Knoxville: U of Tennessee P, 1993.

Wellek, René. *English Criticism, 1900–1950.* New Haven: Yale UP, 1986. Vol. 5 of *A History of Modern Criticism, 1750–1950.* 8 vols. 1955–92.

White, Hayden. *Tropics of Discourse: Essays in Cultural Criticism.* Baltimore: Johns Hopkins UP, 1978.

Wicke, Jennifer, and Margaret Ferguson. Introduction: Feminism and Postmodernism; or, the Way We Live Now. Ferguson and Wicke 1–9.

———. "Postmodern Identities and the Politics of the (Legal) Subject." Ferguson and Wicke 10–33.

Willis, Susan. *Specifying: Black Women Writing the American Experience.* Madison: U of Wisconsin P, 1987.

Wilson, Trish. "Mary Daly." *Feminista* 2.10 (1999). 2 Feb. 2000 <http://www.feminista.com/v2n10/wilson.html>.

Wollstonecraft, Mary. *A Vindication of the Rights of Woman: With Strictures on Political and Moral Subjects.* 1792. New York: Norton, 1967.

Woolf, Virginia. "Addison." *The Common Reader: First Series.* New York: Harcourt, 1925. 98–108.

———. "Beauchamp's Career. Meredith." *Virginia Woolf's Reading Notebooks.* Monk's House Papers/B.2n. 46 (B.6). U of Sussex Library. 2 pp.

———. *The Common Reader: First Series.* New York: Harcourt, 1925.

———. "An Essay in Criticism." Woolf, *Granite and Rainbow* 85–92.

———. "A Friend of Johnson." Woolf, *Granite and Rainbow* 187–91.

———. *Granite and Rainbow: Essays by Virginia Woolf.* New York: Harcourt, 1958.

———. "Hours in a Library." Woolf, *Granite and Rainbow* 24–31.

———. "How It Strikes a Contemporary." *The Common Reader: First Series.* New York: Harcourt, 1925. 236–46.

———. "How Should One Read a Book?" *The Second Common Reader.* New York: Harcourt, 1932. 234–45.

———. "Jane Austen. P & Prej." *Virginia Woolf's Reading Notebooks.* Monk's House Papers/B.2n. 46 (B.18). U of Sussex Library. 1 p.

———. "Northanger Abbey." *Virginia Woolf's Reading Notebooks.* Holograph Reading Notes. 14 (B.4). Berg Collection. New York Public Library. 1 p.

———. "Notes on an Elizabethan Play." *The Common Reader: First Series.* New York: Harcourt, 1925. 49–58.

——. "On Not Knowing Greek." *The Common Reader: First Series.* New York: Harcourt, 1925. 24–39.

——. "On Re-Reading Novels." *The Moment and Other Essays.* New York: Harcourt, 1948. 155–66.

——. "Peacock. Crotchet Castle." *Virginia Woolf's Reading Notebooks.* Holograph Reading Notes. 14 (B.15). Berg Collection. New York Public Library. 1 p.

——. "Phases of Fiction." Woolf, *Granite and Rainbow* 93–145.

——. "Reading." *The Captain's Death Bed and Other Essays by Virginia Woolf.* New York: Harcourt, 1950. 151–79.

——. "Reviewing." *The Captain's Death Bed and Other Essays.* New York: Harcourt, 1950. 127–45.

——. "Richard Feverel. Mer. Vol 1." *Virginia Woolf's Reading Notebooks.* Monk's House Papers/B.2n. 46 (B.5). U of Sussex Library. 4 pp.

——. "Robinson Crusoe." *The Second Common Reader.* New York: Harcourt, 1932. 42–49.

——. *Roger Fry: A Biography.* New York: Harcourt, 1940.

——. *A Room of One's Own.* 1929. New York: Harcourt, 1957.

——. "The Russian Point of View." *The Common Reader: First Series.* New York: Harcourt, 177–87.

——. "Sen[i] Journey." *Virginia Woolf's Reading Notebooks.* Monk's House Papers/ B.2n. 46 (B.14). U of Sussex Library. 3 pp.

——. "Silas Marner." *Virginia Woolf's Reading Notebooks.* Holograph Reading Notes. 14 (B.11). Berg Collection. NY Public Lib. 2 pp.

——. "Small House at A. Trollope." *Virginia Woolf's Reading Notebooks.* Monk's House Papers/B.2n. 46 (B.23). U of Sussex Library.

——. *Three Guineas.* New York: Harcourt, 1938.

——. "Tristram Shandy." *Virginia Woolf's Reading Notebooks.* Holograph Reading Notes. 14 (B.16). Berg Collection. NY Public Lib. 10 pp.

——. "Udolpho." *Virginia Woolf's Reading Notebooks.* Monk's House Papers/B.2n. 46 (B.4). U of Sussex Library. 1 p.

Wordsworth, William. Preface. *Lyrical Ballads.* 1798. Ed. R. L. Brett and A. R. Jones. London: Methuen, 1963.

——. *The Prelude: Or Growth of a Poet's Mind.* 1805. Ed. Ernest de Selincourt. 2nd ed. New York: Oxford UP, 1959.

Worsham, Lynn. "Writing Against Writing: The Predicament of *Écriture Féminine* in Composition Studies." *Contending with Words: Composition and Rhetoric in a Postmodern Age.* Ed. Patricia Harkin and John Schilb. New York: MLA, 1991. 82–104.

Yoder, Leslie K. "Resisting the Assignment." *Writing Permitted in Designated Areas Only.* Ed. Linda Brodkey. Minneapolis: U of Minnesota P, 1996. 284–95.

Ziolkowski, Theodore. *The View from the Tower: Origins of an Antimodernist Image.* Princeton: Princeton UP, 1998.

Index

Elizabeth A. Flynn is a professor in the Department of Humanities at Michigan Technological University where she teaches courses in feminist theory, reading theory, writing, and literature. She is the coeditor of *Gender and Reading* and the founding editor of the journal *Reader* and its editor from 1982–1991 and co-editor from 1991–2000. She has published articles in *College English, College Composition and Communication, JAC, Victorian Literature and Culture,* and elsewhere.

Studies in Rhetorics and Feminisms

Studies in Rhetorics and Feminisms seeks to address the interdisciplinarity that rhetorics and feminisms represent. Rhetorical and feminist scholars want to connect rhetorical inquiry with contemporary academic and social concerns, exploring rhetoric's relevance to current issues of opportunity and diversity. This interdisciplinarity has already begun to transform the rhetorical tradition as we have known it (upper-class, agonistic, public, and male) into regendered, inclusionary rhetorics (democratic, dialogic, collaborative, cultural, and private). Our intellectual advancements depend on such ongoing transformation.

Rhetoric, whether ancient, contemporary, or futuristic, always inscribes the relation of language and power at a particular moment, indicating who may speak, who may listen, and what can be said. The only way we can displace the traditional rhetoric of masculine-only, public performance is to replace it with rhetorics that are recognized as being better suited to our present needs. We must understand more fully the rhetorics of the non-Western tradition, of women, of a variety of cultural and ethnic groups. Therefore, Studies in Rhetorics and Feminisms espouses a theoretical position of openness and expansion, a place for rhetorics to grow and thrive in a symbiotic relationship with all that feminisms have to offer, particularly when these two fields intersect with philosophical, sociological, religious, psychological, pedagogical, and literary issues.

The series seeks scholarly works that both examine and extend rhetoric, works that span the sexes, disciplines, cultures, ethnicities, and sociocultural practices as they intersect with the rhetorical tradition. After all, the recent resurgence of rhetorical studies has not so much been a discovery of new rhetorics; it has been more a recognition of existing rhetorical activities and practices, of our newfound ability and willingness to listen to previously untold stories.

The series editors seek both high-quality traditional and cutting-edge scholarly work that extends the significant relationship between rhetoric and feminism within various genres, cultural contexts, historical periods, methodologies, theoretical positions, and methods of delivery (e.g., film and hypertext to elocution and preaching).

Queries and submissions:
Professor Cheryl Glenn, Editor
    E-mail: cjg6@psu.edu
Professor Shirley Wilson Logan, Editor
    E-mail: Shirley_W_Logan@umail.umd.edu
Studies in Rhetorics and Feminisms
    Department of English
    142 South Burrowes Bldg
    Penn State University
    University Park, PA 16802-6200